Walking the Amazon

860 Days. The Impossible Task.
The Incredible Journey

Ed Stafford

Virgin BOOKS

2 4 6 8 10 9 7 5 3 1

Published in 2011 by Virgin Books, an imprint of Ebury Publishing

A Random House Group Company

The Random House Group Limited Reg. No. 954009

Addresses for companies within the Random House Group can be found at www.randomhouse.co.uk

A CIP catalogue record for this book is available from the British Library

The Random House Group Limited supports the Forest Stewardship Council® [FSC®], the leading international forest certification organisation. All our titles that are printed on Greenpeace-approved FSC® certified paper carry the FSC® logo. Our paper procurement policy can be found at www.randomhouse.co.uk/environment

Printed in the UK by CPI Mackays, Chatham, ME5 8TD

Hardback ISBN 9781905264568

Trade Paperback ISBN 9780753515631

To buy books by your favourite authors and register for offers, visit www.randomhouse.co.uk

Endpapers: This image, provided by NASA, enabled the author to see through the jungle canopy and plan a route avoiding the worst flooded areas. The dark grey is terra firma and light grey is flooded forest at high-water season. (JAXA/NASA/JPL-CALTECH JERS-1/GRFM © JAXA/METI)

For my dad, Jeremy Stafford, for moral courage, mental strength and unquestioning love.

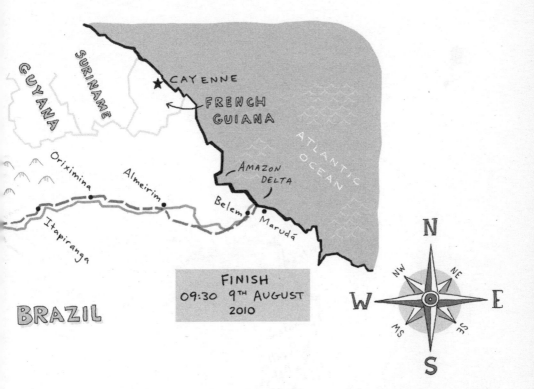

GUYANA

SURINAME

CAYENNE

FRENCH GUIANA

ATLANTIC OCEAN

Oriximina

Almeirim

Amazon Delta

Belem

Marudá

Itapiranga

BRAZIL

FINISH
09:30 9TH AUGUST
2010

N
NW   NE
W   E
SW   SE
S

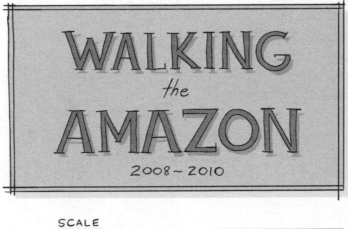

WALKING
the
AMAZON
2008~2010

SCALE

0   300   600

km

- - - PATH

⌣ RIVER

Contents

PART 4: BRAZIL

Prologue

After receiving a very direct warning over the HF radio that we would be killed if we decided to continue our journey, we reach the downriver end of the shingle island in the middle of the Amazon. I drop my inflated pack raft into the shallow brown waters and roll my heavy backpack off my stiff, grimy back and into the rubber boat.

'*Mira, Ed, atrás.* Look, Ed, behind you,' says Cho calmly. As I turn I see five dugout canoes coming towards us fast, full of indigenous Indians. Many of the Indians are standing up in the narrow boats; bows drawn, arrows trained on us. Those who are seated are thrusting hard with big wooden paddles.

Fuck. My T-shirt clings to my body and sweat pours down my temples. My body is still but my heart is quickening, adrenaline pours into my brain allowing me to process the imminent danger rapidly. My perception of time slows down. The carved boats cut through the choppy river fluently. The dangerous scene in the middle distance is framed by a green wall of overhanging jungle beyond. The brown faces of the Asheninka men and women are warlike and fierce, highlighted by lines of bright red face paint. I notice the women are all clutching machetes.

As the boats beach, the tribe leap out and run directly towards us. The men's faces are now taut with anger, eyes wide and white, and the women look possessed. Cho and I are unarmed, with nowhere to run, trapped at the tip of the island like animals. Every sense is now alert and our minds ignore all that is not relevant to immediate survival.

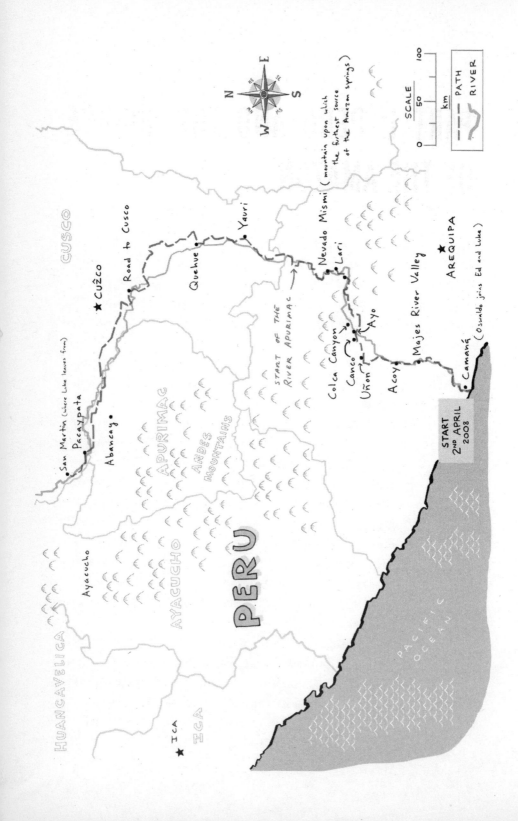

PART 1: PERU AND THE SOURCE OF THE AMAZON

Chapter One

Conception to Birth

A furious cage of heavy tropical rain enclosed the wall-less bar. The extraordinary force of water drowned out the persistent Creole drums from across the muddy street. A cool evening freshness accompanied the rain, cutting through the usual humidity. I sat, beer in hand, with a fellow expedition leader, Luke Collyer, and breathed in the cleansing power of nature. As we reclined in low wooden chairs, a ball of excited apprehension sat conspicuously in both of our stomachs. We'd just come to a decision that could change our lives for ever and we had shaken on it. We had agreed to attempt to walk the entire length of the Amazon River together. My eyes gleamed and I grinned at Luke. 'Fucking hell, mate – this is going to be mental.'

It was January 2007 and we were in the former British colony of Belize, Central America, running conservation expeditions for a British organisation called Trekforce. I'd just relocated our field base from the capital of Belize City to the smaller, more Latin town of San Ignacio near the Guatemalan border. Most people here were 'mestizos', a mix of indigenous Mayan and colonial Spanish, but there was a handful of Creole settlers who were relatively new to the town.

The following morning we stumbled round the field base in our boxer shorts eating egg banjos (fried-egg sandwiches) and drinking imported Earl Grey tea. Surprisingly, when the subject of the Amazon walk came up again neither of us backed down from the gentlemen's agreement. It would have been fairly excusable to blame the bravado on alcohol but, as we scratched our stubble and our balls waiting for the shower, we were both even more animated about the idea than we had been the previous evening.

Two years earlier I had been employed by a British company to set up a scientific research expedition in Argentine Patagonia. I had recently started going out with a girl called Chloë and, both having an itch for travel, we decided to apply for the job together of leading and managing this cold-weather expedition. Chloë was younger than me, with a coarse laugh, a curvaceous body and an endearing passion for doing good and preserving the vulnerable. We were much in love and the scope to do what we wanted and to make our lives in this unknown country was huge. The Argentine Patagonian people had a lovely confidence and humility that we both quickly fell in love with, too. We found Argentine biologists to work alongside and assist and Chloë and I both worked very hard to make the volunteer expedition work.

The expedition was largely a success but at the back of my mind I had a yearning to return to the tropics. Part of me feared the cold, the amount of equipment we were dependent on, and the amount of experience you needed to be safe in the mountains. I started to dream about the simplicity of an environment that I knew a lot better – the jungle. With long, eight-hour Land Rover journeys commonplace, I allowed my mind to wander and dream – what would be the ultimate expedition I could ever conceive of doing?

I had never been to the Amazon, my jungle experience had mostly come from Central America with some short trips to Borneo, but the Amazon undoubtedly had a mystique all of its own. Surely the trees would be much bigger, the wildlife had to be much richer and more diverse and the people would be that bit wilder and cut off from the outside world. It gave me butterflies to think of spending time in the Amazon. Not knowing the geography of the area in any detail, my dreams were restricted to what I did know. There was a ruddy great river that virtually crossed the whole continent from west to east, and . . . that was about it. I had heard of expeditions that had kayaked the entire river from source to sea

– phenomenal endurance feats taking five-plus months – the problem was I was a rubbish kayaker. Sure, I'd done a bit on the canals in England as a Cub Scout but that cold, depressing experience had been enough to put me off for life. What a dull, miserable sport, instructed by overenthusiastic dickheads in stupid helmets.

What I was experienced at, however, were expeditions on foot. After one long Land Rover journey I burst into the Patagonia field base alive with excitement; I was sure deep down that I'd stumbled upon a world first. 'Amazon walk' I typed in; 'source to sea Amazon'; 'Amazon expedition'. The minutes flew by.

I kept searching and searching and began to smile. Unless a trip to the Royal Geographical Society could prove otherwise, no one, in the history of mankind, had ever *walked* the length of the Amazon. This could just be a true remaining world first. I was hooked.

Back in Belize two years on, Luke's arrival in country and his announcement that he was having ideas about kayaking the same river had brought things to a head. I'd never put a timescale on my dream but I'd recently split up with Chloë and was, for the first time in a while, able to think independently without having to worry about, or compromise with, anyone else. I quickly pointed out to Luke that kayaking the Amazon had been done five times before and that a fat Slovenian bloke was currently swimming the low-altitude part of the river. I put forward my idea, a world first, all carried out on foot. Luke thought about it for five seconds. 'I'm in,' he grinned. 'Let's do it.'

We had no idea how long this would take us but we wanted it to be a year. That was manageable in our heads and so we divided 4,345 miles (the length of the river according to Washington's National Geographic Society) by 365 days and came up with the very plausible figure of eleven miles a day. Having spent most of our jungle time on paths and trails, Luke and I naively rejoiced in the fact that we'd be home in just twelve months. How neat and tidy.

Luke was thirty-five; I was thirty-one. Despite being very different characters we shared a slightly reckless desire to 'do something amazing' that ran deep in us. We both wanted to achieve something that we could look back on in future years and be proud of.

I could see that Luke was genuine in his desire to prove himself. He'd never joined the army – something I believed he slightly regretted – but he had led several expeditions since I'd known him and he was generally very well liked. Finding each other in a similar state, with such comparable expedition dreams, was surely some sort of sign. The coincidence was suggesting an exciting course to us and we each allowed ourselves to be easily swept up by the other's enthusiasm.

Luke lost his parents in his early twenties – both mother and father dying in rapid succession – so had needed to become pretty independent. He had 'found himself' when he saved enough money to travel to Australia but while he was away one of his two brothers also died. While in Australia he learned to juggle – everything from machetes to fire – and worked as a street entertainer. On return to the UK he had obtained several outdoor instructor qualifications and had become a keen climber. He had worked for several years in outdoor education for low pay but enjoyed his job. Using his skills he became an expedition leader in 2004, and by 2007 had led four three-month jungle expeditions – all to Belize – the last three to Davis Falls National Park. Luke had a serious girlfriend, Katie, and her family had become his family.

My life had been different. I was born to a sixteen-year-old single mother in the East Midlands and been adopted as a baby by Jeremy and Barbara Stafford. Apart from the fact that my dad had sporadic bad health, I would say we were as happy as any other family. The bits of my family upbringing that shaped me into an expedition leader are, first, that we lived in a small village so I grew up in the country; second, that my parents would encourage me and my sister to make our own decisions from an early age; and third, that my dad influenced us all by his firm conviction that if you say you are going to do something you have to try to do it, and you should not abandon it until you know you have given it your best shot. Dad pushed me into rugby and the Scouts and both had a big part in moulding my character. Their love for me was always evident and being adopted was never an issue or a problem.

My confidence grew when I realised I had a talent for playing rugby. I was six foot one at the age of thirteen and found that I could take the ball from the opposition and run through everyone. What a great sport, I thought, and this confidence spread to other aspects of my life. I left Stoneygate, my prep school, as a prefect and a very proud captain of rugby.

I also thrived in the world of Cubs and Scouts where I was introduced to camping, walking and the outdoors. They were based in a nearby town called Fleckney. My mum and dad both valued education highly and they managed to put my sister and me through private schools. The immersion into Cubs and Scouts was not only a great grounding; it was also a juxtaposition to my private education. Like rugby, outdoor life was something that I could just do. I loved learning the skills needed to live next to nature and become comfortable and competent outdoors. Although Fleckney was in some ways a bit rough, it wasn't geeky – we didn't sit round in a circle saying 'Dib, dib, dib!' and practising our knots. We played murderball, we built things and we made fire.

Boarding school at Uppingham was an experience that undoubtedly shaped my life, too. The school, still officially in mourning for Queen Victoria – boys dressed entirely in black – failed to look at what made many boys tick – and that included me. I soon became disenchanted and rebellious.

Teachers had no background in child psychology and apart from a very few notable exceptions were visibly bored with their secondary role of parenting the children as well as educating them. Each term was about twelve weeks long and I rarely saw my parents while I was there. The elder boys ran the house and 'educated' the younger ones in whatever eccentric manner they deemed right at the wise old age of seventeen. We were lucky enough not to be too physically bullied (that era had pretty much ended) but the environment was not conducive to a healthy, balanced upbringing. For a large part of the first year I, and many boys, lived in fear and confusion.

After nearly four years and predicted to do badly in my A levels, I was eventually expelled for a number of reasons, not least acts of minor vandalism. I have always thrived on danger and adrenaline and sneaking out of my boarding house armed with a wire saw and industrial bolt cutters to cause havoc seemed to be my main outlet at the time. It was completely misguided, of course, but perhaps understandable in an all-boys' boarding house that had a ten o'clock curfew and that failed to address the real needs of many of its students.

I believe strongly that the school mismanaged me and other boys like me. I still feel today that they had a responsibility, *in loco parentis*, to get to the bottom of my behaviour and harness my adventurous spirit rather than simply to label me as 'bad'.

After getting A grades at A level from Brooke House Sixth Form College in nearby Market Harborough, I went to Newcastle University and scraped an honours degree in geography despite living in a thick haze of marijuana for the first two of the three years. Repulsed by the cliquey university rugby team, where to have gone to the right school guaranteed you a place in the first XV, I joined Rockcliffe RFC, a local Geordie men's team in Whitley Bay and savoured the weekly dose of non-student life.

Now a graduate and terrified by the prospect of an office and a desk, I joined the British Army. This might sound an odd choice from someone who had had such an issue with boarding school, but I felt that I was capable of putting up with the regulations in return for a life that was physical and outdoors – a life that played to my strengths. I was always adamant that the military would not change me; I wanted to learn from it but I didn't want to become like so many of the pompous old idiots who had made it past the rank of major. The fear that people sometimes describe when they enter military barracks for the first time never really left me, and although I had some great individual moments in the army, mostly involving nights out in Tamworth, I never quite felt that I fitted in.

In 2002, after four relatively successful years, I'd made the rank of captain but was pleased that my contract was up for renewal and had decided I did not want to extend it. I said as much to my Commanding Officer at the end of a Northern Ireland tour to Crossmaglen, South Armagh. He smiled, recognised my decision was probably for the best (and no great loss to the battalion, I am sure), and so I went looking for civilian work.

After weeks of trying to network in the London financial sector I stumbled across an advert seeking expedition leaders to run conservation projects in Central America. This offered a three-month contract that I accepted; it allowed me to bide my time until the economy recovered and I stood a better chance of becoming a stockbroker. The experience changed my life more than any other: I fell in love with the adventure, the people and the lifestyle. This was outdoor living as a career without the regulations and inherent seriousness of the military. What's more, the whole thing had a purpose that I believed in – my days as a Scout meant that I had a deep affinity with nature and a real desire to conserve the rainforest. The combination of the two made me happier than I'd ever been and dreams of a Porsche 911 and fancy wine bars full of Essex girls slipped away.

*

Five years later, having led expeditions from that point onwards, I was now Country Director of Trekforce back in Belize. I started to plan how Luke and I were going to get this personal Amazon expedition off the ground. We made a list of the different areas that we had to work in. The checklist below gives an idea of all the things that had to come together if this was to work.

1. Research. We need to do enough to know that our trip is, in theory at least, physically possible.
2. Mission. What is the expedition's aim? Is this a purely selfish feat or do we have a deeper purpose to our journey?

3. Risk assessment. We need to evaluate the risks, highlight the dodgiest areas and actively work to make sure we aren't going to die.

4. Evacuation plan. If things go wrong how will we get to medical help or safety?

5. Training. We need to be at a competence level that is appropriate for the task. Are there any areas we should focus on where our ignorance is dangerous?

6. Languages. There are more than thirty languages spoken in Peru alone. We have to be able to converse in Spanish (Peru) and Portuguese (Brazil) at the very least to understand our surroundings and be in control of situations.

7. Accounts. We need to estimate the total cost of the expedition and account for all spending.

8. Fundraising. We need money to live while planning and organising in the UK and we need money for conducting the expedition itself. We need to try to get as many of the individual expenditures as possible sponsored (given to us for free or at a reduced cost) so that the overall monetary cost is reduced to the minimum.

9. Insurance. We need to find a package that is appropriate in the middle of the Amazon that covers our kit breaking or being stolen or lost as well as medical evacuation and treatment costs.

10. Communications. How will we communicate with the outside world? What will work under the jungle canopy? What if it breaks?

11. Website. This will be our shop window to sponsors, charities, the public, and everyone. It's also the way most people will experience the expedition.

12. Charities. Who do we want to help? How will we raise money? How do we work with these charities?

13. Permits and visas. Where do I start getting permits to allow us to visit indigenous tribes in Brazil who are autonomous and yet have a governmental department overseeing their welfare?

How do I legally stay in the two main countries longer than the normal three-month tourist visa?

14. Kit. We need to ensure we are taking the best kit we can find that will survive extended exposure to the humidity and wetness of the jungle and the extreme cold of the mountains. Everything from jungle boots to warm gloves, hammocks to kerosene stoves.

15. PR. How is anyone going to know about us? If no one does, how will we achieve our aims?

16. Filming. How will we record the journey? Where do we start to ensure that somebody someday might watch what we've filmed? Can we speak naturally in front of a camera?

17. Book. Where does one go to try to get a book deal? Can we write?

18. Guide. Can we find one who will walk with us for $7 a day and who speaks English, Spanish and, initially, Quechua?

19. Photography. How will we get great images that can be used to tell our story when we are both rubbish photographers?

By far the most important of the above tasks was getting the expedition funded. With sponsorship everything else would fall into place. Our back-to-nature dream would become a reality only if we addressed that most boring of modern-day worries: money.

As we attempted to put together a proposal document we realised that we needed the expedition to have a purpose for which it was worth giving up our lives. We immediately saw the scope for raising awareness of the need to conserve the rainforest. We would create a website and write regular blogs that adults and kids alike could read, following our adventure in real time. We could describe the rainforest day to day, and how it was taking its toll on us. We could engage people in their schools and offices so that they would start to feel they had a connection with the jungle. Neither of us wanted to be eco-warriors; we were aware that if we branded ourselves as such we might alienate the Brazilian authorities and have difficulty getting permits. So we didn't want a 'Take action now!' campaign, but what we thought we could do was educate and raise awareness. As soon as we discussed this it felt appropriate and worthwhile; we now had a cause worthy of giving up a year of our lives.

For this to be a Guinness World Record we had to be scrupulously strict. We would walk 100 per cent of the journey and never use a motor, a sail or even the flow of the river to propel us. Clearly we would have to cross bodies of water, and for that we would be in boats, but we knew from the outset that every metre of each crossing should be paddled by hand to make the journey truly human-powered.

We also saw the scope for raising money directly for charities. We wanted a rainforest conservation charity as it made sense, as an umbrella charity that was in line with the main mission of the expedition: Rainforest Concern fitted the bill. My dad had died of cancer a few years earlier and my sister had (and still has) ME, so Cancer Research UK and the ME Association were two more charities that I wanted to help as well. Finally, we wanted to select charities that would benefit the host nations, so we found two UK-based children's charities, Project Peru and Action for Brazil's Children, which would mean we could give something back to the countries we passed through without upsetting governments by backing strongly anti-deforestation organisations.

I don't ever want to pretend that the charities and rainforest awareness were the reasons why we chose to walk the Amazon. These were things that we believed in, that were worthy, but the initial drive was far more selfish: the adventure, the challenge and the recognition were at the core of our motivation when we set out. The nice thing was that the adventure was essential for the other parts to work. A nice safe walk that had been done before wouldn't have attracted any media attention and therefore wouldn't have had the same potential for doing good. Equally, we also saw that carrying out the journey for purely selfish reasons was empty and pointless. The selfish and non-selfish goals weren't just compatible; they ended up being essential to each other.

Carried away by our excitement, we thought that this might

make a good documentary so I got in touch with the only person I knew in television, Craig Langman. Craig is a softly spoken bloke who often takes a back seat among more forceful characters. What he does say, however, is all the more worth listening to as a result. 'Of course you are completely crazy,' Craig said, 'I love it. It will make great TV.' He agreed to help us find a production company which could partner with us in the making of a documentary.

Permits and visas were the next thing I looked into and at the time both Peru and Brazil normally gave out only three-month tourist visas. I wrote to Mike Horn, the South African adventurer who had descended the Amazon on a hydrospeed and later in a dugout canoe, to find out what he'd done. His wife kindly wrote back:

> Dear Ed,
>
> Thanks for your mail. We have found it best not to speak too much about your expeditions to the consulates and embassies. Get all your visas as is necessary through the usual methods and take the necessary safety precautions ie global tracking device, satellite phone etc. The authorities do not know how to handle anything out of the norm! All the very best for your adventure!
>
> Best regards,
> Cathy

Such wise words from Cathy and, looking back on it, I wish I'd taken her advice to the letter. But at the time I was adamant that we needed to be above board because, unlike Mike, Cathy's husband, we already had commitments to charities and I felt that, to be safe and insured, we had to be 100 per cent onside with the law in each country.

I contacted the embassies and consulates and started a long and tortuous journey to try to get us extended cultural visas that would cover nine months in Peru and a further nine in Brazil. This would allow buffer time if our journey took more than six months in each country, which I was already beginning to think it might.

Convincing companies that you are worth giving kit to without paying for it isn't easy. We were two balding nobodies who were planning an expedition far bigger than either of us had ever attempted before. The chance that the company would see any return on this 'sponsorship' deal was slim and so we wrote endless emails to very little effect.

I thought one piece of kit that I'd seen used in Patagonia would make a perfect transition to the jungle. Inflatable pack rafts are one-man boats designed to be light enough to carry in your backpack. We knew there would be hundreds of tributaries to cross and so we had to have a workable strategy. Alpacka rafts are made in Canada and so I emailed them asking if they could help. Their response was kind: they had some superficially damaged rafts that they could let us have for US$300 each. This saved us $475 per raft, which I thought was a great deal, and it was the first positive response we'd received. I bought three on my credit card – one for Luke, one for me and one for a theoretical local guide. Hennessy Hammocks then agreed to give us two free hammock systems and Altberg gave us a couple of pairs of handmade jungle boots. Each one of these small sponsorship deals gave us great satisfaction; we were inching closer to making the trip happen.

Despite the success and the accumulation of a bit of kit, however, we were now a couple of grand in the red. We really needed a financial sponsor.

Still planning from Belize at this stage, I received a cautious email from Rainforest Concern:

> Firstly, we want to make sure that we are not encouraging you to do something which is excessively risky to your personal wellbeing. You have backgrounds in expeditions, but we would like to meet you to discuss this further. You have already listed the kind of dangers we would have envisaged, but equally I am sure you can expect progress to be painfully slow on occasion.
>
> Secondly, there is the impact of your hunting to eat. Fishing is one method you might be planning and we would probably be comfortable

with that. However, the hunting of mammals and birds is not
something we would want to encourage for unessential endeavour.
This is something we will need to discuss.

The third question is your potential contact with indigenous people
as this is not always to their end benefit.

All these points were very sensible and the expedition began to take shape as we drew up a no-hunting policy and we started to formulate a plan as to how we would carry food and resupply at settlements along the way. Both Luke and I glossed over the question of indigenous people as we had very little experience in dealing with them and could only come up with the rather feeble 'We are nice people and we will treat everybody with respect'. How naive we were.

Our deployment date from the very beginning had been 1 January 2008. It would give us enough time to prepare, we could spend Christmas with our families, and on paper it seemed like a good solid date. We contacted a Peruvian mountaineering company and they firmly advised us to avoid walking in the Andes between December and March: it would be winter, snow would be heavy and the swollen rivers and gorges might be impassable.

Bugger.

Neither one of us was very experienced above the snowline and so the idea of 'crossing the Andes' was formidable enough without our electing to do it in winter. So we put back the start date to 1 April 2008 to ensure that our time at over 5,000 metres was as comfortable as we could make it. At the back of my mind I already had suspicions that the expedition could take more than a year, so the chances were that we were going to have to endure at least one Amazonian flood season anyway.

It was now May 2007 and Luke and I were becoming good friends, having been very amicable colleagues before, with a strong collective purpose of getting this expedition off the ground.

Despite all our work trying to ensure that we had kit, a purpose and permits, the fact still remained that no one in the world of expeditions we had spoken to could be convinced that it was in fact possible to walk the entire length of the river. The main reason for this was that the Amazon is characterised by a very shallow basin that is prone to enormous flooding. The river regularly bursts its banks and water enters the forest up to 70 kilometres from the main channel. This means that the forest adjacent to the river is flooded above head height for large parts of the year. Not great for walking.

In my simple mind I knew this and thought that we could just handrail the river at a distance that was safe enough away from the main channel. The trouble was, there was no way of knowing the extent of the flooded forest in each area so I scoured the Internet for more information. I eventually stumbled on a very low-resolution image that seemed to show the flooded forest as a different colour from terra firma or solid ground. The image was credited to Bruce Chapman at NASA and so I emailed Bruce to see if he would share his data. Two days later a CD-ROM came through the post at no charge with fantastic images of the entire Amazon basin at high and low water. NASA's project enabled me to effectively see through the canopy from above and get an overview of the extent of the flooded area at peak flood season.

This was a big breakthrough. With this data I would be able to annotate the maps when they arrived and we could plan our route to avoid the worst of the flooded areas. OK, the images were from 1995 but the topography wouldn't have changed too much since then – just a few river-shape changes. We had a workable plan.

We still had the flooded forest adjacent to each of the tributaries that we needed to cross to contend with – that was unavoidable – but now we could use NASA's imagery to cross rivers at points where the floodwaters were at their narrowest. In such circum-stances, we would just have to inflate the pack rafts and advance through the forest in them, with machetes in hand, if the water was too deep for us to walk through. The thought of cutting through undergrowth from our inflatable rafts both scared and excited us. We envisaged nights spent in hammocks above the water and even designed ideas for fire trays in which we could light fires in the crooks of trees above the murky water.

People go to the jungle all the time; in fact, several million people live in the Amazon Basin. The Amazon River is well populated and therefore good for resupplying food and broken gear. There is substantial traffic on the river and so if we had an emergency it would afford our natural exit strategy. These were all positives but our problem was that, once we pushed away from the main river channel to avoid the flooding, all the previously manageable dangers would now be amplified. If we went where there are no people then we had to fend for ourselves. In places, self-evacuation would be long and hard and on conventional risk assessment came out as simply 'unacceptable'. With no helicopters in many areas and no rescue teams, we just had to make the decision that if we wanted to do this journey we had to accept the risks. Thus, an injury or illness that needed urgent medical care, such as appendicitis, snakebite or a serious head wound, would probably be fatal.

Luke had his first success with kit sponsorship when, at the end of May, he got Macpac to come on board and sponsor us for tents and backpacks. This meant a lot to Luke as he'd not been able to designate as much time as I had to the expedition planning due to his work commitments to Outward Bound in the Lake District.

In order to raise money to fund the trip we felt there was a need to increase the expedition's publicity, too. Sponsors would be more impressed if they saw that we were getting at least some coverage in the press. The trouble was that we had no pictures at all of Luke and me together in the jungle. So we piled into a car with my brother-in-law-to-be, Jeremy, and headed to the Eden Centre's humid tropics biome in Cornwall for some 'authentic' jungle shots.

For several hours Luke and I felt very conspicuous standing on the wrong side of the rope amidst the tropical ferns and palms as Jeremy snapped away and every now and then reminded us to smile. Some old ladies with blue rinses decided that, as we were being photographed, we must be famous and we were asked to sign some autographs.

On 1 June 2007 I went up to London to see Ben Major, an old mate from my time leading expeditions in Belize and Borneo. We met for lunch at a coffee shop inside the BBC Television Centre where Ben was now working as a presenter on a children's TV series. He had promised me some maps of Peru from the BBC stores but they were of limited use and provided only a tiny fraction of the fifty-two Peruvian maps I actually needed. I was slightly disappointed but then Ben mentioned a company that might be able to give us some remote medical training (which I definitely needed) so the meeting wasn't a complete waste of time.

While we were having lunch Ben paused.

'Ed – have you ever been to Guyana?'

'No, Ben.'

'Do you know how to set up an HF radio?'

'No, mate, I don't.'

'Have you ever worked with a film crew?'

'You know I haven't, you cock.'

'Do you fancy working for the BBC on a new expedition series as their jungle base camp manager?'

'Let me think about that for a split second . . .' I grinned.

Ben had been offered the job but couldn't take it as he had another children's series to present. He got me the interview at the BBC's Natural History Unit in Bristol and, hardly able to see, having had laser surgery on both eyes the day before, I was interviewed by the series producer, Steve Greenwood. We got on well, Steve was fascinated by the corrective surgery that I'd just had, and within two days I was on the team. I had never done TV work before but it was all behind the camera and they were just looking for someone who could go into Guyana and manage a team of Amerindians for two months in the construction of a remote jungle base camp. Then, when the crew arrived, I was to manage the local guys and ensure that the camp didn't run out of aviation fuel or toilet paper. A three-month contract and a dream job for an ex-army expedition leader – I could do that.

Leading conservation expeditions pays peanuts so the BBC wage was more than I'd earned in years. Luke understood I'd be silly to turn it down. We were seven months away from our Amazon departure date and if I did this series I'd make enough money to enable me not to have to work for the four months immediately preceding our trip. I'd have enough to rent a flat in London where I needed to be to meet potential sponsors and to pay for my living costs. The negative was that it meant leaving all the preparations and fundraising to Luke while I was away.

Meanwhile, Luke organised a meeting with the medical company Ex-Med, and we both travelled over to Hereford, in search of some advice on what to carry in our medical kits and hoping to organise some basic tropical medicine training. Knowing that the guys we would meet were all very experienced military guys meant that Luke and I were pretty respectful as we knocked on the door. Ged Healy, the director, answered.

As we introduced ourselves Ged said, 'Hi, Ed, you're off out to Guyana with the BBC next month aren't you?' Slightly taken aback – and impressed – I confirmed that I was. They had already done their homework on us.

We were led into a room in which there was a half-burned United Nations flag framed on the wall. Luke started giggling and, as he pointed out the brass plaque inscribed with 'Herat, Western Region, Afghanistan, 2004' , I could feel the blood rushing to my face – what were the chances of this?

'Shut up, Luke!' I prayed silently.

'You've got a story about that flag, haven't you, Ed?' Luke chirped as Ged looked on stony-faced.

'What's that, Ed?' asked Ged.

Fuck. With no other option, I launched into one of the most self-deprecating stories of my career. I had been working in Herat in 2004 advising the UN during the run-up to the first-ever presidential elections. I was based in a UN compound in the centre of the city when Ismail Khan, the warlord who was in power in Herat, was removed from office by the American ambassador. As was common in these times the local Afghan population decided to riot and the

UN buildings with their high walls and their light-blue signs outside were obvious targets.

I went out into the compound with a Zimbabwean consultant called Mugs, a vet from the Rhodesian Army. Mugs was a lovely old boy who had seen a lot in his time and was in Afghanistan to make a living to support his family, something that was becoming increasingly difficult to do for a white man living in Zimbabwe.

At first we stood by and watched as the crowd pounded on the huge metal vehicle gates from outside. Then rocks started to rain in on us in the inner compound. This was nothing unusual and so we calmly kept an eye out for missiles that might hit us. Then the missiles turned in to petrol bombs and various parts of the building caught fire.

The fire, visible to the rioting crowd outside, fuelled their frenzy and the pounding on the gates grew more violent and sustained. When a bright UN worker drove a UN 4x4 up against the vehicle gates to stop them bursting inwards, in a thick Zimbabwean accent Mugs turned to me and said, 'Someone should do the same with that pedestrian gate. That's going to go any minute.'

I agreed – someone should. Neither of us acted for what must have been over a minute. We just watched and then, sure enough, the small metal gate exploded inwards and the furious, crazed crowd rushed in brandishing metal bars and petrol bombs.

Unarmed we had no option but to escape down into the basement behind another metal gate where the UN workers had retreated earlier. From the open gates we could see the computers from the electoral planning centre being looted and carried out into the street.

The building was now burning all around us and above us, and if we didn't act we would all be burned to death in the basement. We requested an escort from the nearby US military base and fairly soon two Hummers arrived and forced their way through the angry crowd and into the compound. With one Hummer at the front and one at the rear, all the UN workers and consultants piled into the white vehicles and formed a long convoy. I was driving a white UN

4×4 as we sped up the ramp from the basement through the seething crowd.

This was the first time I'd driven in Afghanistan and I knew that, if I stopped or stalled, the crowd would descend on the vehicle and we would be at their mercy. After time in Northern Ireland as an occupying force, I knew what that potentially meant.

We wound the windows down to stop shattering glass from spraying all over us and we were stoned relentlessly as we sped through the crowd. Rocks entered the vehicle, cutting the arm that was covering my head. People had to jump out of the way of the vehicle at the last minute as I drove like a maniac through the lawless streets.

As the gate was shut behind us in the US military base, the adrenaline started to subside. Reports came back over the radio from the military units on the ground that many of the UN buildings in the city had been burned to the ground.

Mugs and I could not look each other in the eye from that day onwards. Our inaction had caused a catastrophe. Ex-Med had had a medic in the same compound as us and he'd grabbed the burning flag before evacuating the building. And that was what I was now staring at in a meeting in which it had been my intention to impress Ged with how professional and experienced Luke and I were. Christ.

But Ged didn't react at all, leaving me with absolutely no idea what he really felt. As the conversation turned to our expedition, he questioned us about some basic practices. What hammocks would we use? What about water purification methods? What boots did we have in mind? He was testing us – trying to find out if we were competent enough to attempt an expedition such as this.

At a certain point he was clearly satisfied and he asked us what we were after. I told him my wish list and he started to tell us what he could provide. He offered to do a complete disease profile on the Amazon Basin, making up specialist kits for us, and then talk us through what they included. Great, we thought, but we can't afford that sort of service. Ged asked how much money we had for medical kits: £500 each we said. Fine, then we'll do it for that. Slightly bemused, Luke and I both started to glow internally. Amazingly, Ged seemed to be onside.

He moved on to training. We wanted a couple of days of general stuff to help us get out of a tricky situation. Ged offered a five-day intensive trauma course and then a three-day tropical medicine course, too. Our tiny budget in mind, I told Ged that we couldn't possibly afford courses like this. Once again, Ged asked how much we had and we told him. 'We'll do it all for that amount,' he said. Luke and I were pretty dumbfounded at this stage.

He then asked if we had a physician on twenty-four-hour call in case we needed advice. Clearly we had not. He then proceeded to offer this service, too – for free.

Finally, Ged said, 'If you two get in real trouble and you can't move for medical help – what are you going to do?' Luke and I started to churn out our answer about that being one of the inherent risks of the expedition; that we wouldn't have a solution and we accepted that there was a greater risk of death.

'What about if we have a four-man ex-military squad that is on sixteen hours' notice to move that would fly out to any grid reference that you send to us?'

'That would be good,' we stammered, 'but, again, we can't afford that level of support.' Ged told us about an insurance company they had dealings with that, for a price, would include this four-man quick-reaction team in the package.

The meeting came to its natural conclusion and we thanked Ged and his partner and left, still somewhat bemused. We went straight to the pub in Hereford for a celebratory pint. Ex-Med had offered us a tailored medical kit, extensive training, constant medical advice for the entire journey and an insurance package that included the best trained remote medics in the world coming in and getting us out of the shit. We could hardly believe our luck. Grinning inanely, we drank our beers in the knowledge that our amateur expedition had just got a whole lot safer in one short meeting.

On 3 August 2007 I flew to Guyana. The programme was called *Lost Land of the Jaguar* and it was a privilege to work alongside the local Amerindians and the very down-to-earth BBC Natural History Unit team.

My role was to make sure the camp was built for the crew and that the locals were well managed. When the crew came in I became the natural link between the locals and the crew and managed the day-to-day running of the camp.

I returned to England in late October after three months with renewed vigour, ready to tackle the final preparations for walking the Amazon, and I now had the money to rent a room in London. Things hadn't moved on much since I'd left but now I would be where things happened and could sink my teeth into getting the expedition off the ground.

But despite overriding feelings about the expedition still being positive, I started to experience occasional waves of worry. The worry was not about being killed by previously uncontacted tribes or being smashed into rocks while crossing a tributary; it was about not finding a sponsor, not getting our extended visas and not raising enough money for charity.

Although these worries were very real, I had been through enough stressful periods in my life to believe that, just by sticking at it and biding my time, something positive would happen to make our run of good fortune continue.

I moved in with an old mate, James Wakefield. He had a spare room in his Stockwell flat and I set up my office in the attic. I started working in earnest on getting the visas and permits sorted.

In November 2007 Luke and I took part in the Royal Geographical Society's Explore weekend. It wasn't aimed at people like Luke or me but we took the opportunity to network and as a direct result AST agreed to sponsor us and give us two BGAN satellite internet links. Now we had communications – not just satellite phones but broadband internet links that we could use in the jungle. These units were so good that later in the expedition I would use them to do live streamed video interviews with CNN broadcast to 240 international territories. Each was roughly the weight of a hardback book.

Despite all this good fortune the bottom line was that we needed a financial sponsor so badly that if one didn't come in we would have to cancel the expedition. I hated begging companies for money and I wasn't very good at it either. I wrote to hundreds of companies explaining why aligning themselves with Luke and me would be fantastic for their business. I didn't believe it myself and so, not surprisingly, I had no takers. I felt that I should be making more personal calls so I started to feel guilty that I was wasting my time and that, because of my lack of action, the expedition would fail before it had even started.

At 10.30 p.m. on 13 December I was sitting on the couch with my flatmate James watching *Top Gear* and smoking flavoured tobacco through a hookah when the phone rang.

'Ed, would you like to go shooting tomorrow?'

It was an old friend, Saul Shanagher, a pleasantly eccentric individual who was formerly an officer in the Irish Guards.

'Clays?' I enquired, pretending to know what I was talking about.

'No – pheasants,' said Saul. At this point I had that feeling I often get when I envisage a social situation in which I know I am going to be out of my depth and uncomfortable.

'Saul, I'm not posh, I've never shot pheasants before,' I whined, trying to get out of it.

'Well, you've got a tweed jacket, haven't you? And green wellies?' Saul's tone suggested they were standard items in every respectable gentleman's wardrobe.

'Of course I haven't,' I said. 'I've got a hooded sweatshirt, ripped jeans and a pair of Nike trainers.'

'Well, borrow some then, and I'll pick you up tomorrow at six.' The phone went dead.

Luckily, James had been in the army, too, but he was a conventional officer who, unlike me, had collected the full line of appropriate clothing for such occasions. He kindly lent me a tweed jacket, some moleskin trousers and a pair of green wellies. Lifesaver.

Even if I was going to feel out of place I would at least look as if I belonged there. Well, apart from the shaven head and stubble.

The shoot started as I had feared it would: lots of wealthy, highly successful men who worked in the City gathering for a day of backslapping and bragging about the lengths of their barrels. Saul is a good mate, though, and these were his friends and business associates and so I made the effort to get on with everyone. As so often in such circumstances, when you do make the effort and genuinely try to get on with people, the barriers come down and you end up enjoying yourself. They were nice people, of course – they just lived in a different world from me.

The first 'drive' was embarrassing – I didn't hit a thing. 'This is going to be painful,' I thought as we all stood in a circle discussing how many birds we had hit. I feigned the nonchalance of someone who was just there for the laugh and didn't care if I hit anything. I did, of course – I was pissed off.

The change came in the second shoot. I had been assigned a beater to act as a coach and he got me to move the barrel of the gun with the bird, saying, 'Tail, body, beak, bang!' It was a magic formula. I hit bird after bird and, as cruel as it may seem, I enjoyed it. What a feeling to see the feathers burst like a firework and the bird stop in its tracks and drop to the ground with a thud. Bang – I had hit another. Bang – another. This was incredible – I was shocked at how my primal instincts for hunting had come alive. By the time the second drive was finished I had shot nine birds and was brimming with cockiness.

At lunchtime we adjourned to a large manor house where a fantastic meal was served and the red wine was flowing. I was relaxed enough to talk freely about my upcoming expedition and, because it was a quite adventurous and male subject, my companions were receptive to and interested in what I was doing.

At the end of the day everybody said, 'Bloody good day!' to each other, shook hands vigorously, slung their brace of birds into their respective car boots and departed. Before we went our separate ways, one of them pulled me to one side: 'Ed – great to meet you. I didn't want to say anything in the house with the others listening, but your expedition is exactly the sort of thing that my company would be interested in sponsoring. Here is my card. Call me next week.'

'Fuck me!' I thought to myself. 'Did I hear that right?' It was nothing definite, but he had actually approached me to offer me money!

Within a month we had the money and the expedition was 100 per cent paid for and I was feeling like the luckiest man on earth. A guilty day of bunking off expedition fundraising and shooting pheasants had turned into the most profitable day of the year. Luke and I were going to the Amazon courtesy of Jonathan 'Long Barrel' Stokes and his company JBS Associates. It ain't what you know . . .

We did our excellent medical training at Ex-Med and we bought far too much kit with our newfound wealth. We paid for the inordinately expensive insurance (that included the Ex-Med quick reaction team) and we booked our flights. With the Guyana money now gone, we ran up a big bill on my credit card. It was mostly alcohol. We partied hard like men about to go to war and our physical training was completely neglected. Luke got engaged to his girlfriend. We boarded the plane to Peru on 1 March 2008 with overflowing bags, bloodshot eyes and several chins between us.

The Amazon beckoned. Were we prepared for what lay ahead? The stresses, the dangers, the hard work and the adversity? I don't think we had a clue. We hoped we were, worried a bit, then had another drink.

Chapter Two

The Search for the Source of the Amazon

On the plane out of Europe we hid our nerves below our usual self-deprecating humour but, deep down, I think we both realised we'd committed to doing something that would push us further than we'd ever been pushed in our lives. If you believed the experts, we had a good chance of dying. Thinking about the expedition in its entirety could make us both distinctly edgy and stressed and so we focused on more tangible specifics and details, ignoring the ominous shadow of the whole.

We visited some of the major cities along the route by boat and by plane in order to make some contacts (police, expats, local government) and to drop off supplies that we could use when we eventually walked back through. We finally arrived in Lima, Peru's capital, in late March and with the help of a very friendly English-speaking Peruvian called Marlene managed to acquire fifty-two maps from the National Geographical Institute of Peru and two nine-month extended visas (that later turned out to be illegal) from the Ministry of Interior. We waved the lovely Marlene goodbye from the rear window of an overnight bus and adjusted the seats to near horizontal. Our morning destination was to be the coastal holiday town of Camaná from where we intended to start walking from the Pacific Ocean, up and over the Andes in search of the furthest source of the Amazon.

Full of diazepam and having slept for about twelve hours, I awoke to Luke digging me in the ribs and pointing out of the window. Through drug-hazed eyes we gazed with overt amusement and covert apprehension at what proved to be a slight oversight on our part. The sun was still low in the sky, casting long shadows across endless sand dunes. 'Have you ever been to the desert before, Ed?' chuckled Luke as we both started to mock our own incompetence. 'Perhaps we should take a hat,' I suggested, 'some sun screen, too, and maybe a bottle of water.' There wasn't a shrub in sight.

In Camaná we checked into a large pink concrete hotel with an empty swimming pool. No Westerner ever came here – it may have been a tourist destination at one point, but by March 2008 I doubt that anyone would have wanted to spend their precious vacation in this dusty outpost. That evening I couldn't resist going down to the water's edge and seeing the Pacific Ocean, where we would physically start. I can't remember why, but Luke didn't come with me. I got a mototaxi the four kilometres and asked it to wait for me while I took in every detail of the dirty, stony beach, the sewage outlet from the town and the flocks of gulls and vultures.

Drabness aside, I became quite emotional. I was here, at the start of our journey, after years of dreaming and fifteen months of planning. Looking inland, though, I was more than a little apprehensive about the barren hills that loomed behind the town in a haze of dust. I decided to go back to the hotel and study our new maps to see if we were going to be able to follow a watercourse all the way through the desert and up into the Andes.

In general whenever I allowed myself to think about the journey as a whole I could get myself worked up in seconds: partly over-excited about the sheer adventure, partly overwhelmed by what we'd confidently claimed was possible.

First, we needed to meet up with Oz. We had decided initially to walk without a guide. Because of me being ex-military and both of us being expedition leaders we decided we were quite capable of conducting this trip ourselves. But the closer the journey came the more I started debating about whether my Spanish was really good enough, and what I was going to do when we came to settlements in the Andes where only Quechua was spoken, not to mention the other thirty-two languages we might expect in Peru alone. Luke had only a few words of Spanish. Before we had left, a friend had put us in touch with a young Peruvian called Oswaldo Teracaya Rosaldo. Oz was an aspiring guide, twenty-four years old, and he reportedly spoke good Quechua, Spanish and English. Over two short emails I negotiated a wage of seven American dollars a day (bartered up from five) and told him to meet us in Camaná on 30 March 2008. Electronically, at least, we had a guide.

Having lived in Argentine Patagonia, I'd worked with many South American mountain guides before. I was imagining a real character who stood tall and tanned with rugged stubble, a weathered face of experience and a sharp wit. The boy who turned up was stick-thin, had a pudding-basin haircut and was nervously overpolite to the point that his character was invisible. Dressed in a red England football shirt and red nylon tracksuit bottoms, he had virtually no kit and as little English. I took a deep breath and looked for the positives. My Spanish was better than his English so that meant we'd end up speaking in Spanish, and as a consequence mine would improve. Luke spoke to Oz mostly in English – using me as a translator for all but the most basic communication.

We sent Oz out with a fistful of money to buy himself a jacket and some boots. He had worked with that friend of mine the year previously and so I was still fairly confident he would know what he was doing. He returned with a fake leather racing driver's jacket with mock sponsors' badges sewn all over it. It was hilarious, neither waterproof nor warm: I started to wonder just how much mountain experience this boy had.

Luke and I divided the communal kit between the three of us and we watched as Oz stuffed everything into the new canoe bag that we'd given him to keep his kit dry and then tried to force that heavy lump into his backpack. Luke and I looked at each other, worried. You only have to attempt this impossible feat once to realise how absurd it is. He didn't even know how to pack his bag so Luke stepped forward and tactfully gave him a few pointers.

In truth, although things weren't perfect I wasn't too worried. All we really needed was someone who spoke Quechua and who we could communicate with. We had that and we could teach Oz the skills he needed to walk with us. Most importantly, he was keen and excited about this new venture. It had been quite a courageous step for him to travel at his own cost to the coast of Peru to meet two foreigners and so I decided that Oz was OK – and that we were lucky to have a Peruvian to walk with.

On April Fool's Day, the day we'd decided – bizarrely – to leave, we were not ready. We'd not cut the maps down or made many of the last-minute tweaks that were necessary. Over eggs for breakfast we decided to delay our departure by a day, give ourselves some more time and leave, composed, the following day.

On the morning of 2 April we came down to breakfast, this time with our huge rucksacks. It was the first time we'd carried them with ten days of food in each one and we were shocked by the weight. We didn't have scales at the time but, on reflection, I would say they were about 48–50 kilograms. Oz's was less because he and his pack were a lot smaller, but his must have been close to 35 kilograms. Anyone who has hiked with a backpack will know that this weight is clearly daft, especially if you are planning a year-long (or longer) walk across an entire continent.

We knew all this but the problem was that we'd fallen into the trap of thinking about this as an eighteen-month expedition rather than a three-week walk up to Nevado Mismi. We had committed to blogging – which meant a Macbook, a BGAN and a digital camera apiece. We had two tracking devices that were designed to update our position automatically on the website's map – both about the size and weight of a household brick. We wanted to film a documentary so we both carried an HD video camera, five spare batteries, forty mini DV tapes and a basic cleaning kit. We had been given a day and a half's training in how to film by Ginger TV. We were writing a book, so we had several waterproof 'Rite in the Rain' journals and special all-weather pens. We wanted to be able to do radio interviews and to have the ability to make emergency calls, so we had a second BGAN with spare battery and a telephone ancillary to make it work as a satellite phone.

Every bit of electrical kit had a charger; most had cables to connect one to the other. Each piece of kit was in individual rubber dry bags with handfuls of silica sachets to combat moisture.

This was all apart from the kit we needed to do the walk, such as tents, clothes and navigation equipment. Every opportunity or idea that had been put to us we'd agreed to. 'What's another 800 grams?' we had smiled innocently. It added up to a phenomenal weight and we were now reeling at what we had committed to doing.

We said goodbye to the hotel and went out into the street to flag down two mototaxis to ferry us down to the beach. I went ahead with two of the packs in the first taxi while Luke and Oz followed in the next with the remaining pack. I was brimming with excitement and even the weight of the packs couldn't stop me from feeling the sheer exuberance of starting our adventure.

We were here. We did our 'final thoughts' interviews to the camera, and waded into the ocean in our jungle boots to make the journey a true crossing of the entire continent on foot.

Ocean behind us, we walked up the beach, feet sinking into the pebbles under the immense weight and started to exchange looks with each other. We were panting after 100 metres; after 400 we were shattered. We had to walk four kilometres back to Camaná to get to the start of the river that snaked up through the hills and as we approached the town again the sun was already high overhead. We were conscious of everybody pointing at us – the size of our packs was the spectacle – and we tried to walk nonchalantly as if we always did this sort of thing and waved at the laughing masses. As we reached the hotel I had the idea that we could upload the footage of the start and a blog from the hotel's wireless internet while we still had the luxury of electricity.

Utterly exhausted, and in a slight state of shock, it was an excuse that we all leaped at and by the time we'd dumped our packs we thought it was silly not to have lunch there, too. We blogged over lunch and at about two in the afternoon the sun was unbearable outside. 'Shall we stay here another night and leave tomorrow?' I ventured. Again the suggestion was taken up, albeit somewhat sheepishly, as we'd hoped to get well out of Camaná on day one and we'd only done the four kilometres from the beach. We ordered a beer.

'Tomorrow,' I told myself, 'we'll wake up with our expedition heads on.' We had precious little idea of what really lay ahead and it felt now as if we were dithering. We had packed food for ten days – would we need that much or would we need more? Would there be shops ahead? We had a handful of scanty descriptions from various locals but we weren't too bothered. The unknown was part of the thrill.

The following morning we packed again and left the air-conditioned hotel for the last time. We'd decided that we'd start in the dark as we'd felt guilty about the previous day's efforts and our packs actually felt manageable as we strode through the empty streets in the cool early hours of the morning.

The day took us clear of Camaná and immediately into a wide dusty valley with a small river and an equally dusty road to follow inland. We took a break on the hour for ten minutes and kept going as the day grew hotter and hotter and our packs seemed heavier and heavier, the straps cutting into our unconditioned shoulders. There is no doubt at all we weren't fit, but my take on it was that we would surely get fit fairly quickly.

On the map we spotted a village that we wanted to reach on our first night so we put our heads down and walked. Late in the afternoon we arrived at the dusty settlement, receiving strange outsider looks from locals. Half-closed doors quietly shut and children ran away. We asked if there was a shop and were pointed in the direction of a small mud and stick house which sold fizzy pop and sugary biscuits. We drank litres of the cheap colourful fluid and asked the short, kind shopkeeper if she knew of somewhere we could stay.

'*Claro que si!*' she smiled. 'You can put your tents up in our backyard.' She led us back through the dark shop into a fenced-off compound with chickens and livestock.

I think because it was the first example of such generosity this night particularly stuck in my mind. It was exactly how I'd hoped the walk would be; turn up in a place, meet some kind people and stay with them in whatever they had to offer. This first night was a yard full of pigs and chickens and we erected our three small one-man tents. We were utterly shattered from our first day of walking and so decided that we should attempt to shed some weight from our packs.

The lady and her family thus received English novels, bird guides, binoculars, a machete, a compass, spare clothes, daysacks, fishing kit, batteries, extra knives and much more. I was embarrassed at the amount of kit we had brought 'just in case' and it made me realise we'd allowed the magnitude of the expedition to get to us. The family, however, were clearly thrilled and argued good-naturedly over who would get what.

The next day we packed up our tents, and our packs were noticeably lighter, perhaps now around 42 kilograms each for Luke and me. Again we slogged through the midday heat but were struggling pathetically, sweat pouring off us, not making much progress. Luke's watch was showing readings of 50 degrees Celsius in the direct sunlight. His boots were too small and he had already developed quite big blisters so he had no option but to switch to wearing his Crocs (plastic sandals).

The majority of the first week was over flat terrain but the heat and the weight took their toll on us physically. The Majes Valley was wide and fertile and our initial worries about the desert were so far unjustified. The river itself was ice-cold as it was fed straight from the glaciers of the Andes and we trekked through fields of green crops surrounded by brown, dusty mountains.

Then we reached what seemed to be the end of the road. The river was wide and strong and cut right across the valley floor. We had no rafts with us as we'd put them in storage in Cusco when we'd entered South America, ready for the jungle, and so our way forward seemed blocked. However, an old man appeared as if on cue and instructed us to follow him. He led us up the steep valley side following a narrow path along its wall and the drop to our left was both steep and close. We hadn't really quizzed the man as to how long this detour would take from the valley bottom and he just kept on climbing. Then he turned, pointed us vaguely in a direction up the valley, and headed back to his village. Aware we had been led into something of a situation, we had no option but to attempt to follow the faint path as the light started to fade.

Head torches came out soon after 6 p.m. and we were stumbling our way through the dark in search of the next elusive settlement. Poor Oz only had a windup torch that we had bought back in England. We laughed at each other to hide the fact that we were all quite nervous about finding a flat place to camp with water. The valley side was loose with rocks and we dislodged several to send them crashing down the hillside. If one of us had fallen from the path we would have been in serious trouble as the drop to our left was precipitous and the path was no more than a thin goats' track contouring along the steep valley side. Behind me I could hear a sporadic whirring as Oz wound up his torch.

We continued with a feeling of annoyance that we'd let ourselves get into this situation until eventually we started to descend and then heard a dog barking in the distance. We looked into the gloom and saw a dim twinkling light. As we approached the remote dwelling we all hoped that the people would be kind and let us put our tents up.

I later found out it's generally not advisable to turn up at places after dark in rural Peru as people are far more suspicious of those who travel at night. Meanwhile, I approached a house and as warmly as possible called 'Buenas noches!' – good evening. An old woman came out and asked us who we were and what we were doing. When we explained she said that some other backpackers had just come through here – surely we must know them. 'How long ago was it?' we asked. 'About two years ago,' she replied.

Not only did she and her son allow us to erect our tents on a pitch of dirt outside, but they also invited us to sit around their fire inside their tin-roofed shack. We were handed large mugs of a hot, sweet liquid that was wonderful to drink after our anxious evening on the cliff in the dark. I asked, genuinely fascinated, what the incredible fluid was that I was drinking. The woman smiled back: 'Tea.'

We were then given huge plates of freshwater shrimps cooked in garlic and butter. They had harvested them that day and Luke, Oz and I wolfed them down with elated disbelief in our eyes. 'Muchas gracias!' we repeated over and over. After the meal we put our tents up in the dark and crawled into our sleeping bags with that perfect combination of real tiredness mixed with a full belly and the relief of being in a safe place. We slept well that night under a blanket of warm, generous hospitality.

That same blanket was rather snatched away from our stiff corpses in the morning when Oswaldo translated the enormous bill that the lady expected us to pay. Having eaten and slept well we paid, of course, despite knowing that the price was ridiculous; it just meant that in future we had to have that awkward conversation about money before we received any hospitality. If not, we would very soon run out of cash.

One indication of how few people came up this valley was several uncovered Inca cemeteries. Neither Luke nor I even knew that Incas practised mummification until we literally stumbled upon a mummified corpse in the middle of our path and then realised that bodies and heads with hair and skin still on them were scattered across the hillside. It was fascinating and chilling in equal measure; we realised that they must have been exposed relatively recently after a landslide.

The northern end of the Majes Valley led into the mouth of the famous Colca Canyon. Whereas valleys have an open, picturesque feel to them, canyons are not quite as simple to walk through the bottom of. The Colca Canyon is the second deepest in the world – second only to the Apurímac – which we would walk down a couple of months later. Both canyons are, at their deepest, a staggering three kilometres deep from riverbed to mountaintop. Often in the Colca Canyon the river fills the entire gorge between the two vertical cliffs. There are no paths and in some places passing is impossible on foot so we had to plan our route via the mountaintops on either side. The problems with choosing a route along the sides of the canyon over the mountains were that we would have little access to water and we would have to climb and descend thousands of metres every time we crossed a tributary canyon that entered the Colca. But there was no other option.

After our relatively remote adventure in our first week, the northern end of the Majes Valley was starkly different from the sparse stick and mud shacks we had seen. It was connected to the Peruvian road network and suddenly we were back in places with restaurants and hotels and even a tourist information centre. A very pretty girl who worked in the latter, called Señorita Mabel, helped us plan our route through the Colca. She had contacts in the various remote villages in the mountains surrounding the canyon and could contact them and let them know we were coming. How would she do this with villages that are so isolated that to reach them you have to walk or go by donkey? She'd called them on their cell phones, of course.

The first mountain village we needed to get to, perched at 2,700 metres above sea level, and 1,800 metres above Señorita Mabel's tourist information centre, was Uñon. This was a two-day hike and the lovely Mabel asked us if we wanted her to get the villagers from Uñon to send down a man with a donkey to help our ascent. As we had already struggled somewhat we decided that this was quite a good idea as we were about to start doing some serious hills.

At about this time, Luke's and my differing approaches to how the expedition should be conducted became apparent. He wanted to enjoy the expedition as much as he could and so the idea of getting a donkey to carry his kit was very appealing. As it was to me I suppose, except I felt that it wasn't quite right. In my mind I had always imagined us carrying all our own weight in our packs, and so I agreed to the donkey only if it was carrying food and water but we were carrying all our own kit.

Why? Because we had agreed that this was to be a man-powered expedition and I really felt that was the way I wanted to do it. Explorers of days gone by like Henry Morton Stanley went into Africa with huge teams of locals acting as porters and vast herds of animals to carry everything. I like the fact that modern exploration is about getting your hands dirty and putting the effort in. It's what sets it aside from simple tourism because the physical feats are massive challenges in themselves. That said, I compromised and agreed to the hiring of the donkey.

The rendezvous with the animal was organised and instructions had even been sent via Mabel's cell phone to send down a day's worth of food on the animal. We consequently climbed the first day relatively fast as we had to carry only a single day's food. That night, at the proposed donkey rendezvous, we camped and showered beneath an irrigation reservoir. The man-made swimming pool's glacial contents overflowed via a small stone opening to form a steady torrent of near freezing shower water that cut into our bruised shoulders and made us squeal out loud at the sheer cold force.

So far we had seen no sign of any donkeys and by the next morning it became apparent that we had been stood up so we breakfasted on the last of our food – a small plate of spaghetti each washed down with raspberry jam – and set off up the hill to Uñon.

If we had struggled on the flat, going steeply uphill suddenly reduced our pace even more. Each step was an effort and we set ourselves little goals so that we could keep going and stay positive. I'll just get to that bend, that rock, that cactus. By mid-morning, having climbed several hundred metres on dusty tracks, we met two donkeys and their owner coming down the steep hillside towards us. The climb had been relentless and we were hungry and exhausted and wanted nothing more than to pile our packs on to the donkeys. We greeted the man warmly and he seemed to think that this was a great fun day out. He proudly produced his food, as requested – a bag of dry pasta and a freshly slaughtered chicken. Not exactly what you might have in mind on a steep mountainside but Oz started to come into his own before my very eyes. In a flash the chicken was plucked and diced and frying in garlic on the battered old kerosene stove that Luke cranked into life. The pasta was even toasted before water was added and within forty minutes we were wolfing down huge mouthfuls of filling chicken pasta.

With newfound strength, we surprised the donkey owner by turning down the offer of putting our packs on his animals and started to trudge slowly up the hillside with them on our backs. Somewhat superfluous now, the old man and the donkeys followed us, but I was glad that Luke, too, felt that he should carry his own pack. The walk to Uñon was incredibly steep but when we did pause for breath we witnessed beautiful Inca ruins and ancient agricultural terraces from a long-dead civilisation.

We turned into a shallow hanging valley above a steep canyon and were mesmerised by the quaint beauty of Uñon with its neat fields of crops and small clusters of mud-and-stone houses. The climb took a total of ten hours and, thanks to Señorita Mabel, we were greeted warmly by Elard, the village governor. He then took us on a little tour of the village including the bare room in which we were to sleep. The village had no road access but we were amazed to see the Internet in the school as well as mobile phone reception. Everything (satellite dishes, generators, computers and sofas) had been brought in by donkey. There was a pretty pink church overlooking a pleasant plaza with thousands of bees flying in and out of tiny burrows in the dirt floor.

Elard told us how Uñon was having to adapt as a direct result of climate change. The rains that used to fall for four months of the year now scarcely lasted more than a month and the crops were parched and dry. Livestock was suffering, too, and the villagers had to look to new methods to bring in money. The only way the people could envisage surviving now was to push for an extension of the road network to link them to the outside world and the rest of Peru. If that were to happen, the gold mines that were built by the Spanish and kept working up to the Second World War by the Germans could be reopened and bring in an income. Both Luke and I felt sad that this beautiful, isolated community had to be linked to Peru by road after its centuries of isolation and we also felt privileged to be among the last few people to visit it in its romantic hidden state.

To cross to the next village, Ayo, we first needed to climb from 2,700 to 4,500 metres to cross a mountain ridge. Our first guide and his donkey having done their stint, we hired another local man, Hector, to accompany us with his animal. The donkey carried the food and water for the journey and Luke's too small jungle boots. As Luke loaded the donkey he caught my eye; he knew I thought him wrong to load his boots on to the donkey and I knew he didn't care so much about carrying all his own weight and sticking to the agreement that we would make the journey truly man-powered. To me it undermined the essence of the journey and to be able to claim that we had done what we set out to do. Water sources were pretty nonexistent here and so much of the weight on the donkey consisted of two huge 10-litre jerrycans full of water.

Without food and water, and having further cut down all but what we considered essential, both Luke's and my pack weight dropped even more, to 35 kilograms. Even at this lighter weight the thin atmosphere at this altitude started to affect Luke in particular. He was visibly worried about the physical challenge of this leg and he set a very slow pace, adamant that he would not be rushed and that we would get there slowly but surely. Hector and Oz were impatient and kept disappearing off ahead. I stayed back with Luke but was also quietly hoping we could speed up – at least a little bit.

For twelve hours we climbed, '*poco a poco*', little by little, until we'd crested the summit and found a sheltered spot to make camp. By the latter half of the day I was just as slow as Luke and I remember wondering if I had ever before climbed with that weight at this altitude for such a sustained period of time. I hadn't and nor had Luke – these were conditions we would just have to adapt to. We'd now been on the move for two weeks and the cracks were starting to show. In retrospect, the amount we'd travelled was nothing – absolutely nothing – but it was already a longer trek than either of us had ever made before.

At the end of the day Luke and I found a rhythm and it was one of the last times I feel we really worked well together. We would treat ourselves with regular standing breaks and managed to set a steady pace that even left Oz and Hector behind. It felt like a team and we both took strength in the companionship and support we were giving each other. At the summit Hector offered me the plastic bottle he'd been sipping from all day. 'It's for the cold,' he said. I smiled; I had a fair idea what the liquid was and took a long swig. The infusion of medicinal herbs and strong alcohol spread through my chest. It felt like urine warming up a wetsuit.

Luke had been getting on fine in his Crocs and I liked the idea of not wearing socks and heavy boots and so joined him in this unconventional mountain footwear. OK, we both had to stop every now and then to remove cactus thorns from our feet but I found it liberating to have the wind rushing round my ankles and not have soggy, sweaty feet wrapped up in huge leather boots.

Camping at 4,500 metres was cold and Hector made a bedroll for himself from the horse blankets. With frost underfoot we set off early downhill towards Ayo and it was late afternoon by the time we arrived. Thanks to Hector being well liked, we were welcomed and allowed to sleep in the town hall.

Fed up with donkeys and hills, I wanted to change tack at this point and follow the canyon bottom close to the river. We spoke to some locals and they told us this was a crazy idea: the water was high and the canyon bottom was impassable. As it turned out, the alternative route was also dangerous: a thin, winding path up scree and then over a sharp 600-metre-high ridge that would involve lots of scrambling – but this time carrying nearly 40 kilos again (extra food) as it was far too steep for a donkey.

One of the reasons Luke had been a good choice of partner for me was that he was a climbing and kayaking instructor. I had made it clear to him from the start that in both areas he was firmly in charge, as his climbing and kayaking experience far outstripped mine. Luke, looking up at the ridge that we were to cross in the morning, described it as 'death on a stick'.

We set off in the pitch dark and made our way across the valley bottom from Ayo to the foot of the mountain. From there we zigzagged up increasingly steep scree slopes until we reached some near vertical crags at the top. The route we were to take was out of sight and we dreaded what lay ahead. I was back in my jungle boots but Hector's donkey had mislaid Luke's and so he was attempting this very precarious climb in his Crocs.

Hector had gone home to be replaced by Efrain, a wiry man who had brought his pickaxe to cut footholds for us in the semi-solidified scree. He sauntered up the slope with ease as Luke, Oz and I steadily trudged behind with our huge packs. We climbed up steep gullies and traversed slim ledges. It wasn't safe – we knew that – and several times I had rockfall come down on my head. We slowly worked our way through the crags – only once using the rope – knowing that a slip at virtually any point would have been fatal. Handholds would often disintegrate and although not too technical, the climb was the riskiest I had ever undertaken. I was glad that at least I wasn't wearing Crocs. Luke removed his and climbed in his socks for a while. On several sections I offered to share my boots with him by lowering them down on the rope but he declined and seemed confident enough. At one point he was very nearly killed when a rock that he was pulling on came away and almost threw him off balance and down the cliff. Teetering on the edge of death, he held his balance, dropped the rock and didn't fall. Efrain was optimistically holding the rope at this point but Luke weighed considerably more than the little guide.

Undoubtedly the danger clicked us into a hyper-alert state and Luke and I both ended up loving the final stages. Oz, on the other hand, was making it clear that guiding in the mountains might not be his best career option; we had to coach him through several sections as he was absolutely terrified and had frozen.

The route down was not as bad and we arrived in a tiny hamlet nestled in the most inaccessible part of the Colca Canyon called Canco. Canco is an idyllic settlement of only a couple of families who farm the tiny valley bed and raise cattle and crops. Beer in this type of settlement is scarce and expensive; even so, we were delighted to be able to buy some cold bottles to celebrate our survival.

The following day, as we walked up the canyon's southern wall heading for Cabanaconde, I was lifted by the sheer numbers and closeness of the Andean condors that floated on the updraughts of air coming out of the canyon. Such huge birds with near three-metre wingspans charged my soul and gave me strength. I tried to enthuse Luke but he just saw big vultures and trudged on with his head down. Our oversight that day was the cumulative 4,000 metres of climbing that meant we had to spend the night at the side of the road in a ditch several kilometres short of our destination.

The 22 kilometres from Cabanaconde to Lari was again by road and this time it was gently descending the whole day. The Catholic town of Lari was the pot of gold at the end of the Colca Canyon from which we would launch our search for the furthest source of the Amazon. Overshadowed by the high Andes we knew that from here we were just two days' walk from Nevado Mismi and the headwaters of the Carhuasanta, the furthest tributary from the mouth of the Amazon. We had been walking for three weeks and were pretty tired by this stage and needed to rest, so we took a few days to recuperate and make adjustments to our kit before beginning the attempt on the summit.

Luke's fiancée Katie was travelling in Peru and hoping to meet up with Luke when she could. He clearly missed her a lot while we were walking and whenever he found cell phone reception he was on the phone to her or text messaging her. As we knew we would be in Lari for a few days, it made sense that they would see each other. Luke checked into a hotel with Katie while Oz and I slept, bought supplies and then got very bored.

Our three-week trek to the summit through the Colca Canyon

had been inspired by Mike Horn when he descended the Amazon in the nineties on a hydrospeed and, further downriver, a dugout canoe. Mike had crossed the entire continent without the use of a motor and so we wanted to take up his very impressive mantle and complete the same journey, but this time without using the river's flow to assist the descent. If we walked we would be the first to cross the continent via the longest source of the Amazon River, truly man-powered. Mike had set the standard and, as a result, taking a bus to the nearest road to Nevado Mismi was just not an acceptable option any more.

Katie and Luke said a tearful farewell and agreed to meet up again in Cuzco in a few weeks. Luke, Oz and I then set off from Lari to find the source of the Amazon. We had ten days' worth of food strapped on to a couple of tiny donkeys owned by our new local guide, Feliciano. Our maps at this stage were good – 1:100,000 military grade topographic maps – so we entered the Wikipedia coordinates for the source into our GPS and set off. This ascent soon became higher than Luke had ever been before and he seemed to suffer more than the rest of us from altitude sickness. I couldn't understand it as (a) we had tablets for it, and (b) we had gradually risen to this height over three whole weeks and so his body must surely have adapted by now. I am sure he could sense my frustration and he alluded to as much in his blog about summit day when he described me as running ahead doing star jumps while carrying Oswaldo above my head as he struggled on behind. It was fiction, of course, Luke's poetic licence, but I felt his words were full of a real feeling of separation.

After a night in a sheep pen that protected us from strong winds and snow, we crested the ridge upon which Mismi lay and looked for the valley on the north side where we could find the furthest source of the Amazon and the famous white cross. Our Wikipedia coordinates were about seven kilometres out but Luke and I had studied the shape of the mountains enough times that we instinctively knew where we had to look. We both felt as if we had been there before as we used our internal 'force' to guide us down into a wide, flat, grassy valley, hopping over mossy streams until I pointed to the base of a large escarpment of exposed rock and Luke agreed that we could see the cross.

We scampered up the last few metres and everything was exactly how I had imagined it. The 10-metre-high rock face had a prominent shower of water flowing down it and it was obvious to see why the cross had been erected there. It was a picturesque and appropriate spring of water coming directly from the rock face.

We took a few photographs and made some video recordings and then we noticed another cross, an iron one, 15 metres below. It had been erected in 1971 and claimed to be the true source. There was also a plaque from the Instituto Brazilian Brasileiro de Geografica e Estatistica in a separate place. I rolled my eyes at the frivolity of these expeditions all claiming their own official and different sources of the Amazon at differing points on the mountainside – and in fact on the following day we would find a second plaque denoting the fourth 'official' furthest source of the Amazon. We could see the massive snow-covered glaciers above us and knew that they had subglacial streams flowing from them and so we felt there was only one way to cover all bases and ensure we had been to the furthest source of the Amazon – and that was to climb to the summit of Nevado Mismi.

We returned to a flat area and set up base camp on the Carhuasanta Valley floor. That night we set our alarms to 0430 with the intention of being moving by 0500.

At 0545 on 25 April 2008 I looked at my watch and felt a jolt of fear shoot up my spine as if I was going to get into trouble for being late. As I crawled groggily out of my sleeping bag, the dark cold evilly penetrated my thin thermals. The night had been clear and our tents were ridged with ice. I woke each confused occupant one by one.

We had half a mind to leave Feliciano at camp to guard our kit but then decided that (a) no one would steal it even if they made it all the way up here, and (b) it would be great if Feliciano, who had lived at the base of the mountain his entire life, could see the view from the top. He readily agreed.

We were camped at 4,990 metres and so only had 610 metres to go to get to the top. With only the bare essentials, Feliciano in his flip-flops made from old car tyres, we started plodding slowly uphill. Luke was carrying the only pack that had a rope and med kit in it and, as he began to slow down, I offered to carry it. Perhaps this made him feel that he would be relying on me as he declined and kept walking very slowly upwards. It was at times like that that I have to admit the relationship with Luke occupied too much of my brain. I was about to summit the mountain on which the source of the Amazon springs, the sky was the clearest of blues, and the views were phenomenal and all I could think about was 'Why won't he just give me the fucking pack?'

Thankfully, both of us stopped fuming at each other when we realised that the mountain required us to switch on. We were kicking steps into a very steep bank of snow and kept zigzagging up and up in the bright sunshine.

I've not got a phobia about heights but when we reached the ridge and I looked over at the sheer drop below I froze with the camera in my hand – terrified. It was an incredible rush of fright that I had to manage and smile through, mocking my own alarm, to be able to move on up the razor-sharp ridge.

Taking it in turns to kick steps up front, Luke and I led the four-man party up the ridge line to the highest summit on the range – Nevado Mismi – and, despite the previous niggles, as we crested the final part to 5,600 metres just before noon, we all hugged each other in sheer elation.

As a non-mountaineer just the experience of reaching the summit blew me away. Combined with the thought that from here on in we would be walking down the longest course of the Amazon River, living like nomads, carrying what we needed, and living off our wits for up to two years, I felt as if I was the luckiest man on earth. I felt so happy that we had got to this stage and at that point I could distinctly visualise completing the whole journey. I could see us running, bedraggled, into the Atlantic Ocean – the elation of that accomplishment was already there deep in my soul and I knew I would not stop until the job was finished.

Luke was even more overjoyed that he had mobile phone reception and phoned Katie. I felt very conscious that I didn't have anyone I wanted to call, considered whether it bothered me, then grinned to myself, happy to be free to live the next two years exactly as I wanted.

Chapter Three

Descending the Deepest Canyon in the World

Although walking the Amazon sounds as if it should be a piranha-, snake- and jaguar-filled *Boy's Own* escapade, after 200 kilometres we were nowhere close to jungle or even what is known as the Amazon River. Crossing the Andes mountain range was more like an adventure trekking holiday – but we still had to do it if we were to accomplish our mission.

From our base camp on the northern slopes of Nevado Mismi, Feliciano set off back to his home in Lari with his tyre sandals and his donkeys. Luke, Oz and I set off in the other direction following the Carhuasanta Valley. The land was so barren and open it reminded me of a vast version of the English Peak District. The high expanse is boggy in places and because of the heavy packs the walking wasn't easy despite the flat terrain. Trees cannot grow at this altitude and we were descending only a few metres each day as we followed the snaking stream over the flat plains.

One afternoon, 28 April, I can remember becoming annoyed with Oz as he was being cocky about not being tired and I was struggling badly that day. The thing that wound me up was that I was carrying his food (for a reason I can't remember) and so when we stopped for a break I remember dumping my pack, pulling out Oz's food and shoving it at him quite abruptly. I couldn't work out at the time why this had got to me but the evening's diary shows what was really on my mind.

Diary entry from 28 April 2008:

Today I allowed myself to think negative thoughts about Luke. It was very counterproductive because if he was a poor choice of partner for me, I could only lay the blame on myself as I chose him. I became angry at myself, but he is half of Walking the Amazon and the sooner I focus on making the best of the situation and stop wasting energy being angry at him the better. I know I am strong enough to make the exped work with Luke – I just have to be positive and not get annoyed by him. He is – as I have always said – a good person.

On the next day Luke seemed tired. Oz suggested a route (that Luke agreed to) through a field that ended up being very boggy indeed. Oz and I came out the other side laughing at the state of our boots and trousers – it was a sunny day and having wet feet didn't matter. Luke followed scowling and swore at Oz. It was the first time Luke had behaved like this towards Oz. 'Steady on, Luke,' I stepped in, pointing out the triviality of wet feet on a sunny day.

We climbed over a small wall and on to a dusty track. I was in front and turned to see Luke and Oz arguing over who should walk at the back. It was so petty that I have to admit I laughed out loud at them both. Luke flipped. 'How dare you laugh at me in front of Oswaldo!' His livid eyes spoke louder than his words and so I just turned and continued walking without replying.

Soon after, we took a break at the top of a hill and I told Luke that I thought he shouldn't take his frustrations out on Oz.

'Look, Luke – I did it yesterday to a lesser extent – I'm not just blaming you – but we can't let being tired turn into treating each other badly. Perhaps laughing at each other is a good way to stop us behaving like idiots.' Luke still thought I could be more supportive and so after an hour or so's further walking I apologised to him for laughing at him in front of Oz.

I was bored with arguing with Luke. It was happening more and more and we were both becoming more sensitive and touchy.

Banter had disappeared from our group. As Luke seemed very tired, when he suggested buying two donkeys on 30 April I grudgingly agreed. It was half his expedition after all – and we could still say that we had walked the entire length of the Amazon – but I would have liked the expedition not to have been assisted by donkeys. I conceded to make the peace.

On 1 May, after parting with £40 per beast, we collected this aging pair from an old farmer. They had not worked for a year and the method of stopping them running off had been to tie their back two legs together. Once they were released, Oz, who had kept donkeys, tried to attach a rope halter but they saw their opportunity and bolted. We all chased them for several fields until they were eventually caught and could be put on leads. The donkeys were fairly wild but Oz was up to the challenge of training them and seemed quite happy with his new responsibility.

I had to admit that the donkeys would reduce the physical exertion and we would sell them when we got to the jungle. That first day we didn't get far as I had been feeling ill and so we made camp early. After a sleep in the afternoon I woke to find that it was a nice evening and Luke and I had a walk up a hill and sat on some rocks for a chat.

Luke told me he was still hurt by my previous lack of support and so I decided to be completely honest with him. I told him about my frustrations at his not speaking the languages and how he was slowing us down. In my view it was all true but it was the first time I'd let him know how I truly felt. As I saw it, we had almost two years ahead of us and if this relationship was going to work we had to be honest with each other or we stood no chance. It felt good that he knew how I felt. A harsh truth or not, he now knew where he stood and seemed to accept it well.

The air seemed to be cleared after this talk and we all relaxed, ate a great supper of soya meat and powdered potato and practised Spanish and English with Oz. Things appeared to be on the up.

The following day we walked across a huge, flat expanse and then turned right into the small Apurímac Valley for the first time. The

River Apurímac marked the starting point of a network of rivers we had to follow to reach what is actually called the Amazon. After the Apurímac came the River Ene, followed by the River Tambo, followed by the Ucayali, which runs into the Amazon proper. The river was narrow and meandering in a steep valley that might have been in Wales, with scattered rocky outcrops. Heads rose and chatter resumed as the beautiful scenery lifted everyone after a week of desolate plains. In the evening the sunset warmed the vast golden columns of fragmented rock that stood tall and proud above the handsome river valley. The area had been eroded by water creeping into the cracks in the rocks in the day and then freezing at night, forcing them apart. The result was a shattered wasteland of jagged tombstones the size of skyscrapers.

Diary entry from 4 May 2008:

Today was arguably the best day's walking so far. Not the most exciting nor interesting but enjoyable and hassle-free with spectacular scenery in the Apurímac Valley. We swam at lunchtime and even had a snooze on the shingle beach whilst digesting lunch.

As the valley deepened and started to become more like a canyon, the route was increasingly difficult for the donkeys. Paths were either too steep or too narrow for them to pass through and we were forced up and out of the valley on to the flatter expanses on either side.

Sometimes roads went in our direction down these canyon tops and so we followed them. Often we walked over vast expanses of wild grassland with sheep, guanacos and llamas grazing.

On 11 May we arrived in the Quechuan town of Quehue at the end of a long day of walking 25 kilometres. It was market day and the main plaza was full of men in Stetsons and women in multicoloured dresses and brown bowler hats. Oz told me that the traditional dresses and hats worn by the Quechua women were a legacy of the Spanish rule where each landowner would have a particular style for his workers so that he could tell them apart from other workers. It seemed strange to me that this national dress, one so celebrated, was in fact an enforced peasant uniform.

Quehue had an odd feel about it and as we walked through the plaza we were hassled more than usual. Beggars pulled at our packs asking for money and kids pointed and laughed. Unimpressed, and as the donkeys were getting scared of the noisy crowd, we left the town and found a flat field 400 metres north that was just tucked out of sight to put up our tents.

We'd been told people were different around here. There would be far more thieves and 'bad' people who would not help us. Whether we'd read too much into this or we were just beginning to become slightly more insular, we all agreed that we felt far more comfortable in this field in our tents than in a town hall or church building in the town. We polished off our tuna and some bread that we'd bought from town and crawled into our sleeping bags as it got dark at about 6.30 p.m.

For those visitors to Peru who are willing to go slightly further out of their comfort zone than the congested Inca trail, the upper sections of the Apurímac are stunning. At this point the canyon was still less than 2,000 metres deep with forested sides of eucalyptus and fertile valley bottoms where the blue glacial waters bubbled enticingly.

Although we were more content at this stage as a team, I know from my diary that I was starting to yearn for other company. Luke and I had been together for seventy-five days now and I longed for different conversation. Sadly, our interests didn't really overlap and so I would quickly become bored with his kayaking escapades and climbing moves he'd executed on a crag somewhere in England, while he didn't seem interested in topics that appealed to me. We sort of overlapped on films but once we'd discussed the ones we'd both seen – a handful – that was that.

It was a challenge. It just required positivity and looking for the best in each other. But it was certainly a challenge.

On 17 May we arrived in a tiny remote village called Santa Lucia in the early afternoon and sat in the sun in the empty plaza drinking Coke, snacking on the Peruvian version of chocolate Oreo cookies bought in the local shop, surrounded by high mountains on all sides.

The shop was typical of the region: a couple of wooden shelves with warm, fizzy drinks of various hues and packets of sweet biscuits. Sometimes there would be cans of tuna or corned beef and bags of pasta. The shopkeeper was kind and told us of a man who was going in our direction and could accompany us on our way. We jumped at this, as locals always know the short cuts, and set out with Luke at the back with our new friend. Luke soon caught up with me to talk and said that even with his bad Spanish he could tell the man was a bit strange. I fell back to speak to the man and found that he was indeed odd but after two minutes I was bored and so duly sped up again.

When hummingbirds appeared to my right I quickly got out the camera to record the elusive creatures. As I was filming, the man started pulling at the camera to try to see the screen. Hummingbirds, being lightning quick, are not easy to film – even less so when some nutty Peruvian is tugging at your camera.

We started walking again and I palmed mad bloke off on Oz as they could speak in Quechua to each other. After five minutes Oz had become very angry, said the man was mad and that we needed to walk in a different direction from him. He said the man thought that we were cattle rustlers and that we had stolen the donkeys from his village. We detoured further up the hill hoping to escape our unwelcome companion on the parallel path below.

Then he started running up the hill off the path towards us. He blocked our way and picked up a rock, saying we could not pass. Oz's young eyes saw red and he told the man in no uncertain terms how stupid he was being and that we were just tourists. The man pointed at my trekking poles and said that we were armed with secret weapons. As the shouting continued, Luke and I watched, baffled but quite amused at the little Peruvian holding the rock. He was not amused, though, but fortunately a local turned up who was slightly saner and he calmed the first man down.

The man who had intervened was called Estefan and he warned us not to go through the madman's village which lay ahead; they were all like him, he said, and constantly fighting each other.

So, taking his advice, we followed a higher path that was reportedly narrower and more dangerous to avoid the village of idiots. We ended up camping about 400 metres directly above the village and I think all of us were half expecting a visit in the night. We called out jokes between the tents about setting booby traps for the village of pitchfork-wielding madmen but we fell asleep and they never came.

Cusco is a big Westernised city with two grand cathedrals that wasn't on our route but we needed to visit it. It was about 40 kilometres to the north of the Apurímac Canyon, and was where we had cached our jungle gear prior to arriving in Lima. Cusco represented a tempting pocket of Western food and bars that were very appealing after fifty days of walking.

Peru is, on the whole, cheap. There were about six *soles* to the pound and we could generally eat for about a pound or less in places where local Peruvians worked and ate. Cusco was very different. With prices higher than London you can stay in luxury hotels, eat fine food and take designer drugs if you choose in the all-night clubs and bars. Its proximity to the ruins of Machu Picchu makes it the biggest tourist destination in South America and you don't need to speak Spanish to do anything.

My fear was that we would spend too much time in Cusco and get out of the expedition frame of mind. We would also spend too much money and become unfit. I therefore suggested to Luke that only he went up to Cusco while I stayed with Oz and the donkeys in a small village on the Apurímac, and he did the kit exchange and saw Katie again.

But by 20 May we were only one day short of Cusco and were all very tired. None of us had ever walked for fifty days before and the call of civilisation was too strong. I changed my standpoint and suggested to Oz that he and I spend a few days recovering in comfort, too. We palmed the donkeys off on a nice farmer on the Apurímac and headed for the bright lights.

While Luke spent time with Katie, I caught up on the administrative side of the journey – doing the accounts, digitising all the footage that we'd taken so far and couriering the tapes back to the UK. I sorted our kit for the jungle and sent our goosedown sleeping bags, thermals and waterproofs back to England, too. We were realising at this stage the real length of our journey and the real cost. The original sponsorship money that we'd got from JBS Associates wasn't going to be enough to enable us to reach the finish so I approached them for further funds. I became far more worried about money than I ever got on the journey about natural dangers. When I finally made the call to the CEO of JBS Associates, Jonathan, he was understanding and said they would help. The relief was huge but I knew I would have to curb our spending drastically from here on. This meant less time in towns and less buying of expensive kit from abroad. We had to do the expedition as much as possible using what we could acquire in South America.

It's difficult to tell this story accurately without mentioning the differences in Luke's and my attitude towards money at this point. Luke did a tourist trip to Machu Picchu (paid for by Katie) and in my opinion was eating the best food in restaurants (paid for by the expedition). He quickly put weight back on and I began really to resent his presence on the journey. Despite us having got on better in the weeks prior to Cusco, things between us started to turn sour again.

Some friends of ours were travelling through Cusco at the time and so I spent an evening in a bar boring them to tears about my issues with Luke. I doubted my judgement and wanted to know if I was being unreasonable. I actually expected them to tell me that I was making a lot of fuss about nothing. The relief, in some ways, was that they agreed with me and, although they didn't have any solutions, they seemed to recognise that Luke and I were not right as travelling companions.

It was early June by the time we left Cusco. I watched emotionless as Luke and Katie said goodbye to each other – Katie in floods of tears. Their need to see one another seemed to fly in the face of everything the two of us were trying to do. This was a world-first expedition that needed focus and commitment and I felt that Oswaldo was more committed to it than Luke.

We picked up the donkeys, paid the man well for the extended kennelling, and were pleased to be on the move again. I was aware that, when walking, your mind searches for something to feed off as there is often nothing much to think about. Often this energy can become negative and this negativity can end up being focused on your expedition partner. I fell into this trap and, in my head, allowed all of the expedition's problems to be put down to Luke. Some of them were his fault, but, looking back, it is easy for me to see how blaming Luke actually made things worse for me as I felt less in control because the problem was him, rather than me. If I had accepted responsibility for the way I reacted to certain things I would have been in a far better position. It was part of a mountainous learning process for me on how to control my mind; I was still very much in the foothills in this lesson.

On 11 June I woke up having slept right through from 8 p.m. to 6 a.m. Ten solid hours, and I woke feeling more refreshed than I'd felt in months. It was well timed as we had a 1,100-metre climb to start the day.

At about 4,000 metres above sea level we found a small sheltered valley and made camp on a grassy flat by a bubbling brook. May and Cusco proved to be too soon to have ditched all our cold-weather kit and we had a very cold night in our thin jungle sleeping bags and cotton shirts. We'd been looking forward to the jungle so much that we had wished the mountains away by changing gear too early. Idiots.

With long, tough days, often climbing and descending over 2,000 metres, I tried to focus on tangible goals. I didn't like walking with the donkeys so my focus here was getting through the next ten days or so, selling the donkeys, and then the expedition becoming more flexible and fun on foot. This laboured slog with pack animals had become dull and unchallenging; I dreamed of the jungle, hammocks, fishing and fires.

As we now owned our own donkeys we did not have local donkey owners walking with us who knew the way. This meant that we had to navigate, something Luke and I decided to rotate, day on, day off, so that we wouldn't tread on each other's toes and so that the person not navigating that day could relax.

Although I like taking the piss out of the way I go about expeditions, the truth is that I am very confident in my abilities and have high expectations of others, too. In my view, Luke's navigation was too vague, often saying that our destination was 'just over this spur', giving me the impression he didn't know exactly where we were. Had we not been at each other's throats this wouldn't have mattered, we didn't need to be super-precise, but, to me this was – and I hope I'm not being unfair here – another example of him not contributing properly.

Every entry in my journal refers to my fixation with how frustrated I was – and how bored I was about still feeling the same way after so long. Surprisingly, with hindsight, I never saw the obvious way out. I always thought we would resolve our issues or that somehow the expedition would change once we got to the jungle and we'd both be happier.

So the next morning I think I was looking for trouble. Luke came over and offered to run through the route with me and I told him I didn't need to – he was navigating and I'd just follow. I can't remember the exact exchange but it blew up when I told Luke he was shit at navigating.

Luke exploded. I knew it would happen yet I looked on amazed at the angry onslaught of expletives. He was furious with me. Part of the brain-dead me got a buzz from this outburst and I fully admit to creating the situation to cut through the chronic boredom of our failed attempts to get on. It felt liberating to watch some fury come out of him. Oswaldo and the donkeys patiently looked on as they watched two gringos let out all their pent-up aggression on each other. We were both shaking – it was like the most vehement row in a marriage that has gone hideously sour. If we'd been in London we'd have gone our own ways long ago – but the expedition was keeping us in each other's company 24/7– so letting off steam was necessary.

It took us until lunch to start walking. I felt the air had cleared between us and certainly felt relieved not to be bottling up these feelings any more. It had, for me, been a necessarily honest outburst but unbeknown to me it was the final straw for Luke. Although we would walk together for another two weeks, he had made up his mind to leave.

We followed indistinct trails over dusty hills covered in spiky plants; pitched our rain flysheets in sloping campsites covered in sheep and guanaco shit; talked nonsense to drunken Quechua men to try to confuse them; and marvelled at how foul old people's mouths could look after a lifetime of chewing coca and not brushing their few remaining teeth.

As we approached the jungle, Luke had insisted that he needed specialist jungle boots shipped in from the States. We were all shattered and so we left the donkeys with another kind farmer and went to Abancay to pick up Luke's boots at the post office. I had left the logistics of Luke's boots to him as he insisted that they were vital, and so we waited day after day.

The break did mean that we had the chance to relax a little and rest our legs. After a few days, Luke's boots had still not turned up so I told him we had to continue anyway – the inactivity was unbearable for me. We continued along roads for a few days until, at one exit point, Huanipaca, Luke managed finally to take delivery of his boots.

My diary entries show a marked ignorance about the stretch ahead: I thought the jungle wouldn't start until we hit the River Ene; I thought that the valley bottom would open up and we could walk along the bottom by the river; and I believed that the rumours about the Red Zone (the infamous terrorist stronghold and drugs-trafficking centre of Peru) were overstated and that the area would be a cinch to walk through.

As we walked down a huge spur into the canyon we were confronted by two small men who wouldn't let us pass. Conscious that we were now entering the Red Zone, we were respectful and presented our passports and permits but the men refused to budge.

I then had the idea of hiring them to walk with us and they thought this was a good idea and so escorted us on to their land. As we walked and chatted, they told us that there was a land dispute raging over rights to a mine and we had been mistaken for foreign mining surveyors.

The men also bought the donkeys from us. We would no longer need them and would be walking at the bottom of the valley where they couldn't pass. We got only slightly less than we had paid for the beasts and I was pleased that for once some money was coming back into the expedition. Luke was sad to see them go and I have to admit that even I felt my heartstrings tugging slightly as the two men took one donkey each and dragged them away in diametrically opposite directions, separating the aging couple for probably the first time in who knows how long.

The donkeys were replaced by two local lads, Segil and Ruben, who agreed to walk with us for a fee. They were simple farming boys, not used to carrying weight, and asked to stop all the time. We descended into the valley bottom and strung our hammocks in the tropical heat. Luke and I tested out the gill net and caught a trout in about half an hour. The water sparkled with life and the thought of being next to the crystal-clear bath for the rest of the expedition made us very happy. Behind us were the dirty, sweaty months of barren hills; we could now dip into the river and wash off whenever we liked.

The local lads told us that all of the coca fields we were walking through were cultivated for processing into cocaine. The small-scale farmers sell the leaves to the drugs traffickers ('narcos') in the night and then the narcos process the leaves into a moist, cheese-like substance before it is packed out to places like Abancay for distribution to Colombia for further processing and refining.

On 1 July 2008 we had fried fish and noodles for breakfast and the five of us set off down the bottom of the valley. We knew there was a possibility that we would have to divert up and over small spurs if the sides of the canyon became unnavigable, but without the drag of the donkeys we felt pretty confident about tackling any terrain.

Soon enough we reached a section where the water butted straight up to a vertical cliff. Ruben and Oz could not swim and, anyway, the menacing white water river was not an option. Luke made the decision to go up and over the hill to the right and I agreed with him; aside from turning back, there was really no other option.

Heading up the steep sides of the Apurímac Canyon where there was no path was not actually that easy. It was too steep just to walk; we had to hold on to spiky plants and hope the rocks beneath our feet didn't give way. Against the advice of the three Peruvians, Luke decided to head straight up but they followed him nonetheless. Not for long, though – the slope became far too steep and the locals branched left, contouring round the face until they found a ridge that they could climb. The heat was oppressive after weeks in the mountains. Sweat painted our clothes on to our bodies.

I called to Luke to suggest he follow the locals. He didn't respond. 'Did you hear what I said?' I called after him. 'Yes!' he responded abruptly and kept climbing.

The four of us left Luke to his alarming ascent. We skipped across an easy valley and started climbing a rocky spur. At one section a vista opened up to our right and we could see Luke making his ascent. 'Christ!' I thought, 'that looks dangerous.'

Luke was scrambling up a hill where he was reliant on loose rocks and small plants for purchase; one slip and he would have been dead. He would climb two steps and the ground would slide and he would be back to where he'd started. It was painful to watch but we could tell he was completely committed now and to go down would have been even more dangerous – if not impossible. He took about twenty minutes to cover 40 metres and I honestly thought I was about to witness and film his death at any moment. When he'd done the very steep section we decided to start climbing again ourselves. The climb got worse and worse and the crest of the spur seemed forever away.

Luke and I could hear each other if we called very loudly and I asked him how much water he had left. 'I'm almost out' came the faint reply. I was praying that the spur in the distance marked the start of a path that would head down the other side to safety and water. After six and a half hours' climbing, the last three and a half without water, I could see the two locals and Oz, who had gone ahead, against the skyline on the spur above. Luke and I were not together but were at comparable heights still a hundred metres or so below them.

It's difficult to convey how spent I was at this point and the looseness of the mountainside and the weight of my pack had taken their toll. I was falling 10 metres downhill into bushes of cactuses and then not moving out of sheer exhaustion for a further two minutes. I was covered in cactus spines and my tongue stuck to the roof of my mouth as my head throbbed with dehydration.

Oz was shouting encouragement from the top now but I felt so weak I was almost broken, defeated. I started not to care whether or not I got to the top. The next bit is something I will never forget. Oz, who was twenty-four, eight years my junior and about five stone lighter, started heading down the hill to help me. When he reached me he took my pack off me and I struggled to keep up with him as he carried it to the top. The final section took about five minutes and I collapsed in a heap at the top.

I felt embarrassed. I'd been humbled by the terrain, the heat, the vegetation, and the young Peruvians who were looking at me in pity now. Luke had not entered my head for about half an hour but as I lay on the ridge with a mouth that hadn't had water in about four hours of climbing, I started to be concerned for his safety.

Oz then brought up the bad news. There was no path here, we couldn't head down to water in less than a day's further walking. We were stranded on this desolate, barren spur in the deepest canyon in the world.

'Luke!' I called. 'Can you hear me?'

I heard a faint reply. 'I have something in my eye.'

'I'm going to send down Oz to help you. Stay there!'

'Can he bring some water with him?' Luke called back.

I didn't answer.

Oz and Segil, neither of whom had had any water recently either, went down to help Luke. I knew I couldn't help and I was pretty disgusted with myself. I lay under a cactus with Ruben staring at me.

Twenty-five minutes passed before Segil crested the hill followed by Oz with Luke's pack on his back, and then finally Luke himself who collapsed to the ground beside me.

'We've fucked this one up,' he stated matter-of-factly.

'You don't know the half of it, mate,' I said. 'There's no water.'

Luke admitted to nearly fainting several times on the way up. Neither of us felt we were able to keep going but Segil told us there was a town about two hours' walk up the spur. With packs it would have taken us about four hours minimum. Pride now well and truly swallowed, we sent Segil and Ruben up to the town with an empty bag and a hundred *soles* note and told them to buy the shop out of any liquid they could find. They set off at about 4 p.m. and, while Luke and I lay in the dust, Oz went and cut the arm off a cactus with his machete, removed the spines and sliced it up into pieces. Chewing it was incredible as the fluid seeped into our dry mouths. I was soon revitalised enough to sit up and contemplate going and cutting another branch off the cactus. Which I did.

The local lads returned almost an hour after dark and we could see their torches about a kilometre away. They emptied their sack: 10 litres of water in a jerrycan that they'd borrowed, two 3-litre bottles of Inca Kola (yellow) and Coca-Cola, and 10 cans of evaporated milk. We rationed over half of it for the morning and the climb and then set about glugging the life-giving liquid. Never in my life had I appreciated fluid so much. Luke and I had been beaten that day, and we were only OK thanks to the efforts of three young Peruvians. It was an embarrassing and humbling lesson to us both and I don't know to this day why we fared quite so badly in comparison to the locals.

The next morning we all climbed to the town in about three hours and were met by an interested crowd who'd heard about the stupid white men who had run out of water. Despite it only being mid-morning, we checked into a mud-walled hostel with a tin roof

and washed our clothes and ourselves and lay in the sun all afternoon. The hostel owner was great and wanted to help us find new
guides as Segil and Ruben had returned to their village. After much
searching I think he felt embarrassed that he'd not secured any
guides and so he agreed to walk with us. I am afraid I took no note
of his name.

In the next hamlet, high on the canyon side, the kind hostel
owner continued his quest to help us find guides and he finally
produced man called Sergio with a mischievous broad smile. Sergio
was well built: huge chest and thighs and not an ounce of fat on his
short frame. He agreed to leave his new wife and tiny baby to walk
with us. Sergio loved walking and was thrilled to join us – I had no
idea how long he would stay.

The nameless hostel owner, Sergio, Oz, Luke and I descended into
the Apurímac once more. It now had an enormously wide base and
a howling wind was blowing down it. We camped by the side of the
river and Luke and I cooked dinner for the Peruvians. Luke put
together a resupply request list, set up the BGAN and sent an email
to the UK. What transpired following that email was to change the
shape of the expedition forever.

PART 2: THE RED ZONE

Chapter Four

The Red Zone

Diary entry from 3 July 2008:

Luke has decided to go home.

This morning I woke up so annoyed that he had allowed Katie, his fiancée, to send 30 kilograms of kit to Peru for resupply. 30 ruddy kilos! So I asked him to get on the satellite email and try and stop the parcel as it was going to cost £300 to send. When he was on the laptop he read out his list of requested items so that I could give my opinion on what was necessary and what was not. It included 1 x MP3 player. This annoyed me as I had asked him to get me one too and he had only requested one.

So I said to Luke, 'Mate, why only one MP3? You know I want one too!'

'Because I'm leaving the expedition,' replied Luke in a tired, resigned manner.

'What?' I stammered, and listed the people he had made commitments to: the charities, the sponsors, the schools.

'I know,' he said, 'it's one of the hardest decisions I'll ever make but I would prefer not to lose the friendship we've got and become bitter with you – which I can feel happening.'

'Mate – we can talk about this – it will be fine.'

'Ed, listen to me.' Luke had raised his voice. 'Talking about things solves everything for you but for me it doesn't. The comments you said last time still hurt now and I have wanted to leave since our last argument.' [Approximately two weeks earlier.]

'Shit, mate, OK,' I said, shaking. 'If that's what you want then you should go.'

I wasn't prepared for the emotion that then came over me. Pure excitement. I was going to be free to run the expedition how I wanted to; to stay in towns less; to be able to be in charge of all aspects of the exped.

I wasn't sad to see Luke go but I was disappointed that our relationship on this journey had been a failure. I thought he would regret making this decision – throwing away the opportunity of a lifetime – but I had no desire to try to change his mind. Everything was slotting into place and, despite never really planning on Luke leaving, suddenly it all made more sense.

Luke didn't change his mind and we planned an exit for him. I offered him half the expedition sponsorship money so that he could continue walking on his own or with Oz, but he wasn't interested. It was a fairly safe offer – we both knew he just wanted to go home.

We climbed out of the deep Apurímac Canyon again to the town of San Martin. During the long climb my mind was busy with ideas and my newfound freedom. I had to be careful not to show Luke how energised I was about the prospects of the expedition. I didn't want him to change his mind and it would have been thoughtless to act too excited at his departure.

Why wasn't I more sad? Well, in the cold light of day Luke and I had been work colleagues before committing to this expedition. Cumulatively we'd spent probably three weeks working together at the beginning and end of expeditions in Belize and we'd got on very well during that time. But we'd never called each other up when back in England, and we'd never even written each other emails save for the round robins that Luke would distribute to his mailing list.

Even before the expedition started I remember my mind state with regard to Luke. Initially I thought he was the perfect partner: he was an expedition leader, we got on well and, importantly, if we fell out it wouldn't be the end of the world as we hadn't been close friends before.

The interesting thing is that whenever we fell out to the point at which we talked about the subject of not being able to walk together, my default was always that I would have to continue on my own, Luke's that he wanted to go home. That was the difference between us.

Hence the fact that, as soon as the initial shock of Luke's decision had worn off, I felt an exhilarating surge of freedom that I could now throw off the past weeks of negativity and start doing things my way.

Diary entry from 5 July 2008:

Today was a breath of fresh air. I had a clear head and my mind was running opportunities and ideas around in a way that made me feel more alive and enthused in this exped than I have for weeks.

Luke had boarded the bus at five o'clock that morning and I'd got up to wave him off. I could tell he was sad – it felt just like splitting up from a bad relationship – and at that parting moment I think both of us thought, 'We could make this work – let's give it another bash.' But deep down I knew he'd done the right thing taking himself off. I am grateful to him for that.

Looking back, I take a huge portion of the blame for what happened. It was my expedition concept but I chose Luke to become part of it. I believe I convinced him that kayaking was for girls and that we should walk the Amazon. I believe I cajoled him with so much enthusiasm and passion that he ended up committing to something that he never really had the deep desire to achieve. As a result, none of the behaviour or attributes were really Luke's fault – Luke was only being himself. He gave it his best shot and in the end did the noble thing by taking himself off.

Once he'd gone, I ambled back to the rickety bunkroom that we were staying in. Oz and Sergio were just stirring. Sergio swung his feet towards the floor and sat up with a cheeky morning grin that comforted me. I was with two good guys – I wasn't on my own – and we would be fine. Sergio was a kind man with a very confident aura about him. That day he told me how he used to earn much more money than the fifty *nuevos soles* a day I was paying him; he had been a drugs runner. I could tell he had loved the job by the way he spoke of the huge distances covered up and down hills in the pitch dark along winding, narrow paths. He would have a small package (couple of kilos) of base cocaine with him and adrenaline flowing the whole time. Although only twenty-two, Sergio now had a wife and a baby and so he didn't want to continue the dangerous trade. But he had a spark in his eye that told me he was a good man to have with us at this time.

That day Oz bought some food supplies, helped by Sergio, and I started replanning the expedition. It soon became evident that little needed to change. Two of Luke's main roles had been buying food and cooking. Oz took over both without me even asking and the expedition was streamlined.

I took over writing the blogs, also one of Luke's jobs. I wrote to all the charities and sponsors and let them know that Luke had left. Everyone seemed sympathetic and supportive. These things happen on long expeditions.

That evening the three of us sat in San Martin gazing down the canyon, sipping Inca Kolas while we debated our route. We were on the east side of the Apurímac and there were trails high up on both sides. The pain was that they involved descending and climbing a thousand metres every time a watercourse entered the canyon, which was exhausting, and soul-destroying. As part of my newfound solo leadership I suggested that we try something a bit riskier, more fun and actually easier. My idea was to descend into the canyon bottom and follow the river itself. There would be no drugs traffickers down there, we could fish, and we would be walking gently downhill the whole way. No more climbs.

The two agreed – or consented – I'm not sure, with hindsight, whether I'd really sought their opinions. We set off the following morning and went down and down, hour after hour, into the dark depths of the canyon. The dusty upper part was simple enough but lower down it involved us pulling our way through bamboo fields that were tightly knotted together and had us regularly on all fours then squirting out into a smelly bog at the bottom that sucked at my sandals as if I was walking with each foot in a plastic bag full of lard.

Because it was now warm and we wanted to shed weight, we'd sent Luke back to Lima with our waterproofs, and, more amazingly in retrospect, with my boots, too. It shows how much we'd been out in the open on dusty tracks and it also indicates how overwhelmed I was at first with this solo responsibility.

Down on the canyon floor we made our camp by the now fierce river. It was hard to find a flat area on which to sleep and we crafted stone patios on which to lay our sleeping mats. Oz was fantastic with the cooking and now that we'd dumped the kerosene stove he would make a small enclosed fire out of stones – almost like an oven – to balance the pot on and contain the small, efficient fire within.

Oz would always go that bit further to make things taste good. That night we had a starter of a strawberry jelly mix (serves fifteen) between the three of us served as a gloopy sweet drink. Then he toasted the rice and fried the canned tuna in garlic.

As we ate I became aware that Oz and Sergio spoke to each other too fast for me to understand when I was tired. With Luke gone all easy chat was out until my Spanish improved markedly. I took myself to bed fairly soon after supper and did a video diary and wrote my journal. Oz and Sergio stayed up chatting for a while, their tiny voices just audible over the roaring river.

Too tired to appreciate the surroundings the evening before, we woke up in the jagged belly of the deepest canyon in the world. The rocks that formed the 'pebble beach' were up to three or four metres in diameter and a river in full flood would have filled the canyon bottom way above our heads flowing with tremendous, lethal power.

We started to pick our way over the rocks and the problem with my plan soon became obvious. Our packs were just too heavy to allow us to be nimble and we repeatedly risked spraining ankles making huge leaps between boulders. Progress was painful – both risky and slow – but around the canyon corner was a far worse sight. The canyon beach had disappeared and the power of the river was focused between two sheer rock faces.

Realising that I'd led us down into a dangerous route, I started to doubt my judgement and the options spun round my head. The river wasn't walkable and the right face that we'd descended the day before looked too steep to climb back up. That only left trying to climb the left-hand canyon side – the side that the narcos used. We started to climb a spur on the left and immediately bamboo and thorns slowed our progress. Our hands, knees and ankles became covered in tiny black splinters. After three hours we'd moved 200 metres and were exhausted and running out of water.

I asked Sergio if there was a water source above us. 'Yes,' he replied, 'but we can't go there – it's used by the narcos.' I started to get jumpy. What were we doing, trying to ascend a canyon side that had no path at this point, was ridiculously steep, covered in thick spiny vegetation and was frequented by drugs traffickers?

Then, feeling panicky and under pressure, I snapped to another rash decision. I decided that we would have to go back to the river and through the narrow gorge. Oz and Sergio would use the two pack rafts and I would swim behind so as to avoid travelling downriver in a boat. This was a grey area in terms of the rules of my expedition, which were that we should never advance by river, but in the heat of the moment I tried to be decisive. As we picked our way back down to the river my stomach was churning at the prospect of swimming through the gorge. Neither Oz nor Sergio knew how to paddle either and so would be novices on the water, not able to hold a straight line. By the time we'd scrambled down to the bottom it was mid-afternoon. We looked down the canyon and could not see the end of the sheer cliff so I could not gauge the length of the narrow gorge. I got the map out and measured the canyonised part to see how far we would be in the water: two and a half kilometres. I started to feel more and more out of control. I didn't know if we would encounter rapids – there was every chance – and this would certainly put all of our lives at serious risk. What was I thinking? I was swapping one miserable hell for another.

'Mr Stafford, sir, is your village missing an idiot now that you've come to Sandhurst?' In my head I could hear the mocking Scottish burr of my first colour sergeant in army training. 'Take a Condor moment, Mr Stafford.' The latter was a reference to an old cigar advert on British TV that meant take a deep breath and give yourself time to think. I knew that I was failing the others because of the pressure I was piling on myself; I was rushing and needed to calm down and take a deep breath. 'There is no time pressure,' I told myself. I looked at my watch: 2.30 p.m. I decided we would camp. We found a small sandy beach and made a fire. I sat on a rock and poured hot, sweet coffee down my throat. I got the maps out and went through the options in slow time. Once I'd recomposed myself, the only sensible option presented itself to me. I found a spur on the eastern (right) side of the valley that was shallow enough to climb. It would take all day but we could try to rejoin the path we had left forty-eight hours earlier. It meant admitting that the whole descent into the valley had been a complete waste of time and it meant having a huge climb in the morning, but it was the safer side in terms of narcos, and we knew that once we'd climbed out there was a path at the top that we could resume following.

Having found the safer, more sensible route out, I reflected on the day with embarrassment. My confidence had taken a serious knock and I sat at the bottom of the Apurímac Canyon feeling as small and as sorry for myself as I have ever felt. Was I capable of running this trip on my own? Would I get the three of us killed?

I dug out the Cuban cigar my friend George had given me to smoke at some celebratory moment and decided that this was a time for such a comfort. I lit it up and breathed in the smooth leathery smoke. I had made three bad decisions which had put us in two very tight spots. I made a pact with myself not to look for easy options and not to let myself feel pressured into making a particular decision. I had to accept full responsibility for all of our lives from now on and I needed to dig deep and find the composure and confidence required to get us out of this mess.

The following morning I woke up feeling 100 per cent better. Oz immediately found a track on the spur and we reached the path (the one we had left three days before) in only four hours of climbing.

The track contoured back and forth around spurs high on the valley side until we dropped down into the picturesque village of Locmahuaeco, in a valley full of fruit trees heavy with oranges and sweet lemons. In the impossibly pretty village we found a shop that had a new stock of fizzy drinks and biscuits. The young couple who ran it were pleased to welcome their first ever customers and we relaxed immediately in the pleasant surroundings – so much so that we committed the cardinal error of not asking to meet the village chief. The young couple seemed so relaxed and friendly that it didn't seem necessary and they suggested we sling our hammocks between the goal posts on the football pitch.

While we were down on the pitch I used the large expanse to lay out the four six-foot solar rolls and charge the 12v dry-cell motorbike battery that we were using to charge the laptop. Inquisitive kids came and offered us sweet lemons until we could eat no more.

I was just about to start writing my diary entry in my hammock when the village chief summoned Oz and me to a village meeting, demanding to see our permit. We had no permit, of course, so we giggled all the way to the meeting like naughty school kids. Inside the metal-roofed shed I explained who we were and what we were doing. The whole village had assembled to discuss what to do with these outsiders who had just turned up and made camp on their football pitch. Then Oz retold the story for those who didn't understand a word of my crude Spanish. Everyone looked deadly serious, the women more so than the men. The chief took down our passport and ID details and we were told that, as this was the Red Zone, if anything were to happen to us they would be under suspicion. They told us we must speak to the village chiefs whenever we entered a village in future and we apologised profusely and thanked them for their advice. When they said we could go I stepped outside into the dark, relieved that it hadn't been more problematic.

'*Idiotas!*' Oz shouted – far too soon and far too close to the shed. We all broke into a run like kids playing pranks in the street. I needed to take these people seriously – they all lived outside the law here as there was no law – no policing, certainly, and a huge drugs trade. 'Start growing up, Stafford,' I scolded myself back in my hammock. 'This isn't a game.'

In the morning the young couple, recent arrivals in the village themselves and noticeably more relaxed and normal than many of the other inhabitants, cooked us an old hen and some yucca, a local root vegetable. Everyone was all smiles when we left and we started climbing the valley wall out of their community on a wide path. We felt strong after the breakfast but the path was steep and I was having to focus on my walking to keep up with the two Peruvians. At the crest – without really breaking stride – Sergio stretched his rubber catapult elastic between his thumb and forefinger and took aim into the trees to the right. He did this often – launching small stones to the left and the right to little effect. But this time he whooped in delight and shrugged off his pack to retrieve something from the undergrowth. He'd hit a small mountain pigeon and we had meat for supper.

The day was hard and the path split several times. We had to guess the right way each time; eventually the path ran out and we found ourselves picking our way down the mountainside, slipping over and hanging on to roots and branches as we went.

At a small, strong-flowing stream we stripped off and bathed, washing the morning's scum from our bodies. We suspected that the path we had lost was now high above us and so we started uphill following a spur through increasingly dense trees until I realised that we had, after three and a bit months of the expedition, entered the jungle for the first time. Exhausted, I smiled at the familiar feeling of being surrounded by trees. The cool darkness of the shade and the damp smell of the vegetation welcomed me back to what seemed a long-lost environment.

After three hours we had made 400 metres horizontally and 200 metres vertically. We were cutting through dense, tangled undergrowth and crawling under and over fallen trees to make any ground. It was now late afternoon; we had seen no sign of the path and none of water. We made camp, lit a small fire and fried the pigeon in oil. With virtually no water we savoured the succulent meat and had some banana-flavoured sweet biscuits for pudding. Progress had been so slow that we all agreed we could not continue on this side of the river through such mountainous jungle as we hadn't enough food, and according to the map at this speed it could take us weeks to hit the next village. Sergio knew the other side of the Apurímac had a good path all the way from here to San Francisco and so, despite the obvious increased dangers of encountering drugs traffickers, we made a plan to use the paths on the narco side and get out of here as fast as we could.

So we got up, with no water to drink but a slow drizzle falling, and ran almost straight down the hill to the river, one and a half kilometres away down a 650-metre descent. Swinging on trees like monkeys as we crashed down the hillside, we made the river in little over an hour. Lowering ourselves the last treacherous metres down slippery rocks, we finally inflated the rafts and ferried ourselves over to the other side. We glugged about two litres of water each and Oz made up a big pot of noodles that we wolfed down. We could see agricultural fields above us and knew that that meant that there were paths. Paths meant progress and so we started scrambling up the steep hillside.

Diary entry from 10 July 2008:

At one point on this 50-metre ascent I had my arms round Sergio's waist to make him heavier so he could pull Oz up a vertical face that had no handholds. Ridiculous stuff that you do because there's no option. Your life is dependent on a dead tree not snapping or a clump of grass not pulling out of the earth. Once we hit the paths we

*marched quietly up the hill – all suddenly very aware we were in
narco land.*

*Once we had relaxed a little we stopped and sat under a tree and
gorged ourselves on sweet lemons. I ate eight today. Free food that you
don't have to carry – why not?*

We continued up the hill. As we climbed up 800 metres with our
heavy packs I realised how easy it was becoming and how fit we
were getting. We found a fantastic path – maintained to a very high
standard – and rounded the corner into a valley that was covered in
lush green forest. The days of dusty hills were now behind us and,
as if to signal the entrance to the jungle, two troops of howler
monkeys started roaring at each other through the deep valley.
Howlers are the second loudest mammal in the world (after blue
whales) and noise filled the valley as if herds of dinosaurs were
taunting each other, ready to fight. The noise lifted me and I felt
comfort in the fact that I was leaving the mountains, a region in
which I have limited experience, and was entering my favourite
environment in the world – tropical rainforest.

The latter stages of the River Apurímac were still part of the Red
Zone and I slowly became aware that the River Ene was going to be
just as dangerous. Beneath the veneer of peacefulness and tran-
quillity I was aware of the ominous truth: there was a huge amount
of drugs processing and trafficking going on and we were dealing
with narcos on an almost daily basis. Sergio warned me that if we
did mistakenly walk in on an active drugs processing plant we
would be killed immediately. 'No two ways about it,' he said. The
profits were too high for the narcos to be able to risk outsiders
knowing about their locations. If locals were aware of the details of
the processing, they kept quiet. They valued their lives.

With satellite phones, Internet, GPS and modern weapons, the
drugs industry is far better equipped than the Peruvian police, who
don't stand a chance of defeating them. The only successful
operations against the narcos were conducted by the military – and
these were apparently rare.

After a 0530 start, sleeping in a ditch at the side of a road, we wandered into a small town called Villa Virgen at about breakfast time. The town was in the early stages of recovery following a huge party the night before and most people were still awake and blind drunk. The president of the town staggered towards us, face flushed red and eyes bloodshot, and demanded to see our papers. I smiled and asked him politely if he could recommend a good hotel. He looked confused, pointed us in the direction of a hotel and welcomed us to Villa Virgen. We stayed one night and bade farewell to a very smiley Sergio the next morning and Oz and I headed on alone.

Diary entry from 24 July 2008:

We are in Pichari. Oz is very worried about the days and weeks ahead. He is scared of the 'nativos' (local indigenous Amerindians) and the drugs traffickers. I think this fear is understandable and no one thinks the route ahead is safe. Everybody keeps telling us that no one has ever walked through here before.

I am apprehensive but think deep down it's just a fear of the unknown and that things will be much easier than we expect.

Looked at the maps between Atalaya and Pucallpa again today and the remoteness is silly. Hundreds of miles of green with a snaking blue river winding its way through. Whether it is successful or not the next few months will be adventure packed.

I actually do now think it is possible I will die on this trip. I am so committed and focused on finishing though that I think it is a risk worth taking. We have been lucky so far – who's to say our luck won't continue? The thing is I don't want Oz to die – I'd hate that. I've given him more chances today to leave and I can tell he's considering it. I don't want to convince him to stay because if he dies I'll be responsible.

I feel like I'm about to go over the top; that my life is in the hands of fate. Not being melodramatic – that's how I feel.

Spoke to Chloë today. We are very close despite being two years separated. She is the only person I have a picture of here; a photo of us both by a lake in the Fijian mountains. We were very happy that day. Chloë – I love you.

The town in two days is Natividad. Stories are that everyone is armed. They fire shots in the air to call a village meeting. All involved in drugs trafficking. No police. Lots of nativos. Tired. Bed.

On 25 July Oz and I set off walking from Pichari with very heavy packs. We had now got all of the gear Sergio (the Ox) had been carrying and we felt as if we had entered the Red Zone heart. I could feel Oz was scared and we hardly spoke as we struggled with the new weight. After five kilometres a pick-up truck drove past and a man in the back screamed out, '*Aquí se matan!*' – here they kill. Oz looked visibly shaken by the comment and I suggested we take a break. We didn't speak for about three minutes and then Oz said he needed to tell me something. I knew what he was about to say and asked him to wait until I got the camera out and started filming him. 'I've decided I want to go home, Ed. I am sorry – I have too many worries.'

I wasn't that surprised. With just five kilometres made we decided that the best bet was for us to return to Pichari and organise Oz's departure. We hitched a ride on a pick-up and realised we were sitting on top of bails of coca leaves. Ironically, we'd been picked up by a friendly drugs trafficker who dropped us off in town.

Sombrely we checked into a grubby hostel and started to go through the kit that I could carry alone. The medical kit now had about as many drugs in it as there were white people in this area. I eventually got all my stuff in my rucksack down to about 45 kilograms. Cameras, tape stock, computer, satellite links, telephones, solar rolls, a 12v dry-cell battery, chargers, cables, cables, cables and – of course – some kit for surviving the jungle, too. The rest Oz would take back to Cusco and send on to Lima for storage.

I wrote a diary entry and had a rather sleepless night wondering what on earth I could do. I didn't want to walk into certain trouble but I didn't want to give up either.

The following morning Oz agreed to try to help me find a new guide. But as we shyly edged around the town the general consensus was that it was not safe to walk with a gringo. The local population thought that the American military were operating in this area in an attempt to eradicate the cocaine processing plants. As most people in the area had some kind of a hand in the drugs trade they weren't too fond of Americans. With my shaven head and my expedition shirt covered in sponsor and charity logos I looked both American and military.

If we had been in the river, in kayaks, we could have paddled frantically past and not been too visible. But we weren't in kayaks. If the Americans had not recently started to operate in this area we would not have been targets for the alarmed coca-producing locals. But, according to local rumour, they had. I threw away my expedition shirt and bought a cheap T-shirt from a street stall.

The last place we entered looking for a guide was a general store and I bought some fishing tackle as gifts for the Amerindians. The shopkeeper was interested in us and when we told him what we were doing he became very serious. 'You can't go through this area on foot,' he insisted. 'You must get a bus back to Lima and then rejoin your journey at Atalaya. There is no way through the River Ene on foot for a white man.' I asked him what he thought would happen if we tried. His answer required little reading between the lines. 'They will kill you.'

When we told him that I was planning to do this anyway he sighed, and advised I get a permit from the Rondero building. I had heard of Ronderos but didn't really understand who they were until Oswaldo explained it to me. The Peruvian police were not allowed to enter this area and it was, in effect, outside the law. If the police came here they would be killed. The Ronderos were trusted local people who were selected to police the area for crimes other than those involving drugs and they had a hand in the drugs industry.

We left the shop with fishing hooks, lead weights and nylon line and I seriously considered not going and seeing the Ronderos. If they said I couldn't go through then we'd be in an even worse position. Nervously, however, Oz and I crossed the plaza and banged on the metal door of the camouflaged building. I've never really understood why South American paramilitary (and real military) units camouflage their bases. Do they think it means they can't be seen? Ridiculous. We were told to enter and the gloomy room housed one fat bloke sitting behind a metal desk and an old type-writer. He looked at us suspiciously and nodded for me to speak.

I told him what we were doing. Actually, I lied a bit. I knew that he would not want me to walk through here but I also knew that previous expeditions had kayaked through, so I pretended we were on a kayaking expedition and asked if he wouldn't mind typing out a permit for us to pass through. The 'president' (he introduced himself in this way) told us to be careful but clearly enjoyed my respectful request. He said that I had come to the right place and of course he would write me a permit. As he stabbed away at the clunky typewriter I prayed that his permit wouldn't specify our means of transport. After about forty minutes he coughed, signed the permit, stamped it and handed it over. It was perfect – no mention of kayaks; we had official written permission to pass through the area from the Comite Autodefensa (CAD), the Ronderos.

Back out in the bright sunshine of the concrete plaza the small success gave me new hope and the talk of kayaks had given me an idea. 'Would you stay if we were in boats, Oz?' I asked. He said that he would but reminded me that this would break the rules of my expedition.

'We keep being scared of the next part because we are listening to horror stories,' I continued. 'But whenever we get downriver things are never as bad as we had feared. Let's paddle downriver in the rafts – see for ourselves what the situation is like – and if we are both happy we can come back here to walk this section. If you are not happy then you can leave the expedition from where we end up in the boats.'

Oz agreed. This was a longwinded way of achieving my goal but it was a plan and, for the moment, I still had a guide. We would have to return to Pichari to continue walking, but at least we would have an idea of what we were about to encounter.

Chapter Five

The Ashaninkas

The following morning after cow's foot soup and Inca Kola in a grubby café, Oz and I walked down to the water, inflated our rafts and floated out on to the River Apurímac through the morning mist. The 20-metre-wide river was rocky and broken with small rapids and whirlpools. The journey to get to Puerto Ocopa (the next settlement with road access) was 155 kilometres in a straight line and perhaps over 200 as the river meandered. Expecting to arrive in four days, we must have been pretty distracted when we set off as the only food we took with us was three packets of strawberry biscuits.

The first emotion I felt was that, compared to walking, this was great fun. The current was strong and the banks rushed past us on either side. We were moving north very fast.

But then Oz started to behave oddly. He would scream at every small rapid as if he'd seen a ghost. His already shot nerves had now got to the stage where he was almost having a breakdown in his raft. I tried to talk him back to calmness but as we were bombing down a fairly dangerous river with large rapids and potentially dangerous *nativo* huts scattered along the banks my attempts were in vain. He started laughing crazily.

Then the rapids got much worse. At one point I misjudged one and found myself pinned against a rock by the force of the river. The water completely filled my raft in less than a second and I thought I was in serious trouble. Oz was bearing towards me from behind with a manic grin on his face and I waved him away from the path

I'd chosen. As he passed safely I managed to free my raft and to my delight realised that, even full of water and submerged, the raft didn't sink. I paddled out of the rapids with just the top half of my body and my rucksack out of the water – the entire boat was below the waterline.

We passed many indigenous-looking people that day; most of them were armed with shotguns. The majority just watched us, showing no emotion.

We set up camp on a stony beach at 6 p.m. as it was getting dark. Two young boys were fishing with a hook and line and we went to ask them if they had any food to eat. Oz was asking the boys questions in such a panicky, frantic manner that it was somewhat embarrassing and I knew that he really needed to go home. The boys were not too put out by Oz's behaviour and told us that there was a passenger boat passing in the morning. This was the first I'd heard of the river being navigable by boats other than kayaks and canoes and this lifted our spirits greatly. They gave us two yucca to eat and, as I'd never prepared one before, Oz showed me how to chop them up and boil them. We each dined on a big plate of yucca; it tasted vaguely like potato. Oz relaxed a little, comfortable in the knowledge that his stomach was full and that he wouldn't have to get into his raft again in the morning.

The next morning we took the passenger boat to Puerto Ocopa. There I paid Oz what money I could, told him I'd send the rest by Western Union and packed him into a clapped-out taxi to the town of Satipo where he would get a bus to Lima and then another to his home in Cusco. It was all rather dispassionate but at the time I was glad Oz was leaving; his fear was contagious and he wasn't a help to the expedition any longer. He had done an amazing job to get me as far as he had and I owed him a lot. Above and beyond the wages that he had earned I also forwarded him the money to allow him to do his next term at guiding school. The dented taxi disappeared in a cloud of dust and that was the last I saw of Oswaldo.

The expedition was four months in, I'd seen the back of Luke and now Oz, but I could feel myself getting stronger. I was physically and mentally adapting to the new demands of this expedition and I felt truly alive, experiencing new sensations and new scenery each day.

The portly captain of the boat we had come in on was called Ruben and he kindly took me to the local Ashaninka community near Puerto Ocopa in order to search for a new guide. I was looking for a man who spoke the local indigenous language. The village was an orderly arrangement of dusty streets and basic wooden buildings thatched with palm branches. The difference between the Ashaninka village and the colonial settlement of Puerto Ocopa was that the Indians were neat and orderly – while the colonial port was chaotic and filthy. Houses were thatched and often without walls, but the dirt streets connecting them were not too dissimilar to those of a Western village. After about the fifth attempt at finding the right house we arrived at one outside of which sat a middle-aged Ashaninka couple and a young boy. Ruben explained what I was looking for and immediately the young boy smiled widely and said, 'I'll do it!'

'Fantastic!' I said, amazed that I had found someone to guide me. 'How old are you?'

'Sixteen,' said Elias.

It was only a couple of hours before the boat left back upriver and so I repacked my stuff. A fairly light pack for me (minus laptop, solar chargers and other heavy stuff that I would leave in the shabby hotel as we would be walking back this way) and a very light rucksack for Elias. Elias was, I estimated, less than five foot tall. He had broad shoulders and a wide, almost African smile. I bought him some plimsolls and a shirt and we boarded the boat.

On the boat I asked Elias about his family. He explained that the couple I'd met were his uncle and aunt and that he was staying with them because his mother had been killed. 'I am sorry,' I said. 'When was that?'

'On Wednesday,' replied Elias.

I just didn't have the fluency in Spanish to talk to Elias about this as much as I would have liked as it was such a delicate subject – but it would appear that his mother had died less than a week before I met him. Incredibly, with a nail through the throat.

Back in Pichari, Elias and I booked into the same hotel that Oz and I had stayed in twice before. Having left my laptop behind in Puerto Ocopa to save weight, I couldn't check emails and so I rang my friend Marlene in Lima and she relayed all important messages. Speaking to her was comforting and to hear the concern in her voice for my safety made me feel that someone not so far away cared.

I had been anxious and scared for my life at times over the last few days. But when I questioned the validity of the whole expedition I decided that I was simply scared of what I didn't know and would probably be fine. The warnings were almost certainly aimed at the average tourist. I told myself I wasn't one of them. I reminded myself, too, that I had served in Northern Ireland and spent four months in Afghanistan. I could handle this. Especially if Elias could handle it six days after his mother had been killed.

On 30 July 2008, after walking 35 kilometres down a winding, unpaved road, Elias and I arrived in Natividad. After all the warnings, I had built up an image in my mind of this outlaw town being full of armed narcos with wide-brimmed hats and handlebar moustaches. Instead, a quiet couple let us stay in a sort of hostel and I went looking for Oz's sister, Paulina, who was coincidently working as a teacher in Natividad. Paulina was easy to find; she was the only female teacher in town and it was fascinating to see this beautiful female version of Oswaldo. She was very concerned to hear why Oswaldo was no longer with me and told me that I should probably go home now, too. I smiled, tried to reassure her that I was OK about the risk, and suggested we visit the town president so that I was seen to be as open and unthreatening to the drugs traffickers as possible.

Paulina accompanied me to the house of the president but he was in the shower when we arrived. As we waited outside I felt a bit like George Bush hanging around in a Taliban stronghold in Afghanistan hoping not to get noticed. The entire plaza stopped what it was doing and stared at me.

Then I saw the heavies. 'Here we go,' I thought. Four men with shotguns marched purposefully towards me across the plaza with mean looks on their faces. I was in quite a cocky mood so I anticipated their arrival, walked towards them and shook each one by the hand in turn, looking them straight in the eye.

I explained myself and showed them the letter of permission from the Ronderos in Pichari. That letter, I now began to realise, was fucking gold dust.

Slightly confused by the letter, the heavies nonetheless seemed to agree that I had permission to be there. But they demanded to see Elias, who was back at the hostel, and so I was escorted at gunpoint to the accommodation that we'd checked in to. Annoyingly, Elias had not seen the need to bring any form of identification with him, a huge mistake in a country like Peru where it is the law to carry your ID card. He managed to get away with it only because he was a child.

Once through with the letter and Elias, they demanded to see the contents of my rucksack. I took them to my room and showed them everything. I went into silly detail explaining the video camera, how it worked and basically overloading them with information. Before long they got bored.

I had been worried they would confiscate the camera, because the one thing they wouldn't want was people knowing about the narcotics trade in the area. But once they'd seen everything they didn't really know what to do. So they continued looking mean, thanked me for my time and welcomed me to the town. If there was any trouble I was to contact them. 'We are the law,' they told me, in case I hadn't worked that out by now.

After this I walked up the main street and a tall, thin man with a goatee beard slid up beside me. 'Be careful, gringo,' he said menacingly and slid away. Had I not already been warned to be careful here by everybody I would have burst out laughing. The people in Natividad took themselves ridiculously seriously. They were just kids with guns, but that was a fairly lethal combination.

As I went to sleep that night I was surprised to be in a hostel in a

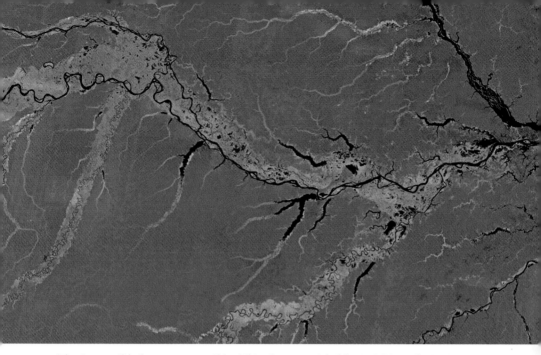

The impossible becomes possible. This data provided by NASA and JAXA enabled me to literally see through the jungle canopy and plan a route avoiding the worst flooded areas. Dark grey is terra firma and light grey is flooded forest at high-water season. JAXA/NASA/JPL-Caltech JERS-1/GRFM ©JAXA/METI.

Oswaldo Teracaya Rosaldo in the Colca Canyon.

With Luke on the summit of Nevado Mismi.

With Luke at
The Source – one
of two crosses
and there were
two further
plaques – hence
covering all bases
and summitting
Nevado Mismi
the following
morning.

The Apurimac
Canyon – the
deepest canyon in
the world.

Two Ashaninka
hunters just
outside Pichari.

Ashaninka mother and daughters making masato, a fermented, mildly alcoholic drink made by chewing yucca and spitting it back into the pot.

Rondero outpost in Pichari, The Red Zone.

Emily Caruso, anthropologist, and her Ashaninka family in Pamaquiari.

The gateway to the River Tambo – this marked the end of the terrifying River Ene.

Donating medicines to the villages along the Tambo – Cho in the background.

Ashaninka men on the River Ucayali.

Andreas and me –
pack raft buddies.

The Dongo
brothers (Alfonso
and Andreas) in
their new T-shirts
bought when
we arrived in
Pucallpa.

A home-made
shotgun trip wire
trap used for small
animals such as
agouti.

Cutting through the jungle.

A village girl in Peru.

Crossing the river, towing the group's bags. This method enabled the local guides' bags to stay dry. © KEITH DUCATEL

Advancing through the floods. © KEITH DUCATEL

Up to my chest in water, wondering how many more months there were to go until I could have a hot bath at home. © KEITH DUCATEL

Mestiso child in a Peruvian village.
© KEITH DUCATEL

Walking into the first flood season.
© KEITH DUCATEL

bed again and I put my camera within arm's reach on night vision in case we were disturbed in the night. We weren't.

We breakfasted at 6 a.m.; then, with fried eggs and bread inside us, we said goodbye to Paulina and walked out of Natividad towards the River Ene. Elias and I looked ridiculous walking together, me at six foot one inch and him under five feet. He looked all the more like a child in his shorts and his brand-new plimsolls.

By mid-morning we had arrived in Puerto Ene. There we met Jonathan, a strong, lean man without an ounce of fat on him who took about two seconds to decide he would leave his wife and kids to walk with us. Jonathan knew the paths and had the confidence of a man who had always lived in the area. Importantly, he was a man with drive and character and he immediately set about motivating Elias and me to walk faster. He led us through the forested paths strongly and the injection of new blood was entirely reviving.

It was now the beginning of August and Elias, Jonathan and I walked through one indigenous community after another in somewhat of a haze. In each settlement we are offered *masato*, a fermented drink that the women make by chewing yucca and spitting it into a bowl. Their saliva is vital to the fermentation process and the resulting product is a slightly alcoholic milky drink. It is offensive to refuse a drink and I hadn't yet worked out that you could politely decline the refills so we drank litres of this rank fermented fluid all day long.

The indigenous communities made me nervous. For their part, the Ashaninka people were equally nervous of me. These were the most authentically unchanged tribal people I would meet during the entire length of my journey and a large part of me wished I'd had more experience at the time so that I could have relaxed and enjoyed the whole thing more. But the expedition was what it was and I just had to adapt and learn and soak up as much as I could. I tried hard to relax but I was so far out of my comfort zone that I never really managed it.

The Ashaninka men and women wore single-piece brown or blue garments called *cushmas*, not much more than sacks, really, that were hand-woven using a traditional method. Both men and women were short, no one over five foot six, and wore lots of beaded jewellery and red face paint, often in a thin line crossing their noses from cheek to cheek. Very few wore shoes and many walked around with a bow and arrow in one hand. Most conversation took place in the Ashaninka language and I spoke Spanish to Jonathan and Elias, trying to get the gist of what everyone was saying. A handful of missionaries had come into some of the communities in the past by boat but everyone agreed I was the first white man ever to enter their villages on foot.

Jonathan had to leave us and head home as he had heard over the HF radio that his daughter was sick. I was sorry to see him go; he'd been a feisty presence and I would miss his energy and impatience to get things done fast. A very atypical South American indeed.

On his last night I lay in my hammock writing my journal when he dragged me out of my dreaming: 'Estafford! Estafford! Come and drink with us!' He had bought a 10-litre bucket of *masato* from the *nativos* and wanted me to drink it with him. When I declined the kind offer from my hammock he slunk up to me and said I had to pay a hundred *soles* (£20) for the bucket anyway.

'*Vete la puta!*' were the last words I ever said to Jonathan. 'Fuck off!'

The next morning as Elias and I continued everything felt very sombre and quiet without our cocky friend. Eventually we reached a community, Pamakiari, which said 'No'. I could not pass. The locals were visibly frightened by my arrival and gathered to share their alarm and shout at me. Elias and I had buckets of water thrown over us and one woman smeared red plant dye all over my face with her hands.

One of the women at the back of the group stuck out in particular. She was much taller, about six foot, slim and white like a Westerner but wearing the same traditional face paint and Ashaninka beaded jewellery. I stared at her, unsure as to what or who she was, and she caught my gaze. She stepped forward. 'Are you English?' she asked in a well-spoken English accent. 'My name is Emily.'

'Do you know where you are?' Emily continued accusingly. 'Do you have any idea what these people have been through?' I was torn between elation at having found a person that I could speak to properly and being embarrassed at my lack of knowledge about the Ashaninkas.

The villagers let us speak but Emily was initially noticeably wary about being overly friendly to me. I was later to find out that she was an Italian anthropologist, and that she had spent months working with the Ashaninkas from a nearby town before they trusted her enough to let her visit and then eventually live in one of their communities in order to study their culture.

She acted as a mediator as Elias was too young to have any influence with the men and women, all of whom were very unhappy about my presence. I was asked if I had a permit from CARE, the indigenous organisation that oversaw the Ashaninkas on the River Ene. I admitted I hadn't even been aware there was such an organisation. I felt stupid, naive and unprepared. The Ashaninkas refused my offers of gifts and sent me down to the river to wait for a boat. I was not allowed to pass. Emily watched me pick up my pack and walk down to the river with Elias. I had no idea what to do. The place they were telling me that I needed to go was Satipo, hundreds of kilometres away, down the river by boat and then taxi. It was the town of I had sent Oz through on his way home.

As Elias sat and waited and I washed my red face in the brown river, Emily came down to the water. She told me that, coincidentally, she was going out to Satipo that day with some of the village elders and that there was space in the boat. We could accompany her.

I could have hugged Emily at that point. She had no idea how close to tears and wretched I was feeling and she was offering help. With Emily, Elias and several Ashaninka elders, I climbed into the little boat and set off back downriver to Puerto Ocopa where Elias lived and where the River Ene accesses the outside world via one dusty road.

Once on the boat, Emily relaxed. Less under the gaze of the

community, we sat together in the well of the boat on the wooden floor and with a smile she handed me a menthol cigarette. I could have kissed her. She'd washed the red Indian paint from her face now, too, and her long curls hung over her confident yet feminine Mediterranean face. The normality of her presence, watching her soft lips draw on her cigarette and the kind way that she started to explain the history of the Ashaninkas made my chest start to glow from within.

There had been huge problems with horrifying violence in this area in the past and the Ashaninkas on the Ene suffered terribly at the hands of the Shining Path, communist terrorists attempting to take over Peru. The government at the time armed the Ashaninkas with modern weapons and they fought back violently. That said, whole generations of Ashaninka males were wiped out and few women over the age of twenty-five escaped being repeatedly raped and beaten during the onslaught. A new threat was petroleum companies that wanted to come and extract oil from under the Ashaninkas' feet – this was already happening on other rivers in the area. On top of that, the coca invasions (colonial Peruvians taking over indigenous lands by force or trickery) were closely linked with illegal logging and it was no surprise that the Ashaninkas looked upon every outsider as a threat.

The water throwing, Emily told me, was a way of turning a serious subject into a light-hearted one – the people were genuinely scared of us but they were kind-hearted and didn't want any trouble. Emily told me that the previous morning a woman had thrown water over a man who had just beaten up his wife while drunk. The message was serious without using force.

Emily said she would introduce me to CARE and help me get a permit from them to enable me to continue my walk. She was putting her reputation and trust with these people on the line for a stranger and in my exhausted, paranoid state I have to admit I was pretty taken with Emily and her long, slim legs.

I took her advice and bought 800 *soles'* worth of presents for the Ashaninka villagers. The bundle consisted mostly of antibiotics, painkillers and hard-boiled sweets, and CARE were convinced of my good intentions and granted me a permit. They had originally suggested taking machetes and shovels for the communities but medication was agreed upon because it was light and we had to carry everything on our backs. They even gave me a guide to walk with from their organisation called Oscar who knew the communities and was trusted. Setting off with abundant gifts, a permit and a trusted Ashaninka guide, I felt that things were back on track. I had spent a few nights in a hotel in a town and I had enjoyed meals out with Emily eating pizza, drinking red wine and chatting about our lives at home. I felt like a new man and was ready for the River Ene once again. With everything now in place, what could possibly go wrong?

Oscar was an Ashaninka of about my age and had the mullet hairstyle of an eighties German footballer. He'd asked me for an advance on his wages the day before. As I gave it to him I thought, 'I'm only doing this because he is part of CARE and I have to trust him.' Oscar was very happy and we agreed to meet at his hostel at seven the following morning.

At 7.01 I banged on Oscar's door in the dark hostel. No response. Had he disappeared? Damn, this was frustrating! I had already paid him and now I didn't have a guide. I asked the hostel owner when he had left and she told me he was still in his room – sleeping. I banged again. Actually, I smashed at the door relentlessly with my fist shouting, 'Oscar! *Buenos dias, amigo!*' At about 7.20 the entire hostel was awake and pretty unhappy with me; then, finally, the door opened a crack to reveal two bloodshot eyes trying to focus on me from the gloom and the stench within. Oscar was absolutely wrecked. The fumes of cheap liquor made me step back a pace. 'Great!' I smiled. 'The boat is waiting! Let's go, my friend!' Oscar grabbed his tiny knapsack and I bundled him into the taxi that would take us to the port. He went straight to sleep but I didn't care. The journey back to where we wanted to resume the walking was two days away by boat; he had plenty of time to sleep off his hangover.

More than thirty hours later the boat pulled up back in Pamakiari. The woman who had thrown water over me was there as I stepped on to the shore. Oscar explained to her that he was here to guide me and that I now had written permission from CARE. Oscar was the important bit really as she couldn't read or write so the paper was meaningless. She smiled at me from behind her harsh black fringe as if to say, 'I'll let you off this time then!' and went about her business.

As it was morning we didn't stay in the community as we could get a fair bit of walking done. The amount of time this travelling back and forth was taking had made me start to worry about my schedule and I wanted to get the River Ene behind me now. We walked through fields of yucca and then on hunters' trails through the jungle. Where we could, Oscar would rope in the services of another man to show us the way to the next community as he didn't know the paths and it was very easy to get disorientated in the green maze of secondary jungle.

Arriving in most communities still made me apprehensive – despite Oscar's presence. He and I got on well enough but there was no real connection and I was aware that his loyalty was with the people rather than me and that I was very dependent on him.

After two days we arrived in a community that looked very civilised with thatched houses surrounding a well-kept football pitch. We dumped our packs under one of the huts and Oscar left to go and seek out the village chief. I sat and waited for him. And waited. I started to get uncomfortable. When Oscar finally came back he looked concerned.

'Put the camera away and come with me,' he said.

'Huh?' I stalled, hearing Oscar but not wanting to comply. If something was about to happen I wanted to film.

'Put the camera away,' Oscar repeated. He looked worried so I obeyed.

We walked out of the centre of the village to a site where a school was being built. Oscar led the way and pointed the chief out to me. As I walked towards him to introduce myself and shake his hand I was soaked with a bucket of dirty water. The girl who had thrown it was shouting angrily in Ashaninka. High-pitched staccato words stabbed at me along with the filthy water.

The next bucket was full of sloppy concrete, followed by two more of the same. As I looked around at all the villagers who were surrounding me none of them were laughing. I felt remarkably calm although slightly pathetic, completely covered in watery concrete. The girl then started pushing the wet concrete mixture into my mouth. The women were shrieking at me, alarmed and angry, but I was sure I could detect sympathy in the eyes of the quiet men as they looked on.

'We should leave,' I said to Oscar, spitting out sand and cement. I shook the hand of the village president and thanked him. We turned and headed towards the river – Oscar was clearly unsettled as we walked but he said nothing. Then, once at the river, he told me that the community downriver was waiting with what I translated as a 'pile of spines' to throw at me.

Oscar explained to me that this was serious because they thought that I was from an Argentine oil company, Pluspetrol. They had received a message the previous day from CARE over the HF radio to be prepared for gringos arriving to steal their oil from below their territory. Then I had turned up.

It was a perfectly understandable mistake on the part of the Ashaninkas. I was white and my timing was appalling. I couldn't help thinking that CARE might have timed their warning message a bit better with regards to me but I wasn't really their problem. Oscar said we could not continue because he had been thrown out of the community, too, and so there would now be distrust between CARE and this community. It was a mess and Oscar said he was not prepared to continue walking with me. I asked him if he would do so on the other side of the River Ene – the predominantly colonial side – but as an Ashaninka he was scared to walk on that side and said that the narcos were too dangerous.

We inflated the pack rafts and first paddled to the far side of the river so that I could mark the position with my GPS. Once happy that I could find the point again when I returned, we started paddling downstream. I was unsettled: I had managed only two further days' walking with Oscar and the all-important permits and was now heading back to Puerto Ocopa again. I was questioning why I was returning with Oscar but my tiredness and the ordeal of having the community so upset with me made the draw of the town enticing. I needed to find someone else to walk with now, perhaps a non-Ashaninka so that I could continue on the narco side. The *nativos* were worrying me far more than the narcos now and so my thoughts were concentrated on the left (west) bank of the river. Once we were a little distance away Oscar and I sat back and just floated with the current.

That night I had a fascinating talk with a man in the port. He told me that the *nativos* in that part were 'bad' and stood in the way of progress for Peru. He was repeating verbatim the propaganda that was being pumped into the Peruvian people by President García. Television advertisements constantly reminded everyone that 'Peru Advances' with shiny happy people extracting oil and other natural resources. It made me feel sick as I knew the Ashaninkas had no part in this prosperous future.

The next day Oscar and I travelled back to Satipo where Emily showed me a map revealing that a whopping 100 per cent of the Peruvian Amazon (outside of the few protected areas) was now allocated for resources extraction of some kind. An astonishing law stated that Peruvians owned their land only down to five metres below the surface. The government was able to sell the drilling rights from beneath the Ashaninka territory to international companies and the indigenous people had no say at all. That is what had just happened on the River Ene. That is what the communities were defending themselves against. I couldn't help but take sides – although the Ashaninkas had thrown me out I completely understood why and started to become quite proud of their fierce defensive spirit.

Emily spoke of other parts of Peru where the oil companies had already started extracting and where native communities had been irreversibly changed. The process was dirty and pollution (largely from spills in transportation) was high, leaving rivers filthy and void of fish. The locals were often compensated with salaries such as $1,000 a month. Enough to live like a king in the communities and to be permanently drunk – which is what often happens alongside a sharp rise in domestic violence. When beer, or, even worse, liquor is brought into communities the traditional values break down completely. Emily told me that after every party in her community about a third of the women would be beaten severely by their drunken partners. Every time.

The Ashaninkas' reaction to me was actually good to see. They only wanted to protect their land and their lifestyle and I hoped they could do both. I wished them well and didn't want to upset them more and so I planned to stick to the western bank for the remainder of the River Ene.

Back in Satipo I was emotionally drained. I put the word out that I was looking for a guide but those who said 'yes' were not quite right or wanted to charge high prices that I couldn't afford. With some resignation I came to the conclusion that I would have to walk alone. I would stick to the river beaches on the left as the water level was low and I would walk with my raft permanently inflated and strapped to my rucksack so that I could make a quick escape if I ran into trouble. It was a risky plan because without a guide I felt much more vulnerable.

Just before I was due to leave, Emily said that the brother of a friend of hers was looking for work. He was a forestry worker and knew the area to the west of the River Ene well. Emily arranged for me to meet Gadiel Sanchez Rivera.

Chapter Six

Gadiel 'Cho' Sanchez Rivera

We met in the dingy kitchen at his brother's house in Satipo. He looked smart and intelligent, had neatly trimmed hair and had ironed his shirt and trousers. I'd brought some maps with me for us to look at. He pored over them thoughtfully, rubbing his African-looking lips, pointing out the areas he knew and the areas we should avoid. He wisely wanted to go in quickly, get the job done and get out. He said he understood bits of Ashaninka as he'd spent a lot of time living in the remote areas where Ashaninkas don't speak any Spanish. He'd been forced to understand the basics in order to communicate with them. We made our plan and shook hands.

Gadiel – known as Cho (rhymes with Joe) to his friends – and I returned to the river via the now very familiar journey: a couple of hours from Satipo to Puerto Ocopa in a taxi then a full day from Ocopa to Quiteni in a passenger boat. We would overnight in Quiteni, on the western, colonial, side then make our way to where I had kissed the western bank in my pack raft and logged a position in my GPS with Oscar. From there the plan was to use a new logging road to head into the mountains, away from the river and avoid the fiercer, less frequently contacted tribes of the lower Ene. The route would still be unbroken but would just take us a little further away from the river than I'd been used to.

From Quiteni I wrote this diary entry:

I'm tired mentally and lacking motivation. Physically I'm fine but

Cho's Spanish seems to be different and I don't understand much he says. He is reasonable and looks fit and intelligent. But he doesn't speak as much Ashaninka as he made out and that's a problem. Tomorrow I need to find another guide that does.

Cho is God squad too and I just had a lecture on why not to put images of Christ up in a church. God gets jealous just like I would if my girlfriend slept with Cho apparently.

I'm really tired of melodramatic people telling us horror stories. It's sapping of energy. Yet again everyone says we are crazy to walk where we are going tomorrow. The Machiguenga 'no entienden' (don't understand) apparently. I just want to walk for fuck's sake.

Cho was about five foot eight inches tall, of medium build but with very little fat on him. As we started walking, him in his plimsolls, he began to sing Christian songs in Spanish at the top of his voice. This made me smile at first, his confidence was evident and he was doing what he liked doing – walking. He invited me to join in but I wasn't yet in a place where I could throw off my anxiety and just sing. Part of me enjoyed Cho's overt confidence; another part soon became irritated by his ging-gang-goolie approach to motivation. 'How is your motivation?' Cho would ask me repeatedly. Such questions manage to make me pissed off even if I'd been fine before. I had just done four months' walking without being jollied along by anyone and I didn't like the upset to my world.

The new logging road led up into the mountains and Cho and I walked hard and fast. I saw my first king vulture with its unmistakable purple, red and yellow head. We disturbed it while it was eating a carcass in the road and as it flew off it reminded me of the enormous condors we had seen months earlier over the Colca Canyon. The logging road had just been completed – perhaps a week beforehand – and no vehicles had passed down it since the bulldozers had finished work. It meant that our escape route from the River Ene had been built while I'd been walking the river. Late in the afternoon we arrived at a small settlement of Indians from the Machiguenga tribe.

To me Machiguengas look, dress and sound the same as Ashaninkas, but the language is apparently different. We asked if we could stay with a family but I could feel they were uncomfortable with our presence. Cho later told me it was because they thought we were drugs runners who were carrying base cocaine in our packs. They gave us a small plate of yucca for supper and asked for fifty *soles* in return which I grudgingly gave them. The whole thing felt wrong and we were glad to leave the next morning.

Cho had been worried about one particular community with whom he thought we would have problems, so he led me up an invisible path into the mountains and avoided the community. His knowledge was invaluable. He told me that the community were 'bad' and they would not have allowed us to pass. He had worked here before and he knew the families that lived in the hills and we could pass here with no problems.

On 14 August 2008, Cho and I walked into a town called Masurunkiari. The town was remarkable because it was modern, with wooden and concrete buildings of two or three storeys, a town hall, electricity and a big school and yet it was 100 per cent indigenous Indian. These Machiguengas had sold their wood and they now had money. They were very open to outsiders and clearly dealt with colonial Peruvians on a regular basis so a gringo wasn't too hard for them to handle.

In two days Cho and I made 80 kilometres. He was a walking machine – his fallibility was revealed only by a big blister caused by his flimsy plimsolls.

After five days of walking with Cho we'd arrived back in Puerto Ocopa, but on foot for the first time. We'd averaged an astonishing 35 kilometres a day down spanking new logging roads. Sadly the logging was horrendous. Cho told me that 10 per cent of what we saw was legal logging and that the rest was completely illegal. In my naivety I asked why the authorities didn't do something to stop the illegal removal of huge trees from the forest here. The obvious answer was that the authorities are involved and benefit nicely from the situation. '*Perú avanza!*'

At a local level the landowners were presented with an amazing deal. If they had hardwood of value then the logging companies would pay them for the wood and build a road to come in and extract it. Landowners were left with a cleared farm now connected to the Peruvian road network and they had money to invest in livestock. With no environmental education, and a government that encouraged resource exploitation as the future of Peru, who wouldn't sell out?

I had now walked for four and a half months from the Pacific, up and over the Andes and had descended the entire Apurímac and the Ene rivers. The infamous Red Zone was now behind me. From Puerto Ocopa, which was as far as Cho had committed to, I still had to descend the Tambo and the Ucayali rivers before the river became the Amazon by name. I didn't expect to complete the Peruvian part of the expedition for another six or seven months.

We sat in a bar below the wooden hostel where I had left my spare kit and had a beer. Both of us were very pleased with our pace and progress over the past few days. Another storm had washed away the humidity and the air felt fresh and new.

If a white man received odd looks round here, one with a black guide got double the number. Peruvians, like many South Americans, were pretty direct and called Cho 'negro' and me 'gringo'. It meant that learning our names was very easy for them. As he quite clearly had some African ancestry, Cho was very used to being identified as looking different from everyone else. We had something in common.

The hotel restaurant pumped out the typical Peruvian pop videos. Anyone who doesn't know what Peruvian music is like is very lucky indeed. Never enter Peru without earplugs. For sheer lack of talent and low-quality music, no other country compares. Oswaldo had tried to teach me about the distinct and different types of music from each region but I didn't bother to learn because to me they all fall under the same category. Utter shite. In the mountains a fat woman in a vast, multicoloured dress will hop from one foot to another as if she's been locked out of the public toilets and she squeals into a cheap microphone as if she's giving birth. In the jungle fifteen ugly men will hoarsely shout slightly different lyrics over exactly the same cheap synthesised beat over and over again. Wherever there is a generator in rural Peru there will be a big box TV, a cheap DVD player and the worst music in the world being pumped out at full volume.

Snapping back into the present from my lapse into despair, I mentioned to Cho that I needed to find a guide for the next section and he paused thoughtfully. 'I will walk with you to Atalaya,' he said. 'It is not far and I know parts of the River Tambo, too.'

Cho and I completed the stretch along the River Tambo together in six days flat. He brought with him the mindset of a hardworking logger. We had a job to do and he wasn't messing around. It could easily have lasted a fortnight if his attitude had been different.

There is a road from Puerto Ocopa to Atalaya that goes straight over the mountains but Cho and I were more than ready to return to walking by the river. We'd only pushed away out of necessity and we wanted to walk as close to the Tambo as possible, through the Ashaninka communities that dotted the river.

The upstream entrance to the Tambo is magnificent. Large forested mountains on either side make a formidable gateway into the new river. The river itself is channelled into an 'S' shape by the mountains, being forced east, before it is then spat out north again. The Tambo marked the end of the mountains.

It's difficult to describe the way Cho and I viewed each other but, despite his confidence and intelligence, I think I was sure I would never see eye to eye with him as we had such different beliefs. My thought was that he was good for the moment until I could find a guide who spoke fluent Ashaninka. There was something else that made me uneasy about Cho but I couldn't work out what it was.

That said, my mood was better than it had been for weeks. The latter stages of the Apurímac and the whole of the Ene had worn me down. I hadn't felt fit, healthy or vibrant; I'd felt tired, old and barely functional. But I was more relaxed now and the towering forested mountains made me notice the beauty of the landscape we were walking through once again.

On 21 August we made camp on a beach after rounding the prominent kink in the river. Cho was uneasy and noticed a local man about 400 metres away. He decided to go and talk to him while I bathed in the river and cleaned the day's grime from my pale, spotty skin.

Cho came back shaken, a state I'd not seen him in before. 'We have to leave,' he told me. 'If we camp here they will kill us.' Annoyed not to be able just to crawl into my sleeping bag, I agreed to move to avoid imminent death. We walked to the house of the fisherman and received the frostiest welcome we'd had so far. Cho, usually jolly and talkative, was silent for the first time and so I took the lead. I showed our permit and explained our adventure. The three men present all had shotguns and they told me they had to accompany us to the community downriver called Cheni.

Cheni ended up being two kilometres away and we all stumbled through the dark together with shotguns trained on Cho and me from behind. I wasn't put out by the aggressive men and made a point of asking their names and being super-friendly. The biggest and meanest man clearly disliked feeling obliged to tell me that his name was Victor. For some reason I was having fun.

Victor told Cho and me to wait just outside the village as he went to talk to the chief. After a short time a tall, slim man with a university-type scarf and round glasses came out to meet us blowing his nose into a handkerchief. His voice was unmistakably camp. 'Weren't you in the Blue Hotel last week in Satipo?' he asked with a Charles Hawtrey (King Tonka in *Carry On Up the Jungle*) smile.

'What?! Erm . . . yes, I was. Erm . . . looking for a guide.' I started to laugh.

'Follow me,' he said and led us to his own house. He dismissed Victor and his heavies and explained that they were crude but it was good to show a strong defence on the outskirts of their territory.

He told us his name was Fabian and he started to enlighten us about the fact that a Peruvian was never the same once he had travelled abroad. He was clearly educated, and had been to Spain where he had friends at one of the universities. He was now twenty-eight and the chief of Cheni. He ordered someone to cook us fried eggs and fresh fish. We were treated like guests of honour and he even put me in a room with a bed in his new concrete house. There wasn't a mattress, but the fact that I was in a bed having showered and eaten well was amazing after the experience of being marched through the dark at gunpoint by Victor.

If there was a future megalomaniac indigenous leader of Peru in the making, I would say Fabian was the man. He knew his importance in the village and thoroughly enjoyed it. He talked of Shakespeare and Beethoven and I found it hard to believe we were in the middle of a remote part of indigenous Peru. Fabian treated us impeccably and we gave the village medicines in return.

Two subsequent Ashaninka settlements gave us slight problems. Poyeni had a group of women with painted faces shouting and screaming at us from a high riverbank as we climbed to the community. We were not even allowed in to explain who we were and had to scramble down again and continue along the beach – avoiding the community altogether.

Then, in Quemarija, we met Jorge, an old friend of Cho's, and he invited us for dinner with his wife, Nelly, and their baby daughter. The couple were lovely but worried about their baby – she had several abscesses on her head and feet. They asked me to have a look at them and I explained that although I was bringing medicines to each settlement I was certainly not a doctor. Nonetheless they were keen for my opinion as there was no medic in the community and no access to medicines either. I gave the baby's father a quarter-dose course of Amoxicillin for his daughter, a pretty general antibiotic, but told him he must consult the medic in the next community before starting the baby on it.

Gifts were important to the Ashaninkas. Their language has only one word that means both 'trade partner' and 'friend'. Medicines, despite being potentially dangerous, were the most valuable thing that I could bring to the communities. I had tried other more ordinary items such as fishing hooks and line, lighters and torches, but medicines were appreciated much more. Most communities had a person who had basic training in uses of medicines and I normally gave the drugs directly to them.

At about 5 p.m. we were still chatting with Jorge and Nelly when a horn was sounded and the village was summoned to a meeting. Cho and I stayed in the couple's thatched house and started to put up our hammocks for the night. A few minutes later we were summoned to the meeting and subjected to a fiery lecture from the village chief who was wearing his official headdress of feathers, which I had not seen before in any community. He spoke passionately about the community's right to make its own decisions and as he finished we were ordered to leave at once.

Confused, we gathered our things together and hoped we could reach the next settlement before nightfall. I asked Cho what we had done wrong – we had donated medicines, shown our permits and we even knew some people in the community.

'He was drunk,' said Cho.

In the communities that were 'more civilised' (as the colonial Peruvians said without a hint of embarrassment) the educated Ashaninka children wanted to learn Spanish and even English; they wanted to become computer literate and wear Western clothes. The more I saw, the less I thought this regrettable. The Ashaninka lifestyle seemed to me to be both unsustainable and meaningless. Unlike their hunter-gatherer ancestors, these families now lived in communities where they sat around all day drinking and growing jealous of each other. With an education they could start to become productive and proud again. Perhaps then the husbands would stop beating their wives up every Friday night.

As we spilled out of the narrow Tambo Valley the vast, flat jungle spread out in all directions. We were leaving the tropical dryforest behind and moving into the far more biologically diverse tropical rainforest. This meant greater animal and plant diversity and the start of the Amazon Basin as we know it. Amazingly, we now only had 380 metres to descend until we arrived at the Amazon's mouth – some 5,268 kilometres (3,274 miles) from here.

Cho and I pored over the maps looking at the featureless expanse of green that lay between the next jungle city to our north, Pucallpa, and us. I had originally allocated a month for this leg but as we studied the vastness of flat rainforest, the mammoth meanders and scattering of oxbow lakes, plus the ominous lack of settlements (and therefore paths), we really didn't have a clue how long it would take. Positive butterflies of exhilarated excitement returned to me for the first time in months. Cho loved the sheer adventure of it and told me he wouldn't go home after all; he would continue walking with me to Pucallpa where he had been born.

In Atalaya I discovered that all the spare expedition equipment that had been in Lima had been taken home by Luke. To give him the benefit of the doubt, perhaps he thought that I would prefer the spare medication and water purification to be taken back to the UK, but it meant that I had to start trying to procure everything from scratch in Peru. Having failed to find iodine or chlorine in Atalaya, Cho and I set out for two months' walking to Pucallpa with no means of purifying cold water to drink. The heated exchange of emails between Luke and me at this point was our last communication.

From Atalaya northwards all of the communities were now Asheninka with an 'e' rather than Ashaninka with an 'a'. Again, to the layman these indigenous villages looked very similar but whereas Ashanikas on the Ene would sit around on reed mats on the floor drinking purple *masato*, the Asheninkas of the Ucayali had raised wooden floors to their houses (and sometimes wooden walls and partitions, too) and sat around drinking white *masato*. The difference in colour came about simply as a result of the lack of a local purple dye that was chewed on the Ene. *Cushmas* – the form of one-piece indigenous tunic – were rarer, too, and more and more the Asheninkas wore shorts and T-shirts with only a few elders wearing the traditional garment. Red face paint was still common among men and women.

On 5 September we stayed with a young couple in Villa Vista. They were half-Asheninka and half-descendants from Peruvians who had bred with colonial settlers and they fed us curried fish and a sweet banana drink called *chapo*, which was so much nicer than bloody *masato*. They kept dogs and an enormous pig that accompanied Manuel, our host for the night, and us for several miles out of the community the next morning.

We were walking on the 'beach' for much of this time as we didn't know the local paths and we thought it was less intrusive to stick to the riverbanks. The going was therefore slow. Some banks were tangled and steep, others were endless stretches of clinging grass that tripped and pulled at our legs. The mosquitoes were out in force and my calves showed more bites than white flesh.

Two days later, in the morning, we entered a community called Santa Luz with no intention of stopping. They accepted our permit from the indigenous overseeing body OIRA without a challenge but suggested that we wait until 3 p.m. (the allotted HF radio hour) to speak to the next community, Pensilvania. They offered to speak to Pensilvania on our behalf.

That day the village was having a *minga*. This was effectively a way to get everyone to work together for free and the person who was hosting the *minga* provided food and booze afterwards in return for the villagers' work. Cho and I accepted an invitation to join in, and worked alongside the villagers throughout the late morning and early afternoon clearing the undergrowth for the planting of a new rice field. We then had the best feast I'd had in a long while: chicken, rice, plantain, yucca and beans.

When three o'clock came round we went with the chief to call Pensilvania over the radio. The response came back crystal-clear. If a gringo walks into their community they will kill him. I heard this myself.

I was sad to hear this. I had so hoped that hostility was behind us and inevitably we worried a little. Cho came up with a plan to stay the night with our friends in Santa Luz and then head down to the river in the morning and use our pack rafts to cross to a large shingle island where we could walk and avoid passing through Pensilvania.

That night we sat in a house in Santa Luz patiently waiting for the chief to tune in his prize possession, a wireless radio. When he finally got a signal with some vaguely recognisable music, I asked him where the signal was being transmitted from.

'China,' he replied matter-of-factly.

The following day, Cho and I set off in torrential rain. As we got down to the river we were shivering in our T-shirts and we inflated the rafts and set off into the grey haze towards the island. On the island the skies cleared and we decided not to deflate the rafts. We carried them under our arms or on our heads, being blasted about by a gusty wind. As we reached the end of the island we put them in the water and lowered our packs into them. Cho indicated behind me with a nod.

'*Mira, Ed, atrás.*'

The scene I describe in the Prologue now began to unfold. As I looked over my shoulder there were no fewer than five dugout canoes heading in our direction – all full of armed Asheninkas. Many of the men were standing up in these narrow vessels and were armed with either shotguns or bows and arrows. The women among them had machetes. As the boats beached, the men and women swarmed on to the island and approached us furiously.

My diary tells me about my reaction more accurately than my memory does. 'Here we go again' was actually the sentiment in my head. I was somewhat vexed by the inconsiderate Indians coming to kill me. Didn't they realise we were pushed for time?

Clearly it must have been a way for my brain to cope. I knew the gravity of the situation but such apathy seemed to be my natural way of dealing with this extreme stress. I slowly and calmly went through the logical ways of calming the tribesmen down. I held my hands open and looked apologetic and unthreatening. I didn't force a smile as I considered it could be misinterpreted as an insult to the seriousness of the matter to the Asheninkas. I showed my permit from OIRA and could see that the chief was too worked up to be able to read it – his eyes could not focus on the paper, although I was later to find out he could read Spanish. Cho and I both seemed to be of the opinion that if we were calm, helpful and non-threatening the people would respond accordingly.

The man I took to be the chief was speaking in angry bursts and gesticulating wildly and demanded that we be led back to their community. At arrow point we got into our rafts and tried to follow the lead canoes but the plastic rafts didn't have the same ability as their canoes to cut through the water and we were inadvertently escaping downriver. We had to use brute strength to stay with the group and were shaking with exhaustion when we arrived at the mud bank that signified the entrance to their community.

All the while with shotguns and arrows pointing at us, we were escorted to a communal thatched hut in the centre of the village and were subjected to a furious lecture from the real chief of the village who had not, after all, been on the island.

The chief was a small, wiry man with a large head housing huge white eyes that were full of what, at the time, I thought was utter evil. With the whole village circling us he ranted on about the insult we had shown the village by trying to pass without permission. They were an autonomous community with their own law which we needed to respect, he scolded us.

At about this time the community's name, Nuevo Poso, was mentioned and I twigged that we were not in Pensilvania. These were not the people who had threatened to kill us.

We were ordered to empty our packs and to explain each item of equipment. Now a familiar routine, I went about unpacking each item slowly and explaining exactly what it was for. The combination of genuine fascination in what we were carrying and the passing of a lot of time seemed to calm the people considerably. Eventually we plucked up the courage to ask about food as we hadn't eaten all day and they granted us permission to go and ask a woman who was barbecuing plantain if we could buy some food from her. She also had some chocolate biscuits which we refuelled on in seconds like animals.

It was the first chance that Cho and I had been able to speak to each other alone and we acknowledged that this incident had been serious for a while. While Cho later maintained that he never believed his life was at risk I feel that his grounding in South American machismo might have something to do with his perception of his memory. I have no doubt that the villagers launched their boats with the intent of fighting had we been aggressors. They were ready to defend their land. It's less far-fetched than it might at first seem when you consider that most of these people had fought violently with the terrorists and had experienced bloodshed and killing first hand.

I was very glad that we were not armed that day. Many people, for the entire trip, told us we were crazy to walk through the forest without at least a shotgun. We reasoned that if people were startled and hostile towards us when we entered a community with just a backpack, how were they going to react to us entering with firearms? We had to look as non-aggressive as we could; a shotgun was out of the question.

The other reason why people usually walked with bows and arrows or shotguns was that they were hunting. We had a non-hunting policy and so the initial reason for carrying a weapon was not there either. We knew we could scare off all but the biggest packs of peccaries (wild pigs) by whooping and screaming at them as soon as we noticed them, and we had a very different opinion to the locals on how real a threat the jaguar was to us. We were much happier to be unarmed.

The village clearly realised that they had to get rid of us somehow and so when we returned they told us that they would write us a temporary permit which would suffice us until we reached the next town downstream. But we had to go by raft – and we could not set foot on the land.

I felt stupid explaining that we couldn't go by raft – and that we had to go by foot as that was the whole point of the expedition. Amazingly, however, it provoked a very positive response. We could continue walking if we agreed to hire the chief and his brother as guides, and if we returned to Atalaya with them to obtain a further permit, this time from the police.

Diary entry 7 September 2008 – Nuevo Poso:

I'm not enjoying myself. I would go home in an instant if I hadn't committed to doing this expedition. Today we managed about a kilometre before being stopped by these Asheninkas.

This lot were bad people. Although I found it laughable when I started that people could be categorised so simply – I've started doing it myself now. You could tell in their eyes that they didn't understand or want to understand.

We were escorted back to their village with never less than four shotguns or arrows pointed at me. Grim faces all round and the women were shouting in that Asheninka panic voice that makes my skin crawl.

It turns out this community has no time for the organisation that oversees Asheninkas (OIRA). They don't trust them so the permit holds little weight.

At the end of the day the chief said he would accompany us to Atalaya to get permits from the police and then guide us to Bolognesi . . . I suspect he realised he could make some money from us. They are not people I would choose to walk with but it seems the only way to continue.

The next morning we all piled into a dugout canoe with a five-horsepower outboard motor and we started chugging back upriver. After a full day in the boat we arrived stiff-bummed in Atalaya. I offered to take everyone (which was quite an entourage of Asheninkas from the village of Nuevo Poso) out to supper. We went for a Chinese – the first I'd had in Peru – and the guys seemed very happy. The next day we went to the police station with the chief and his brother and, because they were local, I thought that one of the Asheninka brothers would explain to the police what had happened and why we were all here. But they stood around nervously and said nothing. It was incredible to see how different these two men were out of their territory and in a colonial town.

'Bollocks. I'll do it, then,' I thought and explained to the policeman that I was a writer who wished to travel the Ucayali on foot to Pucallpa and that I would like him to write me a letter stating that he had given me authority to do so. He took our details and we had the letter in minutes. Not a single question about my motives or method of transport – the permit was granted and the Asheninka brothers were very happy. Now they would walk with me.

The next day we travelled back to their community and the brothers were at once back in their element. They called a village meeting to announce their triumphant return from Atalaya. They proudly told the village that, thanks to their assistance, I now had legal permission to be here and that we would all now publicly discuss their wages for the next few days.

Brilliant.

I reckoned I might be able to outwit them in this bartering considering the Asheninkas don't actually have numbers in their language. Before the arrival of the Spanish, they had had three words to refer to quantity: none, one and lots. With an A grade in GCSE Maths, and a workable understanding of quadratic equations, I reckoned I might have the upper hand.

I paid Cho twenty-five *soles* a day and was prepared to give them the same. 'How much will you pay us?' they asked. The crowd went silent and waited for my response. 'I normally pay fifteen *soles* a day,' I explained, 'but you are the chief and you are the chief's brother so I think I should pay you more. I will pay you twenty *soles* per day!'

'Unacceptable!' the chief said. 'We are the Dongo brothers. We could never leave our families for less than twenty-five *soles* a day.'

'Done.' I stood up and shook them by the hand to seal the deal. Everyone was a winner. The happy brothers were called Alfonso Dongo and Andreas Dongo. Both spoke basic Spanish (perfect Spanish to me but Cho said it was basic) and so we had a four-man team with which to tackle the River Ucayali.

My Spanish was good enough to understand about 30 per cent of meetings like this when people were speaking to each other and not directly at me. It was like being a bit blind and not really having the whole picture at any time. I felt as if there was a haze around me of blurred understanding which made everything that much more dream-like. I was limited to asking direct questions and under-standing basic answers at this stage.

The first community we had to pass through the following day was Pensilvania. 'How are we going to get permission for me to pass?' I asked the brothers. 'They have said they will kill me.'

'They have already granted you permission,' said Andreas, the chief, who explained that Pensilvania's chief had been in Atalaya when we had gone back for the police permit and they had shared a beer together. Andreas had started to earn his twenty-five *soles* a day.

The Asheninka brothers were, without exaggeration, fantastic people. They were so happy to be out of their community and exploring not only the forest, but the other Asheninka communities that they had rarely visited before. It became the Dongo brothers' tour and most communities were entered with ease.

'This is Señor Eduardo – our great friend and famous writer from England,' they would announce, genuinely happy to introduce me. We were hosted well in the communities but they were keen to remind me that this journey would have been impossible without them. When I toyed with them and asked them what would have happened if Cho and I had been alone they would either mime a throat-slitting action or an arrow entering the back of my head and exploding my brains all over the nearest tree. They thought this was very funny indeed.

I had no doubt how dangerous these people really were. They wanted to protect their land against outsiders and so they lived their lives in a constant state of alertness. With the wrong attitude we wouldn't have got through.

Some communities, however, were completely closed – to me, anyway.

I never found out the exact reason for not letting us pass, but many people we spoke to genuinely thought that gringos ate babies.

When you combine myths such as this with the very real incursions from loggers, coca growers and oil companies it's not surprising that some communities didn't want any gringos on their land. The baby-eater myth was ridiculous – but perhaps it was there for a reason. In these instances we were forced to backtrack, cross to the other side of the river and hope the settlements on the far side were more open and understanding.

The current distraction was the *manta blanca* (white cloak), which is the term for the swarms of sand flies and mosquitoes that enveloped us whenever we were near the water (which was quite often). It was difficult to quantify how many biting insects were buzzing around us and biting at any one time, but it must have been tens of thousands rather than hundreds.

'They will get much worse when the wet season arrives,' Cho added cheerfully, 'then they are really bad.'

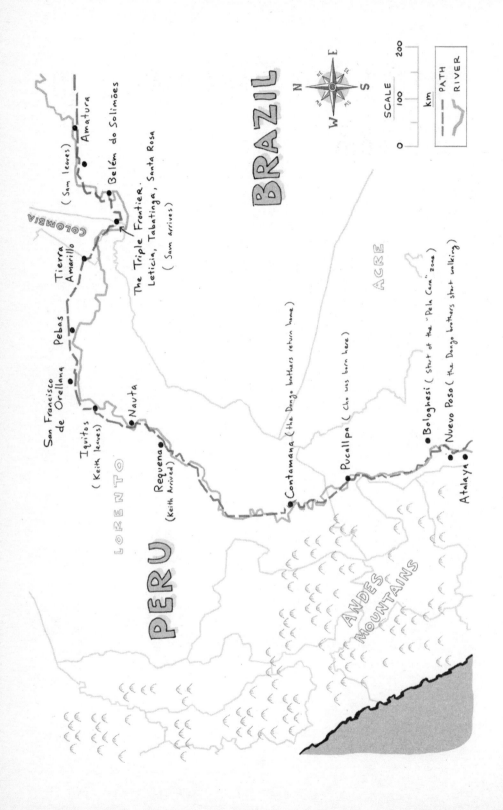

BRAZIL

ACRE

PERU

LORENTO

COLOMBIA

ANDES MOUNTAINS

SCALE

km
0 ___ 100 ___ 200

- - - PATH
~~~ RIVER

N E
NE
W S

Amatura (Sam leaves)

Belém do Solimões

Tierra Amarillo

The Triple Frontier.
Leticia, Tabatinga, Santa Rosa
(Sam arrives)

Pebas

San Francisco
de Orellana

Iquitos
(Keith leaves)

Nauta

Requena
(Keith Arrived)

Contamana (the Dongo brothers return home)

Pucallpa (Cho was born here)

Bolognesi (start of the "Pela Cara" zone)

Nuevo Pose (the Dongo brothers start walking)

Atalaya

PART 3: THE DARK MARCH TO COLOMBIA

Chapter Seven

'Look after your gringo or we'll cut his head off'

As we progressed, some of my thoughts became dark and then darker. I misinterpreted more and more and my whole character began to alter. It started just south of a sweaty jungle town called Bolognesi.

'*Pela cara!*' someone shouted from the top of an overloaded truck as Cho, the Dongo brothers and I were walking down the logging track into the small town. Literally this means 'he/it peels face' or 'face peeler' and so I assumed it was one of the many insults that people shout at me for being different here. Perhaps I'd got a little sunburned.

But no. The same insult was hurled at me a couple more times in the town accompanied by open sniggering. I asked Cho what it meant but his answer was vague (as he'd never heard the term before) and so I was left thinking that the people here were making jokes about scalping my face off.

The river was about 500 metres wide now and to cross with just two rafts and four men meant that the time and effort involved in ferrying and returning for the remaining people was unsustainable. The answer was obvious but took us a couple of days to work out: we had to put two men and both their packs in each boat. One man would paddle while the other made polite conversation and tried to stay still and keep his centre of gravity as low as possible. The total weight in my raft with Andreas, who was admittedly tiny, was about 27 stone, but it was the inability to get the weight low down that gave us instability. We were top-heavy and risked capsizing constantly. After sleeping the night on a braided river beach, we inflated the pack rafts, squashed two men into each and precariously paddled across to a community called Nueve de Octubre. It was smiles all round when we arrived with everyone laughing at how four men could fit in two such ridiculous tiny toy vessels. We had called ahead on the HF radio and so this Shipebo community had been expecting us.

Shipebos were the first indigenous tribe that looked different. The women wore their jet-black hair long but with a universal severe fringe. They all wore a blue shapeless blouse that reminded me more of the colonially instigated clothes of the Quechuan mountain people than the simple *cushmas* of the Ashaninkas, Asheninkas and Machiguengas. Without exception, the men wore shorts and T-shirts.

I was buying farine (pellet-like carbohydrate made from yucca) and sugar in the community shop and, because I had relaxed, I mentioned how nice it was to enter such a friendly community. The Shipebo lady replied that the people's initial reaction when they had heard the message over the radio had been 'Kill the *pela cara!*' but that they had later agreed to let me pass when they found out my purpose and that I had permits.

'What?!' I asked the woman to explain *pela cara* to me and she told me how there had been human-organ trafficking in the area and bodies found without organs.

'The culprits are Americans – gringos like you. The people were scared to hear of your arrival.'

I didn't really know what to make of this – there were many people here who wanted to tell me long stories – but what happened next made things very clear.

As we left the linear village the path linked a row of more separated houses – all occupied by Shipebo families. As we entered the territory of one such family I gave my usual broad smile and waved (to show I'm a non-threatening nice chap) but the owner of the house did not respond – he looked at me, transfixed.

The man then asked Alfonso, my guide, who was walking in front of me, 'Does he steal this?' As he said the word 'this' he circled his face with his index finger. He was still looking at me and looked petrified.

Alfonso and Andreas laughed out loud and explained that I was a tourist but the man didn't join in the laughter.

We walked on and in the next house a woman had had a little too much *masato* and was bordering on drunk. She started shouting at me immediately and it turned out that she had heard that a *pela cara* was coming to take her children.

Again my guides had to reassure her and explain my cause in the local dialect but because she was drunk she didn't understand or calm down. We moved on quickly.

There were many people here who thought gringos stole babies and killed people for their organs. Whether there was any truth to the origins of this illegal trafficking I didn't know, but that was somewhat irrelevant because the Shipebo people believed the stories.

The result was that we were warned several times that if we were found by indigenous people after dark, and they saw that I was white, they would kill me without asking any questions. We managed this risk sensibly by planning the route thoroughly and always having a community within reach at the end of the day.

It was hard not to let this get to me. Cho, Alfonso and Andreas were happy entering communities but they were not the focus of attention. I was. I was also still handicapped at this stage by the amount of Spanish I could understand and obviously the Asheninka brothers spoke to each other in Asheninka and the Shipebo people to each other in Shipebo. The guides enabled me to continue but my lack of understanding and my subsequent anxiety sent me deeper into my own world of sadness. I hated being feared and became emotionally exhausted trying to prove that I was a good person in each community before people would relax and accept me. The fact that we never stayed in one place more than one night meant that all the hard work had to be repeated night after night as the river was packed with these remote communities. To stay outside the settlements was far more dangerous because we would be seen as hiding and therefore give cause for even more unnecessary suspicion in the defensive tribes.

Everything became harder. Putting my wet clothes on every morning became a mental obstacle, walking became laboured and I found enjoyment in almost nothing. I didn't see the jungle we walked through; I didn't taste the bland fish soups or the tough *paca* (rodents) that we ate. I was, I am sure, depressed and yet deep inside me I had a voice asking me, 'Are you physically moving forward?' 'Yes?' 'Then everything is OK.'

I had completely subordinated pleasure for my long-term goal. I existed in a manner that was less than human. I went to bed early and didn't chat to the guides. I withdrew from putting up blogs until I had unusually confident days, scared of the outside world seeing what I was becoming. When I did blog I tried to hide my true melancholy. I carried myself like a nervous teenager and I looked at the floor. I couldn't call my family or friends because I knew I had lost perspective on the expedition and I couldn't face their normality or their humour. I was thoroughly miserable and many nights I let myself cry silently in my hammock, tears streaming down my face in self-pity.

From the base level of unhappiness I did get glimpses of a world that had humour and goodness in it. Cho wanted to learn some basic English and could now say 'Let's go wash!' to me at the end of a long day. It was a small thing but it made me smile. The Asheninka brothers could see me struggling, too. Andreas, who had become my pack-raft buddy, would look me in the eye when we had the privacy of being face to face in the bath-like boats and ask me if I was OK. He had a kindness to his face now and his mannerisms made me smile. He would point with his lips to indicate what he was talking about and he and I formed quite a close bond as we relied on each other when crossing the difficult currents of the river.

On 11 September 2008 we arrived in Diobamba, an Asheninka community where Andreas's and Alfonso's uncle lived. Alfonso had also picked up a tortoise as a gift for the community about half an hour before we arrived and so for two reasons we were welcomed more warmly than usual. The family with whom we stayed was headed by a single mother of about thirty-four whose husband had died. For an Asheninka she was tall and athletic with the graceful feminine curves of Florence Griffith-Joyner. Most noticeably, she was very confident; she looked me straight in the eye and smiled widely. The Dongo brothers teased me that she wanted me for a husband – and from her manner they were not making this up and a surge of unexpected excitement and warmth rose in my body. The attention, in my weak, self-doubting state, caught me off guard and I wasn't composed enough to do anything but smile and thank the lady as she brought food and drink and entertained us magnificently. She had the most generous laugh I have ever heard in a woman and deep inside me a switch flicked and I began to crawl back into the land of the living.

The tortoise that I had thought to be a gift of a pet was clinically opened with a machete like a can of beans and ripped from its shell. The shell was then rubbed with salt and barbecued as an entrée for us to pick at while our hostess cooked up a tortoise casserole. We were also given a plate of giant armadillo meat to devour and I could feel my strength returning physically and emotionally.

Despite this incredible hospitality my mental state was too distorted to be healed by a single incident. From my hammock I remember listening to the Dongo brothers who, in my state of half-sleep, I was sure were plotting to kill me. There was an Asheninka word that was very common that sounded like the Spanish word *matar*, to kill. Part of me knew I was being paranoid, but not enough of me to get a grip and to stop my brain racing in my hammock.

Walking the river beaches meant we had to cross the river several times a day. The walkable beaches alternated from one side to the other with the meanders. As the river was low this was still faster than cutting a path through the dense undergrowth in the forest.

On the first proper day of these multiple crossings the Dongo brothers were in a boat together and they worked out that if they didn't paddle hard, the river would take them further downstream and they wouldn't have to walk as far. Their logic was understandable but both Cho and I failed to stop them doing it time and time again as the day went on. The problem was that I had committed to walking the entire length of the river and Alfonso and Andreas were gaining 500 metres downstream with every crossing. Because staying together was important, Cho and I were gaining ground on the water, too.

We could see each other getting agitated about this. We were here to walk the Amazon and neither of us wanted to do it anything less than 100 per cent.

'Cho, we have to tell them that from here downwards we absolutely cannot let the river take us downstream and that, if it does, we must walk back to opposite from where we started on the other side.'

'We need to do more than that,' replied Cho. 'We need to go back and do today again.'

For the first time I saw the depth of commitment that Cho had now decided to give this venture. His values dictated that today was unacceptable. We smiled at each other, shook hands and made a plan that in the next community we would hire a boat and return to rewalk this section of the river.

It was a lesson for me. A niggling doubt or guilt that had been manifesting itself in me all day was replaced with a pure, clean feeling of doing the right thing. It would slow us down by a whole day and it would cost money, but it would mean our consciences would be clear. This was an instinct that I would become used to relying on as the weeks passed and I learned for the first time in my life how really to start living based on what felt right or wrong.

From Bolognesi we hired a boat at great expense and redid that section of the river. Once they understood what we were driving at, the Dongo brothers bought into the concept completely.

As we intended to be back in Bolognesi by nightfall we stashed all our gear there and just had with us minimum kit: water bottles and a GPS. But the river took longer to walk than we expected and night began to fall. We were forced to make camp on a beach where a man was fishing. He lent Alfonso a hook and line and the skill with which, when faced with the prospect of no supper, Alfonso pulled out fish after fish was phenomenal. We shared our catch with the fisherman who let us use his fire to cook on and gave us some chewy tortoise to eat. As it grew colder, Cho found a small plastic sheet about a metre by two metres with which we made an improvised shelter. Lined up like soldiers under it, with the roof covering us from our knees to our chests, we prayed for a warm, dry night.

At ten o'clock the wind picked up and at eleven the ominous patter of raindrops started to drum on the crisp packet of a covering above our heads. As the storm matured we drew in our knees and sat up in the line we had formed, now soaked to the bone by the driving rain slamming horizontally into us. Sleep was unthinkable so we just sat together shivering in the darkness waiting for dawn. The wind and rain subsided in the early hours and we had small snatches of sleep as we tried to warm up our damp clothes by staying as still as possible.

From this point on we had a firm rule. If we crossed any river in a pack raft or other boat, we would have to walk back to a point perpendicular to the point at which we had embarked. That way we could never be accused of using the flow of the river to advance us.

One thinks of the dangers of the jungle as coming from jaguars, snakes and electric eels but it was the insects that were driving me mad. Regularly we cut through wasps' nests concealed beneath leaves, and, when the shout '*Avispas*' went up, we would scatter in different directions into the undergrowth so as to reduce the number of stings we each got. I learned to stop steadying myself on trees or plants as I passed, since tiny ants would run up my arms and bite me, leaving small, wet sores.

Diary entry from 20 September 2008:

We are in a world of shit. We've not made the community we were aiming for; we've got no water and so we've not eaten, drunk or washed. The mosquitoes are the worst I have ever seen. Climbing into my hammock I let about 30 into my mosquito net. I keep thinking they are all dead and then one more appears to swat.

I can tell they are biting me because I get a juicy red blood splat on my hands when I clap them but I am not reacting [not coming up in bites]. Perhaps I am building up a resistance like the locals. There are millions of mosquitoes outside the net. MILLIONS.

Today was bad. The guides are guessing our direction. I do not understand anything. There are no paths.

4.30 a.m. additional entry:

I just got up to urinate and looked down at my stomach and there must have been 40 mosquitoes sucking my blood. I wiped them off with my hand leaving a large red streak of fresh blood across my belly.

Sleep was now becoming a problem, too. Despite having almost twelve hours of dark hammock time I would lie for hours worrying and thinking about how we could get through the next part. At first I used antihistamines to aid sleep, but it led on to using diazepam, tramadol and even morphine to enable me to get enough sleep to move forward. I received one email from Chloë, my ex, simply asking if I was taking drugs. She knew me so well that she could tell from my blogs that I was not thinking straight. She was right. The alternative was more unbearable for me, however – the hopeless despair of seeing the sun rise when I had still not managed to stop my brain racing.

The next morning Cho was, as usual, the last to be ready. He hadn't yet developed a system for organising his kit quickly and the normal routine was to wait for him for another twenty minutes after the three of us were ready. I had a snipe at him about this when we finally set off and his response was to hand me a bottle of fresh rainwater that he had cleverly collected in the night. As I gulped the liquid down, my first drink after an entire evening and night without fluid, I felt a huge pang of guilt for snapping at Cho. He'd collected enough for the brothers and himself to have a litre each. What did twenty minutes' waiting really matter anyway?

It's hard to justify why I'd not really been navigating. The previous weeks had been all down the river channel and so it hadn't been necessary. I assumed that the Dongo brothers were so adept at jungle walking that I could simply switch off and follow them. But as the day progressed I could tell we hadn't been keeping to the same direction and I started to at least check our direction with my compass.

For half an hour we walked north and then for half an hour we walked south. Still unsure at this point if this was part of the brothers' plan, I just observed until it became evident they didn't know which way to go.

I started to talk to them and to indicate the direction that in theory we should be travelling and showed them that the river was on our left. I was amazed to see that they really were disorientated. I was to discover that this was because the last two days had been overcast and they hadn't been able to use the sun to keep track of our direction. They had never seen a compass before but from that point on I made sure I kept them going in one general direction, which for the first year of the expedition was north.

It made me switch on more to navigation, too. Now that I had a competent team around me there was no excuse for sloppiness and I needed to take control and always to have a good idea of where we were in relation to the river so that if anything happened we could evacuate. I started to realise that when the guides confidently stated 'The community is this way!' they were giving me their best guess rather than a statement of fact, and that I still had to check the navigation the whole time.

This actually helped me start to pull myself together again because, as the only person in the team who could navigate without the sun, I was key to our progress.

Fellow explorers, adventurers or walkers of any kind might be surprised at my lack of concern about navigation until this point, and in mitigation I can only say that the walk had now turned into an existence rather than an expedition. We were just walking, loosely following a river, and my perspective and handle on many things had shifted a lot due to my preoccupation with matters such as safety or financial worries.

The Peruvian riverine Amazon – the forested areas that are strongly influenced by the river – can be nasty and dense. The canopy was low and there were very few large old trees left. Thorns and brambles filled the gaps between trees and walking without a machete literally to open a path was unthinkable. Often the forest floor resembled a half-drained lake bed, and exposed roots and vines lay twisted and gnarled over the sucking, thick mud. Locals were able to slip through tiny gaps with the ease of panthers while my backpack snagged on every overhanging bit of vegetation sending dirt and ants down the back of my grimy neck as I fell behind the group, getting more and more frustrated.

The Asheninka communities were much easier to stay in than those of the Shipebo. The *pela cara* myth was taken far more seriously among the Shipebos and things could be frosty and awkward. Conversely, the Asheninkas would turn our arrival into an excuse for a reunion party with the Dongo brothers, who perhaps knew a couple of them, and would be more than happy to have a night on the home-made sugar-cane rum.

Reading my diary, though, I know that I wasn't yet completely comfortable.

Diary entry from 26 September 2008 – Selva:

> I'm bored with being the butt of jokes that I either don't understand or just aren't funny. Maybe I'm just too tired but half of the jokes are about how crap I am at walking and the other half are about killing me. 'Look after your gringo' they would say to Cho, 'or we'll cut his head off.'
>
> Cho laughs, the Dongo brothers laugh and the community laughs. Everyone but me. I don't really enjoy anything at the moment except eating, and being clean after I have washed.

I so wish my Spanish was better. In the evenings I am just too exhausted to learn or to concentrate enough to translate. So I allow the noise to pass without making the effort to translate and I end up understanding less and less.

For some time I'd been questioning whether my walk was selfish. Was I causing upset here unnecessarily and could the resulting distress be avoided? Had I really thought through the effect I was having on the people I met?

The indigenous people in this part of the Amazon wanted to develop. They wanted electricity, torches, satellite TV and mobile phones – without exception. The communities that I walked through would be unrecognisable in twenty years' time. This was not a case of uncontacted tribes that needed to be left to lead their isolated lives – it was, rather, a case of poor communications and gossip and rumour causing ignorance and unnecessary fear.

I came to the conclusion that my walk was a positive thing for these communities, whether or not they were initially upset. Although such communities had to live in a state of high alert to protect their land, ignorance of the outside world is never a good thing. Not all white men were the same and, although I admired the defensive spirit of the indigenous people here, it was good that they had met a gringo who did not want to steal their land, timber, children or body parts. It was good that they had met one who smiled stupidly and waved at them – and bought farine and sugar in the local shop.

By this stage I had slipped the timeline yet again and was now forecasting that the expedition would take two whole years. The big jungle city of Pucallpa marked a quarter of my journey completed and was a landmark that I had dreamed of reaching for months. On 28 September we had been walking for nearly six months and two days, but I was still three days short of Pucallpa. Mark Barrowcliffe, a British journalist, was due to arrive to walk with us so that he could write an article for the *Guardian*. As Mark had no Spanish he was coming in with Marlene from Lima and I was going to have to go ahead by boat in order to meet him. Once we'd picked him up we would all return by boat to start walking from where we had left off.

The whole experience did me good. Being out on the river allowed my eyes to focus on things further than 20 metres away and the idea of a night in a bed was heavenly. I desperately wanted to get an air-conditioned room, that little bit of extra comfort that would have guaranteed a solid night's sleep, but, with the Asheninka brothers and Cho in tow, I could not afford to spend so much.

It was great to see Marlene again. She's a lovely woman, not really very Peruvian and quite alternative; she laughs and swears like a trooper. Mark was quite nervous at first, I think, and I was equally apprehensive about him coming in. I think we picked up on each other's nerves and moments after his arrival I was telling him about the *pela cara* threat and the miserable time I had been having.

He had a wife and a baby daughter and he was seriously considering whether walking with me through these areas was a responsible thing to do. I felt it was my duty to point out that he had to accept that he would be walking at his own risk and that the tribes were unpredictable and anything could happen. That didn't help.

Marlene was pretty gutsy to walk with us. Totally unprepared, she managed a day of winding, slippery paths and was on her arse for a good chunk of the day before she took the boat out.

Mark walked with us for three days and was pleased to be leaving by the end. For him the jungle was a baptism of fire. For me it was great to have a fellow Brit to talk to about sport, schools, TV and all things British. We were very different but enjoyed each other's company and Mark helped me see how far I had come. To witness him take his first steps in the jungle made me look like an absolute professional. I looked after him for three days and forgot to worry about myself. It was just what I needed and I saw that I had become pretty efficient at what we were doing by then. Seeing the jungle through Mark's eyes made me realise that I was comparatively comfortable and at home in the trees.

On the last day Mark looked at a raging river and laughed: 'For one hellish moment I thought we were going to have to cross that!' I smiled and he knew instantly that we were. We all linked ourselves together, faced upstream and edged across as the force of the water threatened to throw us backwards.

I don't think Mark ever really relaxed. He seemed to be nervous of the people and the jungle and I felt for him in this alien world. As we shook hands to say goodbye Mark thanked me and I hoped he had had a good experience. I don't know if he realised how much he had helped me psychologically and how grateful I was for his visit. Cho and I now had new trousers and shorts, too, as Mark discarded his freebies from outdoor clothing suppliers. We waved him off, the pair of us now looking like fresher Boy Scouts.

The cost of hiring boats to collect and drop off Mark, hotels, flights for Marlene and more expensive food in the city had set us back almost £1,000 over just a few days and so, once we hit Pucallpa properly, on foot this time, we just sped on through and didn't look back. We needed to be somewhere cheap.

As we walked, each of us had his own kit and a proportion of the group kit that we had to carry with us. Pots, boats, laptop, satellite phone, EPIRB (emergency position-indicating rescue beacon), cameras, tape stock, batteries etc. were split in a way that I thought was fair. Andreas and Alfonso had said that they would walk for another seven to ten days to the town of Contamana, at which point they would turn back.

On 20 October we spotted something very bright red and yellow up ahead and thought we were arriving at a logging camp on the river. As we walked closer, we could make out that the colours were actually two helicopters parked on a helipad, and that the camp was far too smart to belong to loggers. We paddled across the river to the camp and smiled and waved from our inflatable boats. The camp workers looked foreign, Argentine perhaps, and were bemused by the two rubber rafts with an Englishman, an Afro-Peruvian and two Asheninka Indians waving at them.

We were greeted warmly enough by the French manager of the camp who explained that they were conducting seismic surveys to try and find oil. They'd not found any and the camp was in the process of being collapsed over the next few weeks. I tried to dredge up some French from my seven years of schooling but couldn't even remember 'good afternoon' so we spoke in Spanish. The Frenchman was kind but fairly uninterested in us and said we could stay in the workers' tent at the back.

Despite being the only structure on the camp that wasn't air-conditioned this was luxury to us. We were given a safety brief (I had to pinch myself that I was still in Peru) and shown the hot showers and flushing loos at our disposal. It was phenomenal what money could do to convert tangled jungle into a sterile camp; the men lived in luxury with their own gym, bar and restaurant. We were fed huge plates of fried chicken and rice with tomatoes and charged up everything we owned on their twenty-four-hour generator.

After breakfasting well, we had to sneak through people's gardens to continue walking on that side of the river and soon arrived at a Shipebo settlement called Holandia. Holandia seemed deserted and so we walked straight through to a village called San Juan, where we were met, detained and escorted back to Holandia by men with shotguns.

In Holandia the chief of security was very old and I've not taken such an instant dislike to anyone since a lunatic Australian professional golfer my sister was dating. He told us that a man had gone missing and that we were under suspicion for murder. This was, of course, far too ridiculous to take seriously, so we didn't.

In my diary I seem to have referred to the old man as 'Mr Wanker' and it would be a shame not to stick with that entirely appropriate name. Mr Wanker wanted to pick every hole in us that he could and thought he was being very clever. He announced that my passport was not valid as the Queen had not personally signed it. He told me it was up to me to prove that Mark Barrowcliffe was back in England and not hiding in the bushes nearby (Mark's name was still on our permits).

After two hours of questioning me on my own, he then said he would like me to explain every item of equipment that was in my pack. I have to admit my patience was wearing a bit thin and so I asked him why he didn't ask the chief of San Juan who was sitting next to him holding the full inventory that we'd compiled together four hours earlier when his village had detained us.

No – I had to empty my pack again. During the torturous process Mr Wanker flicked suspiciously through the pages of Mark Barrowcliffe's comedy novel *Lucky Dog* as if our detailed murder plot might be contained within it. The serial number of my laptop was even noted down. Better safe than sorry.

But it wasn't just me. Mr Wanker spent over two hours more on Alfonso, then Andreas and, finally, Cho. Luckily I had a book to read. The whole day was taken up with interrogation about the missing Shipebo who had probably got drunk and wandered off and fallen asleep somewhere.

Thankfully not everyone in Holandia was like Mr Wanker. Two families offered to cook us food and in the confusion we were entertained twice and ate two enormous candlelit suppers.

The next morning, after we had been put up in the police station (wooden shack), the real chief of security arrived and we learned that Mr Wanker had been a mere stand-in. The younger man took one look at us, smiled, asked us if we were going to visit the hot springs in Contamana and bade us farewell and good luck. He did spoil it at the end, though, by saying that it was obligatory to donate fifty *soles* to the Holandia police force to repair the roof of the station – after that, we were free to go.

At the end of the day the guys chatted to the very attentive young girls in the street. I shouldn't judge but these girls were early teens, thirteen or fourteen, and none of our group was under thirty. Most girls of fifteen or older were usually married with kids so I was the only person who found the situation strange. Any man who wanted a single available girl went for one of fourteen or less.

We left Holandia at six the next morning with the intention of making up for lost time. The route to Contamana was flat and we strode out on the increasingly good tracks that eventually became paved roads. At 7 p.m., in the dark, we checked into a hotel in the built-up town. This was no longer a wooden shack kind of town: buildings were constructed in concrete and brick, the plaza was green with neat flowers and there were litterbins that were actually being used.

Alfonso and Andreas Dongo, our faithful Asheninka brothers, left us at this point. They had a good night's sleep, washed and put on their smart polo shirts, slacks and aftershave for their journey back upriver to the community they had left forty-seven days earlier. They were so far from home now that their influence was waning and so it was the right thing to do. When I went into their room to pay them and say goodbye I felt sad to be splitting up this team. Apart from my dark moods, it had been a phenomenal forty-seven days and I know we would not have got through the fearsome communities without their help. We shook hands and the brothers went out into town and bought a brand-new outboard motor for their community. I was left with a warm sensation that I was saying goodbye to real friends.

That night I read back my journal from the day we had met Alfonso and Andreas.

This lot were bad people. Although I found it laughable when I started that people could be categorised so simply – I've started doing it myself now. You could tell in their eyes that they didn't understand or want to understand.

Who exactly didn't understand?

Chapter Eight

Depression

On reflection, I must have been struggling so much with the expedition itself that I had shut out the possibility of such things as pleasure and light-hearted chat. I ignored most interaction and activity that wouldn't directly help me advance. My gut told me I had things out of perspective; I knew I was being antisocial but I withdrew nonetheless.

Part of the stress was caused by financial concerns. JBS Associates were now giving me a monthly allowance of £1,000 but that only covered half our outgoings. I was up to £9,500 on my credit card with a limit of £10,000 and had no way of paying the interest. My mortgage still had to be paid in England and the tenant had just announced she was moving out. I know that the jungle was stunning in places because very occasionally I stopped and took it all in. Jungle-covered hills clustered together like green egg cartons and steep banks gave way to vine-covered cliffs towering over small streams. No one walked through here because it was so dense and without a machete progress was almost impossible. Detours around natural obstacles such as impenetrable swamps were common as we struggled forward and backtracked with our leaden packs.

Cho soon found a new Shipebo guide, Pablo, another kind-faced individual, and I had a good feeling about him. I advanced him 150 *soles* as he wouldn't have come otherwise. The problem was that men always needed to leave their women with enough money to live on while they were away. I could see their point.

Pablo, Cho and I walked through the boggiest forest that we'd encountered to date. Having experienced slight trench foot from my original pair of jungle boots I had switched to what the Asheninkas were wearing. Plimsolls. They would be temporary until Altberg could make up some new boots that drained better and so my ankles were now exposed and I felt naked walking through the jungle. The lack of ankle protection left me vulnerable to sprains, thorns, scratches and, most importantly, snakes. But the plimsolls were so thin and simple that they allowed me to walk through bog and not suffer from trench foot.

This deep in the jungle snakes were ever more present. If you walk down jungle trails they are a manageable risk. If you are cutting through dense vegetation knowing that most of them are semi-arboreal (they live in trees) then the risk is much higher. Like all animals they wouldn't attack us without reason as we were too big to eat, but the chances of us disturbing one and startling it were greater than ever. Increasingly, when we passed pit vipers on the forest floor I suggested walking round them rather than killing them, as the locals tended to do. We were often in areas through which no one else would walk now so the chances of someone following us and being bitten were very slender indeed. The snakes could live on.

Every day in the jungle I had a strict routine for sorting out my feet. I would Vaseline them in the morning before my socks went on and then I would put on my clean (but damp) socks from the day before that I'd washed in the river. Then, at the end of the day, I would wash myself and my socks before supper, powder my feet and walk around in sandals or Crocs for the evening, allowing my feet to breathe and dry out.

This method worked perfectly throughout the expedition except with the first pair of Altbergs, which were too thick and the drainage 'valves' blocked up with mud. Subsequent boots I requested had the valves replaced with simple eyelets that had the advantage of draining fantastically well but the disadvantage of collecting sand from riverbeds. These boots would need to be washed out regularly if the area was sandy and we were crossing numerous rivers. The consequences of not doing so were red-raw, cheese-grated feet and subsequent infections.

It was only at this point that I judged it safe to tell Cho that I wasn't religious. I hadn't lied before but I'd avoided being direct. He took it well and I could see that he saw it as a challenge to convert me while we were walking. Pablo had to return home to protect his daughter from the unwanted attention she was getting from a man in their village. He'd heard the news over the HF radio and he was replaced by Jorge.

Jorge was very different from every local that we'd so far hired. He wasn't indigenous but, rather, a Spanish colonial Peruvian. He was a bit older than the others, about fifty, with a huge belly and the calm, relaxed manner of a favourite uncle.

On 9 November we also picked up Raul, a local man of similar age who was stick-thin yet strong and muscular. I was worried about money and didn't feel in control of the finances. Employing a man who didn't know where he was going was infuriating as it was a direct reminder that I was wasting my money. Raul had claimed to know the paths and so we set off as a team of four. As we started to go wrong and to go round in circles I became irritable and made it clear to Raul that I wasn't impressed.

In a village called Nuevo Delicia, as the four of us sat eating sloppy rice and rodent, I took it upon myself to bring up the subject of guides.

'We need to find a new guide tomorrow morning,' I announced. Everyone looked down and continued shovelling food into their mouths. 'We need to find someone who knows the paths so we are not going round in circles all day,' I continued. I thought Cho and Jorge were in agreement but everyone clearly felt for Raul, who said nothing.

Cho ventured, 'What happens to Raul?'

'He goes home,' I said, 'we've paid him for today.' I was very aware I was talking about Raul in his presence. 'Is that OK, Raul?' I asked.

'*Si*,' said Raul.

That night I finished reading *The Book Thief*, an amazing story of courage in 1942 Munich. I lay in my hammock crying – the book reminded me about all the people I loved and about what mattered in life and what didn't. It made my walk look absolutely trivial compared to wartime suffering, and I realised that I needed to keep reminding myself that I had to relax and think of others rather than live in this insular bubble of blinkered determination.

I slept well with the help of the cheap diazepam that I was now reliant on to enable me to shut out the money worries and get a decent night's sleep.

At the breakfast table in Nuevo Delicia a rat fell from the rafters above us on to the table and made us all laugh, but there was an air of uneasiness. Raul wasn't pleased about being let go but, rather than admit this, he proceeded to tell me all he could about the route ahead which we would now be taking without him. The more he talked the more I realised how knowledgeable he was. I stared at the map pensively.

'Cho, do you think I've made the right decision about letting Raul go home?'

'You're the boss,' said Cho.

'But I'm asking you for your opinion, Cho.'

'OK,' Cho began, 'I think you are being too impatient. I think that this walk will take time and that you need to relax, and when a path turns into brambles and thorns for two hours you need to take a deep breath, smile and accept it as part of the adventure.'

All this time Raul and Jorge were listening and everyone, including me, knew that Cho was right and that I had been put in my place. I felt pretty humiliated and turned to Raul. 'Sorry, Raul. I was too hard on you yesterday. If you are happy to, I would like you to continue.' Raul said nothing but I could tell he had accepted the apology and would stay on.

Somehow the revelation of my inadequacies and the ensuing honesty seemed to change things for the better. We walked well and in my journal entry the following night I made comments about the fact that we had the makings of another great four-man team such as we'd had with the Dongo brothers. On breaks we would share cheap cigarettes and they would teach me to swear in Spanish. We started to laugh and, notably, I began to feel much more a part of the team.

The next day we passed through a colonial settlement. There were fewer and fewer indigenous communities now and the reception we were getting became warmer and warmer. I would occasionally hear the cry of '*pela cara!*' but now it seemed more in jest than anything else. It was lunchtime and Jorge, never slow to point out the chances of eating a decent meal, suggested that we stop for one. An eighteen-year-old girl appeared – the most beautiful person I had seen since arriving in Peru – and my heart pounded as she served us rice, beans and plantain. Her name was Sonia and she asked me personally if I could stay for a few days. I explained why I couldn't and left the village with my three companions mocking me but with a spring in my step.

Many of the communities we passed through still had problems with alcohol and it's sad to report that in most of the settlements there were several drunken men in the middle of the day, smashed out of their minds. Not singing or even getting into fights: simply so blind drunk that they looked insane and were completely out of it. The people were still very indigenous-looking. Despite all of them speaking Spanish, there had been little direct interbreeding with pure Spanish stock here and the tolerance to alcohol was correspondingly low, as with the Amerindian tribes.

Our marching order was often Raul, me, Jorge and then Cho at the back. Raul carried only a light daysack and enjoyed macheteing, I navigated from just behind him and Cho and Jorge brought up at the back. On one path between communities Cho called us to a halt. '*Mira!*' he said, 'Look!'

As I tried to focus on what he was pointing at in the undergrowth I saw the ominous presence of a fer de lance (a pit viper), coiled and ready to strike. The snake was half on the path and so Raul, Jorge and I had all stepped within inches of the now very agitated serpent. The saying goes that the first person wakes a snake up, the second aggravates it and the third gets bitten. Cho had been number four and had seen the movement as the snake recoiled ready to strike defensively.

A bite from a pit viper such as this could be very serious indeed. Fer de lance has become the common name for many species of vipers in the *Bothrops* genus. They have predominantly haemotoxic venom, which causes a breakdown in the cells and massive haemorrhaging and necrosis. A bad bite would mean death from all organs and tissue breaking down and failing. You would bleed from your hair follicles, eyes, ears, nose and your fingernails before dying a gruesome death.

As it was on a path and could easily have struck a passing villager, Raul killed the snake unceremoniously with a sharp blow to the head with a long stick. Conservationist or not, I agreed it was the right thing to do in the circumstances.

At the next village – now feeling pretty vulnerable in my plimsolls – I adopted Raul's and Jorge's style of footwear and I bought myself some rubber wellies and football socks. I liked this combination immediately and loved the ease with which I could empty the boots out after crossing rivers. I would put them upside down on sticks at night and in the morning they would be bone-dry and quick and pleasant to put on compared to soggy shoes or boots with gritty, muddy laces. The one drawback was that when I waded through dirty water I would also get thorns and spines in them. These came in over the top and would need to be removed as soon as we were on dry ground again. Not a great hassle as the wellies were quick to take off, swill out and put back on again, but it wasn't the perfect system.

Life with Cho, Raul and Jorge became routine as the days turned into weeks. We would wake up with the light at 0530 without the need for an alarm. My hammock, which had been awkward and uncomfortable all night, suddenly became the snuggest, cosiest cot imaginable as I considered the wet clothes I would have to put on.

Once my feet touched the ground I was on autopilot. Everything followed the same pattern, day after day. Although my T-shirt, trousers and socks would have been hand-washed in the river the evening before, they were wet and invariably still somewhat gritty. The humidity meant there was no chance of anything drying overnight and so they had to go on in that state. Once they were on, of course, it was fine. And before too long I started to sweat anyway so the garments never actually dried. Later in the expedition, Cho and I would develop a washing line system over the fire to dry our clothes every evening.

In villages we would often eat a soup made with cockerels' testicles and old hens for breakfast. It was nutritious enough – if a little bland and repetitive. I would usually leave the guides to chat as my brain would take a while to warm up.

I would dress my infected feet and take antibiotics to stop them turning into tropical ulcers. On went the Vaseline layer and the football socks, lastly the black wellies.

Villages here often didn't have areas set aside for defecating. People would just go a little way into the jungle and take a shit. This process was both haphazard and pretty unhygienic and, although there were enough insects and worms to break down a bit of faeces, even a family's worth, once you got a whole village without toilet facilities of any kind things became pretty smelly and dirty.

My moods were as variable as those of someone who was depressed. Perhaps I was. Sheer elation at seeing a bearded saki, a distinctive looking monkey, might be followed immediately by frustration at having to backtrack four kilometres because we'd hit a marsh that couldn't be crossed by boat as there were too many spiky trees. Covered in scratches, ant bites and sores from my pack, my mood could then be transformed to one of pure happiness by stripping off and having a wash. Of course everything was relative but I could get that feeling of cleanliness from washing in very stagnant oxbow-lake water that was brown and full of weeds and grasses.

I made the mistake, after being lifted by some positive messages, of looking for a boost to my morale from the blogs. This form of pick-me-up was totally unreliable and to live in hope of receiving nice messages was terrible for maintaining a constantly positive mindset. Sometimes the messages would not come at all, and at other times they would be angry and negative, calling me irresponsible or worse.

Music was, throughout the whole expedition, a fantastic way of escaping. I went through about seven cheap locally bought MP3 players, none of which lasted long. The only problem with the music was that after a day of my brain being half switched off, coping with the monotony and the tedium, I would turn on this stimulus and get so excited in my hammock that again I couldn't sleep. For hours I would listen to the sounds of civilisation, or normality as I knew it, and the Western world.

Diary entry from 13 November 2008, San Ramón:

Apprehension does my feelings no justice at all. There are no longer any river beaches and the paths are muddy or flooded. Soon I will have to venture further from the river just to find hard ground to walk on.

Raul is very worried about 'trampas' (traps). We've entered an area where the local method of hunting is home-made shotguns set up with tripwires across small paths. The targeted animals are large rodents such as paca or agouti and the crude barrels blast huge gaping holes in the animals at nearly point blank. At about six inches from the ground, it we tripped one they would remove an ankle and no one seems to keep records of where they are set. There is every chance we could walk into a whole field of these traps that might as well be anti-personnel mines. Walking at the front is becoming a less popular job.

Diary entry from 17 November 2008, Puerto Vermudes:

I had to stop the group at 2p.m. because I was so tired. My legs felt like jelly and I was almost crying with tiredness. It's funny, I've spent a large part of my adult life abroad but I've always been in a group of other Westerners. The military, expeditions and risk consultancy work never put me in situations on my own for an extended period of time. This is the first time I have been completely immersed in a country and its people. It's been four and a half months since Luke left and since then I've had a couple of nights talking to Emily but that's it. [I had clearly forgotten Mark Barrowcliffe's visit at this time.]

I should listen to the others and try and interact more but I am so tired that my Spanish isn't advancing. I just let the noise go over my head and switch off.

With hindsight it's hard to justify such behaviour. Why didn't I just find the extra energy to make the effort, to interact more, to learn more words each day? I also noted in my diary that the chief of Puerto Vermudes was called Juan Rojas, that he was kind and that he fed us *caimitos*, sweet, slimy, round green fruit that stuck your lips together if you didn't know how to eat them. I also wrote that he had five children, the most confident, polite kids I'd come across, and that one of them had offered to guide us for the next four kilometres to the next village and had given us all mangos from his school rucksack. He was six years old. Huge amounts of goodwill and generosity were going on around me but I couldn't focus on that good. I was stuck (by my own stubbornness and commitment) in a place that I didn't want to be and so I was still very down.

Jorge, my fat guide who has been with me a week now, is fifty years old and is enjoying the walking. I think he thinks that I am less intelligent and less capable than I am. I know that my poor Spanish probably doesn't make me sound that bright but recently he asked me what rank I'd reached in the army. He was amazed when I said captain. 'But not in the infantry?' he asked. 'Yes,' I replied, 'an infantry captain.'

I knew that I was a shell of my former self and wasn't that surprised by Jorge's reaction.

Diary entry from 19 November 2008, San Roque:

Had a big debate today with Cho about religion. I had always steered away from this subject because I knew we would not agree and I needed him as a guide. I don't think he minds that I'm not religious. I don't think it will change this but it is interesting that he thinks that I am going to hell because I don't believe in God. I explained to him that I thought religion was a clever way of controlling people devised centuries ago and that it was no longer necessary. I borrowed a bit of material from Eddie Izzard and asked him to 'explain dinosaurs'.

It's nearly 12.30 and I must sleep. Things will be OK.

On 20 November we were drawing ever nearer to the jungle city of Iquitos where we wanted to break for Christmas. With still 300 kilometres to push we decided to cross from one apex of a meander to another. Direct line of sight it was seven kilometres, whereas following the river channel would be twenty-four. So we set off with Raul up front. He opened the path all day carrying only a tiny daysack. Cho, Jorge and I took turns going number two, opening up the path a little more for our rucksacks and Jorge's belly to fit through.

We started walking at about 7 a.m. and the first hour was, as always, cool and fresh – or, that is, cooler and fresher. By 8 a.m. we were sweating and the mosquitoes were out in clouds, too. Walking at third or fourth in line was the worst. Clouds of mosquitoes would descend on us and bite constantly. The number of bites we were getting was absurd. With Deet (repellent) being too valuable to use all the time (it sweated off so quickly) we would save it for breaks when eating, when we wanted some peace from the infuriating whining in our ears. That meant that while walking and standing and waiting around, which happened a lot as we were cutting through the undergrowth, we were constantly under attack.

At any one time I had five mosquitoes biting the back of each hand and couldn't see those biting my forehead and the back of my neck. I conservatively estimated at the time that I was getting at least ten bites a minute. When you multiplied that by the length of the eight-hour walking day that came to 4,800 bites a day, 33,600 bites a week and a whopping 145,600 bites a month. They were often not nearly that bad and so my estimated number of bites for the entire expedition would actually only be around 200,000, but it still explained why our bodies no longer reacted to the bites.

Armchair explorers around the world must be throwing down their copies of the book in frustration shouting, 'Why didn't they use a mosquito head net?' or 'What about gloves?' I had both with me and never used either. Partly because I was the only person who had them and I didn't want to be the smug gringo behind his fancy kit, and partly because they just seemed such an alien way of dealing with the situation. The men I was walking with were tough and accustomed to the jungle and so it was important to me that I be the same. In a similar way that I was pleased to have got rid of my ridiculous permethrin-impregnated expedition shirt and was happy with my locally bought wellies, so I enjoyed experiencing the Amazon as the locals did, without the flashy gringo trappings. There was pride to be taken in doing the walk in the manner of the people who lived there.

To keep Raul on track when he was cutting required a careful balance of giving him enough leeway to choose his own 'path of least resistance' through the tangled wall and keeping him roughly on a bearing. I often had to risk upsetting his pride in his 'inbuilt compass' by reorienting him and setting him back in the direction we were meant to be travelling in.

At this time the floods started to worry me. Lakes were fine, if time-consuming, as we could inflate the rafts and paddle across. Thickly vegetated marsh was harder as the rafts were vulnerable to puncturing and so we often had to cut floating bridges out of palms and vegetation to cross somewhat precariously vast expanses of deep, weed-overgrown water.

I was realising at this point that handrailing the river at the edge of the floods was far more simple in theory than in practice. The flooded forest was sporadic and unpredictable and the Peruvian maps we were using were forty years old. The flooded forest was the most tangled environment you could imagine. Vines and roots created a web of gnarled wood in front of us, covered with every type of biting ant. We hauled ourselves over high roots and under low branches, accumulating scratches, thorns and cuts at a worrying rate.

My feet had blisters on the outside of both of them from my rubber boots, which were slightly too small for me, and being under filthy water for most of the day meant that I had finished a course of antibiotics and they were still as infected as ever.

So, at 5 p.m. on 20 November, we decided we weren't going to reach the other side of the seven-kilometre crossing and made a hasty camp. We had only half a litre of water each and, with no stream nearby, we retreated fast into our mosquito nets without making a fire to eat our personal rations of half a tin of tuna, a handful of farine and some sugar. I mixed all three together with a dash of my precious water and regretted it from the first sweet, fishy mouthful.

The following morning we broke camp early and in an hour we could see the vegetation opening in front of us. The light was now streaming in and when we broke out of the tree line we expected to see signs of life on the river. But the river had changed its course and we had arrived at a dry oxbow lake.

After a short walk around the edge we met two locals who laughed at our mistake and told us that the river channel was now four kilometres further on. They had a little plot of land with plants and a small hut and we were invited in for chicken broth and plantain. After the previous night's sludge the meal was very welcome and we all ate a big plate each and glugged down some of their collected rainwater before setting off again.

Two hours later we arrived in Tahuantinsuyo, a small village with a football pitch and a shop. A kind lady cooked us pork ribs and we forgot the discomfort of the previous day as every bit of our minds focused on the wonderful fat of the salty ribs.

When I arrived in a town everybody would stare at me. When I went for a wash everybody would stare at me. When I got changed out of my wet clothes everybody would stare at me. Even in my hammock, reading by my head torch, it would not be uncommon for fifteen to twenty people to be sitting staring at me. Even where a community had 'Direct TV', the Peruvian equivalent of satellite television, I was apparently far more interesting.

This would have been OK if it had only been for a few days, but after eight months it was wearing thin. I became ever more insular as I wanted to hide from the staring. I was praying just to be left alone. But my antisocial behaviour had to be overcome. I needed the help of these people to continue. It was their land I was passing through and their villages I was sleeping in. This just wasn't the jungle expedition I had envisaged. I longed for Brazil, the vast expanses of rainforest and the absence of people.

When we did make conversation, when I made the effort, the topics were always the same. 'You are crazy, you will not be able to walk that far. You will be shot by Indians or a jaguar will eat you.'

But over time I did start to enjoy the company of our team. Jorge was kind and considerate and Raul would laugh at our predicament constantly. When I was sitting down on a break the mozzies would bite through my trousers, targeting my balls, which, of course, I found annoying. Raul found this hilarious and we started to form a bond forged by black humour.

With the increasing conversations with Cho, often about religion, I began to feel more included and Jorge and Raul became a tight working unit much as the Dongo brothers had been before them. Jokes were, predictably, all racist and sexist but not in a spectacularly bad way, just in the bantering manner of a group of people who have never considered political correctness in their lives.

On 24 November 2008, still 246 kilometres from Iquitos, I got up at 0345 to do a live link-up with my old Sandhurst mate Ben Saunders, who was giving a talk at the Royal Geographical Society on expedition communications. I was in a small town called Tamanco at the time and I set up the Macbook so that the Skype camera was pointing at some shrubbery in the town plaza. It was fairly dark when we chatted prior to his talk and then, when we went live just after dawn, it looked suitably jungly.

This was the first time I'd used the BGAN and Skype to do an interview and it worked well. To speak live from the rainforest was such an incredible thing to be able to do, considering we were carrying all our equipment on foot.

It was great to speak to Ben briefly and I was sad to be cut off after only a couple of minutes. He hadn't a clue how I'd been struggling mentally and what that shot of normality had done to revive me.

Cho was fairly sullen at this point. It can't have been easy to walk with someone who was finding it all so difficult but he would often mock me in towns and tell people that I wasn't religious just so that he could see their reaction. He kept telling me I was going to hell. So were all gay people, apparently. At least I'd have some company, I'd tell him. The blunt humour and archaic attitude towards women, gays and different races was a frustrating world to be immersed in. Everybody just thought so differently from me.

As it was the wet season and we were in and out of water all the time, our boots were constantly filling up; this meant that we'd grab our heels with our hands and do quad stretches to empty out the water without removing our boots. Although it worked most of the time it still meant that any water remaining would warm up and slosh around in our boots, leaving skin soft and vulnerable to cuts and fungus.

I decided to take a gamble with my boots and cut two holes in the insteps in the same place as I had had them in my jungle boots. Being waterproof was now irrelevant as the water was always over boot height but the guides looked on in despair at my modification.

It worked like a dream. I could now step out of deep water and continue walking without having to stop to empty my boots, and after a minute they were considerably dryer than they would have been if emptied as my weight was constantly forcing out more water. My skin improved no end and my blisters started to heal. This system also meant I could wear my trousers over my boots to stop any crap such as thorns and spines entering over the top.

It became my favourite boot system when real jungle boots were unavailable: wellies with holes in the instep and trousers cut off just below the top of the boot so that they stopped stuff entering but not so long as to get muddy and grimy round the ankle.

Diary entry from 27 November 2008:

I think I actually enjoyed today. I would more without Cho but I realise that I have to have a focus for my negative energy and that Cho is currently it. I don't think I am mentally very strong. I have determination, which is why I will finish, but I have little control over my moods.

I've cut down on the drugs I'm taking. I'm now just taking omeprazole for my stomach and doxycycline for malaria and feel much better as a result. I've stopped taking diazepam and antihistamines for sleeping and my head is clearer.

I'm so missing having a friend to chat to or a girlfriend to confide in. I miss having a drinking partner.

Diary entry from 1 December 2008:

Today was a day from hell. We left Bagazan without a local guide at 7 a.m. Everyone had been scared of walking with a 'pela cara'. We had hoped to reach a lake by mid-morning but progress was slower than ever and we made six kilometres all day. The forest was varzea [this translates as flooded forest], painfully slow and the mosquitoes were unbelievable.

I had to have a system of using my cap to swat mosquitoes constantly. First I would swat my other hand, then my neck from the left, then my left ear, then my forehead, then my right ear, then my neck from the right. Then I would repeat. We have completely run out of Deet now.

Then I walked under a branch and knocked an ants' nest down on to my pack and thousands of biting ants covered me and my rucksack. I was up to my knees in flood but had to throw off my pack, strip down to the waist and pick them off one by one. I can smell ants now. It's unmistakable and it's earthy and stale and the smell of this nest was pungent.

We found the lake at 5 p.m. and saw a house on the far side. We paddled across and the people allowed us to stay (after a little persuading) in their school. I'm very tired – that was the most unpleasant day of jungle trekking in my life. That's with about two years of my life spent in the jungle. All jungle is most definitely not the same.

It's going to get worse though as the waters rise. I really don't know what we'll do. We'll have to push even further from the river. This varzea is impossible.

When people mention 'pela cara' now they get a standard response: 'Sorry. I am bored with talking about this. It is only the uneducated that believe such stupid stories.'

The final paragraph sounds so blunt and rude to me now. I can remember the sentiment completely, though – I was so bored with pretending that the people's stories were worth listening to. I was so bored with such ignorance. It wasn't their fault but the more I thought about it the more I thought that it wouldn't hurt to tell them they were being stupid. But I could have done it more politely on occasions.

Diary entry from 4 December 2008, Magdalena:

Today we woke up at 5.30 a.m., packed everything away, and after shoving down some farine and sugar in water we started walking. The skies decided to unleash a huge downpour and so we were soaking wet all day. I was conscious of every cut and wound and every slight rub turning into a sore.

At the moment I have an open wound on my left heel; sores around my waist from my pack waist belt; and cuts on my hands from falling over. It's impossible to keep any of them clean or dry.

After two hours of following Raul through the mud we bumped into a settlement of thatched huts that turned out to be called Elmer Fawcet. It was five kilometres from where it was labelled on our map but a family was gathered in one of the huts sitting round a bubbling pot. They invited us up and we climbed up the thin wooden plank to escape the torrential rain.

'What's in the pot?' I asked. 'Mono,' replied the mum. Monkey.

Just pleased to be out of the rain we accepted the family's invitation to eat and I was pleased not to be given the head. The 'monkey' was in fact a kinkajou, a nocturnal arboreal mammal like a racoon. It was boiled seemingly without seasoning and was tough and tasteless.

Jorge sucked at the skull and had juices flowing down his fat chins.

The man and his son agreed to guide us to Magdalena with their shotgun in the rain and we cut back and forth over the tiniest of bridges and walkways through floods and swamps. Without their knowledge we would have been the whole day at least struggling through the maze, but in the end it took only two hours.

At one point on that two-hour dash through the swamps the man's son pointed out something I had never seen before. A thick, muscular, brown body was snaking through the shallow water. '*Puta madre, Cho! Una anaconda!*'

I grabbed my video camera and started filming this mythological serpent. It wasn't big for an anaconda – perhaps 3 metres long with a girth of 15–20 centimetres but it was the first anaconda I had seen in the wild and I was keen to record it.

The boy's father asked me if I'd finished filming and I smiled when I told him that I had. 'What a sighting!' I thought. He then stepped smartly forward and cut the anaconda up into pieces with his machete for his dogs to eat.

Diary entry from 6 December, Requena:

OK I'm depressed. Quite badly so. I have fleeting moments of happiness but they are all short-lived and basically I'm unhappy.

We arrived in Requena yesterday, I felt OK but tired, bored of walking, bored of my guides, bored of the expedition. It's all compounded by having such good access to the Internet. A life of beers and girls and friends and love is just on the other side of the screen and yet I've never been so lonely.

I need to think less about the outside world and focus on the task. I need to take confidence in my own abilities to deal with the jungle. I need to be emotionally independent from everyone.

What do I need to concentrate on to become happier? Language: I still have three months left in Peru and could be reading Spanish every night. I could be doing Portuguese lessons on my MP3 player too so that I will not have this whole problem again once I enter Brazil.

I need to be in control. I need to become stronger each day rather than weaker. I need to do press-ups and exercises to ensure I improve. Mentally I need to focus on the positives, what we have achieved so far.

I need to stop thinking about the women that have been in my life. That is not constructive and is getting me down. I need to accept that not having a relationship is the sacrifice of this journey.

Keith [photographer] arrives tomorrow. It's important that he gets a visit with a positive explorer who loves what he's doing. 11 p.m. Lights out.

Chapter Nine

Recovery in Iquitos

At about seven in the morning Cho knocked on my door. 'Ed, Kid is here!' (Keith is unpronounceable to South Americans). 'What? Eh? Thanks, Cho,' I mumbled through the door and lowered my bare feet on to the cold tiled hotel floor and padded softly out of my room.

In the corridor I saw a tall Brit with a shaven head, a broad rucksack and a grin to match coming through the door. 'All right, Ed? How are you?' beamed Keith, in a London accent. 'Fancy a fag?'

I'd never met Keith Ducatel before. He was a friend of a friend who had found out about my expedition and wanted the opportunity to come out to the Amazon and take photographs. I had seen an example of his work and he was very talented indeed, but somehow I'd got the impression he was younger, perhaps because photography was only a passion of his rather than his main job.

The bloke with the fags now standing before me had an aura of cheerful excitement about where he was and what he was about to embark on. In his late thirties, he was relaxed and unfazed by the complicated journey he'd just undertaken to get here. Immediately I started talking.

It was like some sort of release. To have someone come in who was my own nationality and approximate age was such a relief. We went and did a few admin tasks about town together and just chatted nonstop. I was so excited to be able to communicate with someone again that I found myself smiling. To be able to express subtleties, to be able to make jokes, to be able to relate to someone. Positivity, energy, humour and life started flooding back into my being.

The very same morning that Keith arrived we reorganised his pack and started out of Requena. Jorge, Raul, Cho, Keith and I made us a party of five and yet, because none of us was local, we didn't know the local paths and had to ask for directions at every village. As a result we came to a large tributary that had been bridged but the bridge was down. A big section in the middle was missing and the waters below were strong and fast.

We couldn't swim it, that was for sure, but before I'd even contemplated inflating the rafts and ferrying people across, Raul and Jorge, now very relaxed into our journey, started cutting poles from nearby trees. In seconds they had ten long, straight poles and were cutting vines to use as cord for lashings. I watched with the utmost respect as these guys rebuilt the bridge without a second thought and without a nail or a hammer. Keith used the opportunity to get used to the conditions and take photos of men working completely at ease with nothing but their machetes to assist them. In ten minutes the bridge was crossable, not just by us but by anyone else who wanted to cross in the months ahead. Keith was impressed and I was proud of the capable, no-nonsense team I had around me.

We entered a community called Santa Rosa, where the village children crowded round us and watched fascinated as we pored over the map, planning our route, sipping cheap orangeade. The communities here weren't pure *nativos*; they all considered themselves to be colonial and spoke nothing but Spanish. Only a couple of hundred kilometres from the huge city of Iquitos now, they were all pretty relaxed around Westerners and we were treated almost kindly. We bought a kilo and a half of smoked armadillo and continued walking.

Keith and I chatted a great deal while walking and my sanity just kept on being restored. I found I could now cope with any problems with ease and we would laugh like old friends if one of us fell over.

It was emotional for me to go through this return to normality. I felt happier than I could remember; the contrast with the depressed, lonely months was stark and the walking became adventurous and fun again.

Keith managed well with the weight of his pack, too. He'd done some training in England but he'd had to join a group that had been walking together for months and he never moaned once. He wasn't acclimatised and he poured with sweat, his T-shirts showing the ridiculous amount of salt he was loosing as he sweated. His back and arms were covered in bites – bites so big and angry and abundant that they would have got the toughest of people down – but he just smiled, looked for the positives and kept snapping away with his camera in a cloud of mosquitoes.

The one drawback was that he smoked. He didn't just smoke, though, he clearly *loved* smoking. As an ex-smoker I could see the absolute pleasure he gained from taking a break, sitting on a log or a rock and inhaling deeply the calming smoke. It didn't take long for me to crack, and for the next few weeks the whole party, Cho included by the end, would ensure we always had cigarettes when we left a village. The smoking represented a distinct shift from just continuing, to being able to relax and enjoy the journey, as friends who all shared in a simple pleasure.

Sometimes we would hire a local guide who knew the paths to the next village, perhaps only for a few hours, and so we were fluctuating between a five- and six-man team. This was costing me loads and, despite being very happy that we had a team that worked, I knew that as soon as I could I would have to say goodbye to Jorge and Raul. For the moment, partly due to the comfort of having these older men as part of the team, they stayed and I just took solace in the fact that we weren't merely going forward, we were advancing well and actually enjoying it, too. I would just have to find the money.

My confidence started to grow and grow during this period. There is nothing like coming from complete self-pitying brokenness and then rebuilding yourself simply on the strength of knowledge about your capabilities. I could now compare myself to a normal Englishman and in addition I could skip over slippery logs, I could handle a machete and I could lead a team.

In military training at Sandhurst the first five weeks was an intense period of nervous sleep deprivation. It made many people drop out as they lost focus and lost sight of their reasons for joining in the first place. We watched the platoon slim down as those without the drive to continue left. But those who stayed all had times of feeling broken, low and pathetic. And then, very cleverly, the army training system would take these half-broken men and rebuild them. They would start to become good at military skills such as marching, shooting and navigating and their confidence would grow. The training was designed to create men who were proud and confident in themselves as soldiers, rather than in what they had done in their former lives, and the difference they achieved in a year was remarkable. Young, scruffy students became British Army officers who were confident and capable.

I could see the parallels in what I was putting myself through. I had been cocky prior to the journey and my confidence had come from others complimenting me or commenting on my abilities. That false confidence had now been stripped from me and I was rebuilding myself based on nothing but my actual abilities. No opinion, no blagging or pretending, no hiding and no bullshitting. I was learning my trade again based on nothing but natural ability and the sense of rejuvenation at coming out of the other side of this was empowering.

Having Keith to watch over helped me, too. He had little experience of the jungle save a week-long trip with a mad drunken Brazilian. I taught him how to look after his feet, how to tape up sores on his hips where his pack rubbed before they became broken skin, and he became proficient at putting up his hammock and organising his kit.

I told Raul and Jorge that we could walk together until Nauta, where I would pay them and give them the money to take a boat back home. From there Cho, Keith and I had a few days of walking in the direct sunlight on the highway that stretched south of Iquitos. Jorge had a chest infection and Raul had been coughing, too. Being wet all day long was fine for Cho, Keith and myself in our thirties, but Raul and Jorge were around fifty and they were beginning to show signs of physical deterioration. Jorge was also becoming slightly contrary and less helpful. This was just fatigue, I think; he'd been solid for weeks. Raul had an offer from an American to sell 350 trees from a plot of land that he had claimed, so he had hopes of making his fortune. Had this not been the case he said he would like to have continued further.

Looking ahead on the map, I was becoming worried about the upcoming flood season. I had always thought I would get across the border into Brazil before the waters rose but now that looked impossible. The outcome meant that the Peruvian (south) side of the river would be completely flooded as it was very low-lying and that I had to consider the option of going through Colombia on the northern bank. The very name 'Colombia' filled me with apprehension and I remembered reading about kayaking expeditions that had been shot at from the Colombian side. We wouldn't be kayaking past at speed, however; we would be walking.

We were still a week or so's walk from Nauta, the town at the start of the highway, and we had a lot of jungle to cross. From a camp on a river beach on 15 December 2008 I wrote the following:

> We stupidly pushed north-east away from the river and were fooled by false 'horizon' [river] after false horizon. Each time we thought we were arriving at the river the trees opened to reveal a marsh, an old river channel, or a swampy lake. Some were crossable but others required huge detours. The river had changed position recently and we were not sure of the exact location and making estimates based on boats that we could hear through the vegetation kilometres away.
>
> We crashed through cane and rushes covered in tiny spikes that were almost like hairs that penetrated through our trousers into our knees and shins. At 5.40 p.m. we finally reached the river with only twenty minutes of light left; without saying a word we all cut poles for erecting

tarps and mosquito nets on the beach and we had a quick wash in the twilight before a supper of water and farine with sugar.

I remember the night well because Keith and I shared a mosquito net on the beach and he had an iPod that could play movies. We watched *The Deer Hunter* with one headphone each until we were both too tired to keep our eyes open.

I woke about an hour later to see Keith on all fours on the sand outside the net vomiting again and again. Raul showed his caring side and got up and sat by Keith until he'd finished being sick then Keith came back to the net and he too fell asleep.

In the morning Keith was clearly still feeling ill but there was no option but to walk. We had no food left and needed to reach a community to resupply. Keith summoned all his energy and we walked all day until mid-afternoon when we eventually found a community with a shop and some boats.

Keith, who had developed malaria on his previous week-long trip to Brazil, had a recurrence of the illness and was in no state to walk. As his Spanish was all but nonexistent, I asked Cho if he would take him in a boat ahead to Nauta. Cho and Keith had struck up a good relationship and Cho was happy to help. I would walk with Jorge and Raul and we'd meet Cho in Nauta. Keith would rest up in a hotel in Iquitos for a few days.

The change in dynamic was fun again. Walking with the old guys was different and calm and we put in huge distances each day. I was happy that the civilisation of Iquitos was in sight and that we'd be there by Christmas. Somehow Christmas in a town with a bed was a light at the end of a very long, dark tunnel and the break was going to be the most appreciated one I had ever had.

Sending Cho off with Keith again made me realise how much I trusted him. I still found him annoying at times but he was honest and dependable, and I realised I was grateful that he was still with me.

Raul, Jorge and I arrived a few days later to find a very refreshed Cho in laundered clothes and new jeans waiting for us in a small hotel in Nauta. Cho, like many Peruvians, had the habit of combing his hair across his head like my grandpa used to and he looked very smart in an old-fashioned way with a pressed shirt.

Jorge, who had become a bit tetchy, now asked to be paid and was very annoyed when I deducted the money that he had wanted to be advanced to him for beers. He sulked like a child and when Raul, Cho and I went out for the last time together for beers he stayed back at the hotel. When we returned later in the night he had gone without saying goodbye to any of us. But times were hard and money was very tight.

Raul left the following morning, too, but he and I parted firm friends and kept in contact sporadically by email over the following months. Cho and I marched north towards Iquitos. We looked at the 101-kilometre stretch and foolishly told ourselves that we would do it in one straight go; all day and all night just to get it done. In fact we had underestimated our state of exhaustion and the walk on hot asphalt took four whole days.

On the last day a tall, broad man rode up to us on a motorbike and pulled off his helmet, shouting in American-accented English, 'Ed Stafford! Is it really you?'

'What the—?' I thought as this larger-than-life, slicked-back grey-haired character bounded towards us, hand outstretched and a broad smile showing well-kept teeth. His name was Rodolfo, Rudy for short, and he'd read an article in the local paper about our walk. I'd never been recognised before and so was amused at Rudy's reaction to us. He offered us supper at his house when we arrived in Iquitos and we gratefully accepted.

In fact Rudy went much further and, although he and his wife, Mati, were travelling to Lima for Christmas, he offered us the keys to his house and the free run of it while we were in town. Rudy reminded me of gangsters out of the old films; he told me that he could leave his motorbike outside his house because the local kids respected him. Rudy loved to impart manly advice: 'Whenever my football team – Universitario – wins, I buy the whole street drinks, and you know what? No one fucks with me.' He had lived in

America and had very American ideas and had returned to his home country Peru with a high regard for money and status.

Rudy continued, 'I went into the bank today and it was empty. There were five tellers and I asked the first if I could withdraw some money. "You need a queue ticket, sir," said the Indian man. "I am the only person in the bank, you fucking pussy," I said. "I will find you in the street one day, you pussy!" The teller threatened to call security and so I repeated, "I will find you", and I walked out.'

Rudy was loud and crude and swore in English all the time. But he was good fun and we enjoyed his extremely kind generosity while we recovered our strength and enjoyed the tourist city of Iquitos.

On his way in to get to us, Keith had flown through Iquitos and had met a beautiful English-speaking girl called Yvonne. Keith had a girlfriend back in the UK and so wasn't interested in Yvonne but he had seen the sorry state that I'd been in when he arrived and so he decided we needed some R&R. Cho, Keith and I piled into the city to meet Yvonne and her friends in one of the touristy bars. This was a different Peru, one that was foreign to me; fashionable ladies with make-up and perfume – it was startling for my senses that were by now just attuned to the jungle. Yvonne had a friend called Ursula who spoke no English but who I enjoyed chatting to and so I agreed to meet her again the following day in the plaza.

'You can drive a motorbike, can't you?' smiled Ursula who was mid-thirties, worked out every day and had an incredibly toned body.

'Umm, I never have,' I admitted, 'I'll go on the back.'

Ursula told me she needed to pick up her dog from somewhere and I agreed to go with her. She was tiny, not much over five foot, and it was only when I climbed on the back of her bike that I became conscious that, in Peru, the culture is so macho that a man on the back is an amusing sight. I tried not to be self-conscious as Ursula darted through the streets and pulled up at a shop. She told me to wait and reappeared with a poodle that had just been trimmed. 'Hold this,' she instructed and I obeyed and I took the manicured dog in both hands.

Because it was carnival time the local tradition was to throw water-filled balloons at passing cars and bikes and this was when I started laughing at my predicament. A week earlier I had been wading through swamps with machete in hand and now I was on a motorbike, drenched by water bombs with a flustered poodle and a tiny, beautiful Peruvian woman projecting me through the streets of this crazy town at high speed.

We stayed for Christmas and a little longer after because I had made a decision. One of the greatest things that I have Keith to thank for is opening my eyes to Cho. The two of them had got on so well from the beginning because Keith had put loads of energy into trying to get to know Cho. As a result I was now seeing sides of Cho I'd not seen before and qualities that I'd missed completely. Combined with also having a few nights out with Cho, our friendship strengthened considerably.

Cho wanted to continue into Brazil and so he needed a passport as he'd never left Peru before. We filled out all the forms and Rudy helped us, too, and waited for Cho's passport to arrive from Lima.

Rudy introduced us to some very helpful people such as Dr Oto, the main military doctor in town, who was able to give us great advice on increasing our anti-venom quantities for vipers and how better to administer it.

I had to admit that the looming apprehension of Brazil and the unknown was lessened by the knowledge that Cho was going to be walking with me until the end, and that we were now better prepared and experienced than ever.

What wasn't working was our Brazilian visas. With only a few months left before we hoped to enter Brazil, Iquitos was the last place in Peru that we could have been issued with them. I felt infuriated that my expedition might be put in jeopardy by a fat, lazy man in Manaus who I had already paid to sort out our visas. When I expressed my concern at the lack of visas and FUNAI permits, the response that came back from Manaus was offhand and unhelpful.

The delay over Cho's passport application meant that Keith ran out of time and had to return to England without doing any more walking. He got some amazing shots and recovered from his relapse into malaria and so was happy enough with his trip. I would always be indebted to him for coming out, paying all his own expenses, being the friend I needed to help me get control of the expedition again, allowing me to see the good in Cho and, on top of all that, taking some great images that we could now use to build a new website and use in the press. Several mornings in Iquitos we had been sitting up drinking whisky until the sun rose, talking rubbish or arguing about our different tastes in music. I knew I had found a lasting friend in Keith and both Cho and I were sorry to see him leave.

From Iquitos to San Francisco de Orellana we followed muddy roads that turned into muddy paths through mainly agricultural fields and secondary forest. We would inflate the rafts whenever we got to rivers as the water was now high and we seemed to be crossing water constantly. Many of the villages were well kept and almost twee to walk through, pretty wooden huts behind neat fences and grass trimmed by the cattle and sheep. It was an easy introduction to walking after the excesses of a fantastic Christmas in Iquitos.

From Orellana everything changed. We paddled across the vast Napo River that came down from the north and hit a band of the lowest lying forest we had seen so far. Looking back, I can now see immediately on Google Earth that we were crossing a river delta and that it would be flooded, but I hadn't realised the stupidity at the time and was used to walking by the river. The next 25 kilometres were to teach me a lesson. They took ten whole days to cover.

The first day, we immediately hit thick vegetation and deep water. Imagine the thickest of bramble bushes, knotted with razor-sharp vines and spiky palms. Then imagine sinking the whole thing in a swimming pool full of muddy water and having to make your way through that swimming pool using just your 18-inch machete. In the thicker parts five metres could easily take five minutes and in the first ten-hour day we covered 2.4 kilometres. The water at times was up to our nipples and we couldn't see our feet or anything in front of us under the water so we had to feel our way through the spines. At the end of the day there was nowhere to camp. Nothing but trees and floods, and the only option was to push out of the tree line, inflate the boats and head downriver looking for a patch of land or a settlement in which to stay the night. We marked the position we'd got to with the GPS so we could return in the morning to the exact spot and set off downriver. After a half an hour of paddling we found a group of houses on a unique patch of higher ground and asked the inhabitants if we could stay. They agreed and we gave them some rice and tuna to prepare and put our hammocks up in their hut with their children.

On 25 January 2009 we paid a local man ten *soles* (£2) to take us back upriver to where we had got to the day before. He dropped us off but still wasn't sure what we were doing. 'You're going to *walk* back?' he asked, stupefied.

And we did. But what a day.

It was 0930 when we started walking and we had with us Cho's smaller pack, two machetes, a compass, a GPS, a video camera, two packets of fags (Keith's legacy had not yet been stamped out) a lighter, a head torch, an EPIRB, one kilogram of farine and 500 grams of sugar.

The moment we set out the land started to drop. We were wading up to our waists at first, but then deeper, to our chests.

I observed things that I never expected to: how light a machete is when you hold it under water all day; how slow you have to walk if you don't want two-inch needle spines sticking into your knees and shins. The spines were horrific; I was in wellies and they went straight through – no messing. Under toenails, into kneecaps. When extracted, they left the immediate area with a dull ache that almost always became slightly infected.

We took turns up front and we took turns to lose confidence. I realised that it really was all in the mind and that it was positivity that made the walk exhilarating and challenging. In my moments of negativity, when stung, spiked, bitten, or all three, I was left almost in a panic attack wondering how I could get out of this spiky hell. I had to calm myself down on such occasions.

Cho would have his moments, too. I could feel the times when I was stronger and had more courage than he had. But each time he recovered well.

It was anaconda country and there were plenty of piranhas and I was still amazed that we never got a bite from one. At the time we were fairly sure that there were no caiman this close to the main channel although I later learned that there were probably plenty all around us. In truth, of course, none of these animals wanted to attack us. We were too big to be eaten by all but the largest of black caiman (and jaguars out of the floods) and as we progressed we felt less and less threatened by the wildlife. There is a pressure when writing about the Amazon to extend the myth and write about the place as if dangers lurk under every log. But the truth is that, although there are potential dangers, the likelihood of becoming prey is far less than people imagine. The fear of the unknown is the biggest cause of such rumours and embellishment and, in truth, the times Cho and I walked through the jungle I felt we were safer than if we had been walking through London dodging traffic and pickpockets.

Late in the afternoon the flooded forest became too deep to walk. I tried carrying the rucksack above my head but my face was half submerged and it wasn't working. Rather than panicking, I found that challenges like this now brought out the best in me. Fully recovered, my brain was now working at its absolute best when faced with real, tangible pressures from the wild. We just had to adapt and find a way of continuing. With a situation developing, a plan would form in my mind to allow us to do just that. Cho would inflate the pack raft in the river and take the rucksack and paddle in the river while I would have nothing more than a machete and I would swim from tree to tree in the forest. The boat would have been punctured in seconds in the mass of thorns and so Cho had to be on the river. Cho agreed grudgingly as he always wanted to walk when he could, but the only person who physically had to walk (or in this case swim) was me.

The line between the forest and the river was blurred. There were no banks (they were well below the surface), just a massive sheet of water cutting straight into the jungle.

The plan wasn't a sensible one. Swimming isn't one of my strong points and wearing wellies and carrying a machete I was gasping and spluttering my way through the forest. I could tell Cho was concerned. At each tree I clung for a few seconds, gasping for air, before plunging into the floods again with as much swimming grace as a petrified cat.

Eventually we reached an area of very high ground and climbed a river cliff using tree roots and getting covered in mud. Muscles quivering and sapped of energy after my swim, I deflated the boat and pushed on. We'd waypointed the village downstream, Siete de Julio, with the GPS the night before and so we knew we had only 300 metres to go.

That last 300 metres took us an hour and a half and four or more water obstacles before we emerged, bedraggled and bespiked, into the village.

We washed, put on dry clothes and felt human again in seconds. We were given a meal of a fillet of fish. I was sure it had been cooked in butter but Cho insisted otherwise. He was right: the fish had been cooked in its own wonderful natural oils and we washed it down with rice, yucca and Inca Kola.

The following morning was serenity itself. The forest was calm and quiet and although we were chest-deep in water the forest was open enough to allow us to pass with little cutting. The mosquitoes were not too bad either.

From our map we could see a tributary river called Atuncocha coming down from the north ahead of us and we could see that on the far side of Atuncocha was a lone contour line. Due to the angle of Atuncocha coming in from the north-west, it was decided that we should head away from the main channel of the Amazon and head north-east directly towards this tributary.

At 4 p.m. we decided that, as we hadn't seen any land above the water for the past two hours, we should stop when we found some and make camp. We were far too far inland now to escape down-river in the boats – we were camping in the floods, no matter what. We were still about 700 metres short of Atuncocha and the situation looked ominous. The forest closed in and became brambles and thorns and we could not have erected our hammocks there had we wanted to as all the trees were too thin to bear our weight.

At 5 p.m. I found a piece of land above the water that was six foot by three foot and I thought it would have to do. Soon after, though, Cho found an island in the forest that was 10 foot by 15 foot and that was where we made our camp (see my diary sketch below). Our hammocks were over the water but it was only ankle-deep. Importantly, we had land on which to make a fire and cook. If the river rose in the night, though, we were in serious trouble. In the dark the only option would be to inflate the rafts and rise with the water, keeping in one position by securing ourselves to a tree. It would be too dark to move at night, the forest was too thick to move through in the rafts, so we would have to sit it out until dawn.

Writing that reminds me of what an amazing time we were to have ahead of us. The waters still had six months to go before they were at their highest in Brazil and high ground seemed to be running out fast. Every day I questioned whether this expedition was possible.

Diary entry from 26 January 2009:

If the water was ANY higher this section would be unwalkable. Sometimes only our heads are out of the water and often we have to backtrack and choose different routes because the water is too deep. Now it is fun – I wonder whether I will still think so in a year's time.

We woke up on 27 January and although it had rained in the night the water level was the same. I dropped out of my hammock into six inches of water, naked except for a pair of jungle boots. I found my wet T-shirt, my wet trousers and my wet socks all still dirty as we had not washed as usual the night before, and cursed myself for not having been more composed.

The island of solid ground was a haven for animals and every crevice of my rucksack was inhabited by spiders, bugs, beetles, millipedes and ants. We broke camp and immediately the waters became deep again and the vegetation dense. We prepared ourselves for hours of hacking through matted thicket up to our chins in brown sludge when we caught a glimpse of a bright light ahead. Sun was streaming into the forest and we opened up on to an oxbow lake. The lake was inhabited by every spiky plant imaginable and so we inflated the rafts and gingerly worked our way across, cutting through the prickly vegetation. The lake was deep but on the other side it went straight into the forest and we had to stay in the boats, crawling under branches and over giant lily pads with armoured thorn-covered rims.

The precarious navigating was like playing that game where you have to pass a wire hoop along a wire course without touching it and setting off a buzzer. At any moment I was expecting to burst the rafts and plunge us into brown, sludgy, caiman-inhabited water.

Eventually the vegetation opened up and we spilled into the river that we'd been aiming for, the Atuncocha. We'd been walking for a day and a half from Siete de Julio to reach this canyon and to make the three kilometres felt like a real success. Our eyes revelled in their ability to focus on things far away and the space around us on the water felt reviving. We whooped like Americans and paddled across the canyon to the long-awaited high ground denoted by the lonely contour line.

Santa Rosa de Atuncaña lies at the mouth of the Atuncocha on the banks of the Amazon's main channel. On arrival we were welcomed and invited to stay in a house on the tallest stilts I had seen so far – perhaps five metres off the ground. Everyone came to and from the house in their dugout canoes. A drunken man offered to guide us to the next village, Roca Eterna, but by morning he was so plastered that we left him and continued on our own again.

We left Santa Rosa, heading for Roca Eterna, with no food and no idea how far away our destination was as it didn't feature on our map. We suspected it was about three days' walk but the village shop had nothing – so we left with no more than a soggy bag of salt.

The morning was slow as the high ground was so overgrown and tangled that we had to push away from the river and into the more open flooded forest. We glided through the mysterious world with everything reflected in the waters, hardly making a sound as we floated along, rucksacks buoyant on our backs behind us. The waterproof rucksack liners were absolutely invaluable; without them we couldn't have walked in this manner. They were thick 100-litre roll-top canoe bags and everything was bone-dry inside them, despite the rucksacks being half submerged for most of the time.

At 4.30 p.m., having walked just over a kilometre and a half, we decided to GPS our location, inflate the pack rafts and paddle downriver to Roca Eterna. Cho had got very cold while wading and was struggling more than I was as a result of being constantly submerged in water.

We planned to return in the morning to continue walking – but at least we would return having eaten, dried out and bought supplies. It annoyed me, this going out and coming back into the walk, but there was no other way I could see of doing it. Little by little we were chipping away at the vast mileage still ahead of us and at least we had a workable system that enabled us to continue.

As we drifted away from the banks on to the main channel of the Amazon the sun was strong behind us and I turned my cap backwards to protect my neck from burning. Ahead a rainstorm was approaching malevolently. The wind picked up and the waves grew bigger and, as the dark wall of rain hit, Cho started singing religious songs at the top of his voice. It was the sort of rain that smacks you in the face, like diving into a glacial lake. The individual drops stung like hail and I turned my cap to the front again to protect my eyes.

The Amazon is three kilometres wide at this point and to be in the middle of it, in a four-foot inflatable dinghy that has a safety label on it which reads 'Do not use if there is a risk of drowning' while waves crashed and the wind howled, was exhilarating to say the least.

I tore myself out of my self-conscious English shell and joined in the singing. Not knowing any religious songs in Spanish I sang, for some unknown reason, 'Don't Cry for Me, Argentina' at full pelt. It seemed appropriately dramatic and it didn't seem to matter that Cho and I were singing completely different songs. We were three metres apart but could hardly hear each other over the rain.

We grinned at each other and it felt as if we were winning. Small and vulnerable in the midst of the colossal storm, we were sticking two fingers up at the Amazon, and the past week of wading through murky waters.

As the rain passed and the wind dropped, we sat back and floated for a while. We could see Roca Eterna perched on a lonely hill and, as we paddled calmly up to the row of dugout canoes, we were met by about twenty kids with inquisitive faces. They helped us pack up the boats then we climbed up the riverbank, drenched to the bone, to the village to meet the chief, Marcus, who we'd come across two days earlier in Santa Rosa.

Once again out of the rain and the wet, we sipped the hot 'Yerba Louisa' drink, a sweet herbal tea, with genuine appreciation.

The average of 2.5 kilometres a day made pretty gloomy reading when I did the maths that night. We could be walking for up to seven years from this point! Even when I took out the inevitable roads and the dry seasons, I determined that it could take a further three years from here if we continued in the way we were going.

There was only one thing for it: we had to change our tactics and head well away from the river. We had to be far enough away from it that the floods would not affect us.

We finished the flooded section to Roca Eterna over the next two days and then walked an additional day on hard ground to Oran. Oran was a town rather than a village and had hardware stores, places that served food and bars that served beer. We checked into the only hotel, which gave us a shabby room with a sad bed but it did have electricity in the evenings from six to nine o'clock. To wash we still had to walk down to the river but having my own space for the first time in weeks was a luxury.

We took a day – 1 February – off to wait for the journalist Matt Power who was coming to walk with us for a bit to write an article for *Men's Journal*. Cho and I pottered around Oran, charging and cleaning kit, drinking beer and watching women's football in the plaza.

The other person who was coming was Ursula (poodle- and motorbike-owner) from Iquitos. I had promised her that she could come and walk with us for three days and she was arriving at eight o'clock the following morning on the fast boat from Iquitos. Matt was due to arrive six hours earlier on the slow boat at 2 a.m. Cho and I decided to wait up for Matt.

By the time he turned up, Cho and I had had a few drinks. Matt stood in the bows of the boat as it came in and leaped down on to the grassy banks with a big grin. He held out his hand and in a New York accent asked, 'Mr Stafford, I presume?'

'Hi, Matt. Let's go for a beer,' I replied.

Matt was excited and we chatted away for a couple of hours

before deciding we should get some rest before tomorrow's walk. Then, what seemed like only seconds later, the alarm was going off and I knew that Ursula was almost here. I dragged myself out of bed.

I was regretting asking Ursula. Hosting Matt was one thing – it benefited the expedition and got us much-needed publicity – but Ursula's visit was less logical. She arrived in skinny jeans with a fully made-up face and very tight T-shirt and tottered off the boat. This was going to be interesting.

We found an old boy called Mario who agreed to guide us. Mario had warm, trustworthy eyes and carried his gear in a flour sack with a strap over his forehead. He could walk twice the speed of any of us through the forest despite being sixty-two. He knew the hills behind the town and we wanted to head up into the higher ground in order to speed up our progress. Mario led us through cleared fields of grazing buffalo. I hadn't laid down any ground rules and Ursula wanted to hold hands. I could feel Matt's eyes on my back as I walked through these pristine fields of foreign livestock, holding hands with my miniature Peruvian Shakira. He must have wondered what on earth he had just flown down from the States to write about, but he just smiled knowingly and followed in his full Gortex Pro outfit and matching gaiters.

We vaulted buttress roots the size of stretched limos reaching out over the trail and trickling streams as clear as bottled water. Despite our guests, we made about 15 kilometres each day. Ursula walked well considering what she was wearing and that she was so far out of her comfort zone. She walked for three days, pretty much all on paths through the jungle, through small streams, over log bridges until we arrived at a community called Sanalillo. It took us three days to reach Sanalillo. Mario normally did it in a day.

On the third day we opened up into a field that had been recently slashed out of the jungle and the stumps of the felled trees were still smouldering. The Yawa village was having a *minga*, where everybody works together, and the inhabitants were working the field and drinking the infamous *masato*. The red-faced Amerindians welcomed us without hesitation and after three days of hill walking the fermented liquid tasted wonderful. After a night in the local school I organised a boat to take Ursula home.

Matt was joined by a larger-than-life ice-hockey-playing photographer called Pete McBride who came in to add some images to Matt's article. The two of them enjoyed the walking and Matt relaxed considerably in Pete's company. Their energy bars and Western ideas seemed almost foreign to me now, slightly brash and overdeveloped.

Despite our more considered route we still had to cross large areas of flooding as we neared the small jungle town of Pebas. We would be up to our waists, then past our chests and then we had to load all the packs into a raft and swim through the shiny black water.

'Holy shit!' called Pete in waist-deep water. He had spotted something big in the water nearby. I turned to look and saw what appeared to be a huge catfish with a broad, wide mouth and a snaky body about two metres long lurking in the depths between Pete and me. The eerie thing was the complete lack of fear the weird fish had of us. I called to Bernabet, the young guide, to see if he knew what it was. 'Aguila,' he smiled, electric eel. I asked him if it was dangerous. 'Not if you don't upset it,' he replied.

When we reached Pebas I found out that these Amazonian electric eels could indeed be very dangerous. They can produce up to 500 watts, a potentially deadly strike for a human, although the most common way of dying was said to be drowning after being knocked out by the shock. They are an apex predator, the king of their food chain, hence their complete lack of fear because nothing hunts them. I looked ahead at the next four months of flood walking that we had before us and smiled at the ridiculous situation.

At Pebas we said farewell to the Americans, who had achieved everything they'd come for, and had offloaded loads of fancy kit that Cho and I split between us – head torches, trousers, even second-hand socks. Cho and I were more than grateful for the Yanks' chuck-outs; then we turned our attention east towards Colombia.

Chapter Ten

The Drugs-Trafficking Trail to Colombia

Pebas is an odd Peruvian town. With no road access, it is completely dependent on the river and it has a large population of gays. Somehow gay groups within Peruvian communities have to be much more ostentatious and extravagant than in other countries. Perhaps in such a macho culture you have to go to extremes if you want to buck the trend. The result in Pebas was teams of the campest volleyball players mincing around the court in the town plaza that directly overlooks the Amazon. The striking thing was that they moved like women as they walked about and interacted with each other, but the moment they started playing they were skilful men hammering the ball from one side to the other with impressive strength. At the end of a punishing rally they would snap back into camp mode and congratulate each other with theatrical kisses and girly giggles.

The self-installed Lord of Pebas was a famous painter named Francisco Grippa, Pancho to his friends. Francisco lived in an absurdly lavish mansion overlooking the whole town and he allowed every single traveller who passed through Pebas to stay in his house for free, much to the annoyance of the town's only hotel. Francisco said he did this because, although he was Peruvian, he was proud of his travels and enjoyed meeting the people who visited the town. If his guests chose to, they could buy one or more of his huge, brightly coloured paintings of the Amazon that hung in his vast gallery.

Francisco was a bit of a player as a young man and his current wife was young and beautiful. Stories of the parties that he used to host in his castle-like residence were still the talk of the town.

He had hosted Martin Strel, the Slovenian long-distance swimmer, when he had swum past the year before and he enjoyed playing a little part in our folly, too. He was kind to us. We stayed with him for a few days while we talked to as many people as we could about how to get to Brazil from there on foot. We had pretty much resigned ourselves to the fact that we were now going to go through Colombia and many people warned us of the dangers of the FARC, the infamous Marxist-Leninist guerrilla group, and the drugs traffickers.

Francisco's loyal housekeeper, Warren, found us a very professional-looking guide called Juan Rodriguez da Silva. Juan was a logger who had spent time in the military and he was the strongest Peruvian I had met in my entire time in Peru. He had arms and legs like those of a bodybuilder and I would never have believed he had never been to the gym if I hadn't known that there wasn't a gym for 500 miles. He had got that strong from hauling vast planks of wood huge distances in the forest. Juan was keen, interested in the walk and spoke knowledgeably about the areas between where we were and the Colombian border.

There were trails for much of it, he said, many of which were used by loggers and drugs runners alike. I immediately liked Juan: he was professional and intelligent and, like many ex-military men who we had walked with, he had travelled outside his hometown which gave him an experience and wisdom that was missing from people who had never left their own patch.

We set off with twenty-one days' worth of food, the most we had carried so far. Our packs were very heavy and Juan was carrying a large flour sack with cloth webbing around his forehead. The pouring rain was now the norm; I couldn't remember the last dry day we'd had.

I'm not sure if there was any one particular reason but Cho and I immediately found the going very tough. We had heavier packs with twenty-one days of food; we were not used to hills after having done so much flat walking, and Juan was easily storming ahead. Cho was feeling it more than me and I began to be slightly concerned about his health. He'd been having stomach pains in the night, too, and had occasionally vomited blood. Either way, both Cho and I were struggling ridiculously and it was clear that Juan was slightly frustrated and surprised by our inability to walk fast. We had to ask for several breaks, something that neither of us really took any more, and we were confused by our own weakness.

We passed a small fishing village where one of Juan's friends, Boruga, was working at the side of the path. Juan turned and asked me if I thought that another person to share the weight would help and I jumped at the offer. Boruga, real name Moises Soria Huane, was asked and immediately agreed to join us. He said he needed five minutes to say goodbye to his wife and kids for three weeks. Boruga and Juan had worked together as forestry workers before and they were both very accustomed to carrying weight and being away from home in the jungle. They were both incredible with weight and as Cho and I had the group kit (communications, cooking and medical equipment) they took much of the food between them. In retrospect, these were the best guides of the lot over the whole journey; they were both ex-military, both loggers. They were absolute naturals in the forest, more skilled even than the Dongo brothers, and they were both very strong. Despite the heavy weight on their backs they walked fast all day long without the slightest problem. Pound for pound, I was the weakest by far; these men were all between five foot six and five foot nine, whereas I am six foot one, but they were a much better shape and build than me for carrying heavy weight through the close jungle.

After just a couple of days, though, through relentless rain, Cho was getting worse.

The air felt cooler and the constant wet seemed to be bad for Cho's health. One morning we woke up in one of the last jungle villages before we were to start our big crossing of unpopulated rainforest. I had got up early and Juan and I had gone to look at the route we had to depart on. The water was clearly too high to leave that day, the paths were all washed out to chest level or deeper. Juan and Boruga didn't have the same rubber dry bags as we had so they couldn't swim through water with their bags on their backs without soaking all their kit. We decided to wait a day and I went to tell Cho the plan.

I made two basic errors in planning this leg of the journey. Firstly, I took Juan's timings at face value. When he said the route would take twenty days I wanted to believe him as it was such great news. Clearly I should have estimated the timings against the maps, but I didn't.

Secondly, I let Cho and Juan calculate and buy food for the leg. After seven days of walking we had only three days of food left. At this point I estimated that we still had fifteen to twenty days of walking between us and Colombia.

We were heading away from the river, much further than I had anticipated, and as a result we had gone off our 1:100,000 maps that just covered the riverine areas. I did have a 1:1 million map of this section of Peru but the river had not been plotted accurately as it was an aeronautical navigational chart. Trying to get anything accurate out of a 1:1 million map is difficult, to say the least. Google Earth would have been the obvious answer but there was a stinking big white cloud over the whole area blocking all the jungle below.

We cut the rations and started scavenging from the forest. After two days on very low rations Cho turned to me as we entered a likely campsite and said, 'God provides!' 'Yeah, right,' I said to myself, thinking this was the start of another lecture on God, only then to see what he was talking about. A large red-footed tortoise was nestling in the leaf litter. Red foots are categorised as 'least concern' by CITES (the international agreement between governments that protects endangered species) and are not threatened species and, as we were low on food, no time was wasted worrying about ethics.

Boruga butchered the tortoise while Juan made the fire. I

absorbed their skills attentively. Juan's fire-lighting technique was different from most as he didn't use any small sticks at all. He found dry wood that was two to three inches thick and he made a base to raise the fire off the wet ground by splitting the logs in half and laying the dry inner side face up. Next, he shaved one of the logs repeatedly to produce dry shavings that he piled up on the platform. Then he just arranged the large logs around the outside of the shavings like the spokes of a wheel and lit the fire using a lump of resin he'd chipped off a tree with his machete. The result was a roaring fire in about ten minutes even though it had been raining solidly for days. The Boruga-fried tortoise liver cooked in garlic and oil was nothing short of breathtaking.

Incredibly, the next day we found another tortoise, wild tomatoes, various nuts and wild bananas. Boruga continued to impress, proving also that he was an able fisherman. He disappeared when we made camp and returned with a little smile carrying catfish, trout and crabs. He taught Cho as much as he could, too, so Cho started to enjoy fishing and began to become proficient from this point on. We were thriving and morale was high despite having three days of food to last the next two weeks. Our carried food totalled:

4 kg of rice
2 kg of salt
13 packets of Ramen instant noodles
1 small sachet of monosodium glutamate.

No sugar, tuna, farine, coffee or milk powder. Our only hope was that one of the abandoned logging camps that we were trundling through would be occupied and we could negotiate some food with the loggers. The one main thing we struggled to source from the jungle was carbohydrate, which is why these loggers always carried a big bag of farine and not much else.

I wasn't experienced enough to know the difference between false corals and coral snakes but we saw several red-, black- and yellow-banded snakes of some size near the rivers. The old saying 'Red next to black – friendly Jack. Red next to yellow – kills a fellow' referred to the coloured bands but it originated from Central America and didn't apply here. All of these snakes were potentially lethal and their venom was neurotoxic, which meant that it attacked the central nervous system and the lungs until the victim suffocated to death.

We were normally safe from coral snakes because they have small mouths and short fangs that could not penetrate a boot. One evening, however, when I was washing in a river I casually threw my soap box into a convenient hole in the riverbank, only to see a coral snake wake with a start and slip out of the dirt hole at lightning speed just inches from my bare fingers.

We had not encountered anybody at all in the six days since our departure but when we saw fresh footprints we knew we were not alone.

The laptop had run out of charge at this point and I was still trying to use solar panels to charge it. In the constant rain and rare sunlight this was impossible. We followed footprints for the next two days, never catching a glimpse of who was ahead of us. At the back of my mind the fear of drugs runners was niggling at me and yet I felt I was in good company. But we needed to acquire food.

On 2 March 2009 we set up camp well above the river on high ground but we could see the residual leaf litter of recent floods and knew that the water had risen about three metres recently, almost reaching our camp. Boruga disappeared for a while and returned nonchalantly smoking a cigarette. We'd run out of cigarettes five days earlier. He told us there was a logging camp ahead and that they had food. This was great news but we'd already made camp so we decided to stay put and pass through the camp early the next morning.

When we got there, lots of very tough Peruvian loggers were eating breakfast and joking loudly. We were immediately given plates of spaghetti and ham and cups of sweet coffee. In our reduced rations state, the food gave more pleasure than I thought it possible to get from a meal. We ate fast, loving every mouthful. The loggers had an admirable code of looking after each other and we were treated very well. These guys were not in the least concerned by my presence; they were just amused at what I was trying to do.

They lived a very comfortable life although, it has to be said, at the expense of the forest. With refrigerated motor boats and shotguns they would hunt everything that moved so that they could eat well while working and take out meat to sell, too. That day a woolly monkey had been shot and I watched as the almost human-looking body was chopped up and put in the cooking pot. The scene was made all the more dramatic as the monkey's infant offspring was watching, screaming incessantly. I did eat a piece of the tail for interest's sake. Unlike many indigenous communities that live in the forest, it was clear that these men's presence was not sustainable.

The loggers informed us we had reached the end of the path but navigationally, the next bit didn't seem hard at first. We had hit the River Apicuari and all we had to do was follow it until it rejoined the Amazon. Easy in theory until you see how much the river meanders. This was still an area obscured by cloud on Google Earth and I estimated the 100 kilometres would have turned into 200 kilometres if we literally walked along the river's edge.

Clearly we wanted to walk in a straight line, but if we pushed away from the river we had no way of knowing when or if we would encounter it again. I felt blind and just wanted to be lifted above the canopy to see the shape of the river so we could put together a plan. How could we make an accurate map?

As we pondered the frustrating problem it suddenly came to me: we would hire one of the boats from the loggers to take us down-river. I would have the GPS recording the whole way so that we could sketch a detailed map of the river. We would buy food at the Yawa community of Platanal and then return to the logging camp in the same boat. Two problems solved, food and map, at the minor expense of some long days in a cramped boat.

We sat in the canoe for three days and two nights solid to

complete the round trip, but the plan worked. We bought ten more days' food in Platanal and estimated we would return there on foot in eight days. We could now plan the walk to stay away from the tangled riverine jungle at the river's edge for most of the day and return to the river at night to make camp, wash and cook.

The time in reconnaissance had been well spent. It was long-winded, but we were back in control and I was pleased that we were overcoming difficulties and still going forward. In fact, we arrived in Platanal on foot in just six days and chatted to the Yawa Indians about our journey, while charging the laptop and BGAN in the sun. I managed to get seventeen minutes of internet time – enough to blog and answer the main emails – but my mum lost out as the screen died just before I pressed 'Send'. The tiny window into the Western world had shut again.

Once we were back in Platanal, an old Yawa man called Vicente asked, 'Why don't you take the path to Colombia?' I rolled my eyes at this apparent contradiction. I explained that the loggers had told us there was no path. He informed us that there was indeed a path but that it broke away from the river and went due east towards Colombia to a border post called Tierra Amarillo on the River Loreto Yacu.

We hired Vicente as a guide and took six days' food for the five of us, heading directly east towards Colombia. We knew that we would be relying heavily on Vicente's knowledge of the paths as they were old and completely closed in places. He was meek in comparison to the loggers and spoke softly but he knew the path and we advanced 13.3 kilometres in the first day – the furthest we'd walked in weeks.

We reached a new river and started snaking, doing vast sweeping bends that meant we weren't getting very far, but the river was extremely sinuous. We took the decision to attempt to walk from one meander apex to another in a straight line, but that is easier said than done when you can't see more than 15 to 20 metres ahead of you and don't have a map of the river. We headed away from the banks to attempt a more direct route and soon rejoined the river, easily identified because it was the only one of its size in the area.

Juan was up front, in his element. Never flinching in the rain, he cut and slashed with his machete making slow but steady progress. After about an hour, we saw fresh footprints and an opening in the forest made by machetes, the first signs of human existence we had seen since leaving Platanal. My thoughts immediately turned to drugs traffickers and, even though I was soaked to the bone and covered in sweaty grime, my senses heightened notably.

Then Boruga started to laugh. 'Look over there!' he pointed. 'That's where we had lunch!' We all groaned as realisation dawned. The footprints and machete cuts were our own. I hadn't checked the compass in over an hour and just followed Juan blindly. We had come full circle. Somehow, when we'd crossed from the apex where we'd actually picked up the river further upstream, thinking we were moving on we had turned and hacked our way back to where we'd started. Juan, who'd been cutting like a machine for an hour, was the most crushed by this farcical error. We made camp and Vicente told us he would return home the following morning.

At about six o'clock that evening I heard a loud bang. 'What the—?' I sprang out of my hammock and looked around the gloomy, twilit forest. Bang – another shot – and Cho ran off into the trees. Vicente was the only person with a shotgun and he was not in camp. 'He must have gone out hunting,' I thought. Despite being intrigued I had just washed and had no desire to rush through the forest in the dark in my clean, dry clothes and flimsy Crocs.

When they did come back the news was bad from my perspective. Vicente hadn't just shot an animal – he'd shot a bloody tapir. All species of tapirs are listed as either endangered or vulnerable and this massive herbivore is such a gentle giant that I couldn't help but feel sad.

Vicente was a Yawa hunter and he just saw the tapir as food; I understood his point of view. My issues with it were that it was far too big for us to carry and so only a fraction of the animal could be used and the rest had to be left on the forest floor to be eaten by other animals. It was a pregnant mother the size of a small cow and the fact that we'd been involved in its death annoyed me. Now that it was dead, however, I was absolutely sure we should make the most of the meat and carry as much as we could. Juan, Boruga, Cho and I set to cutting up the beast, salting and smoking as much of the meat as possible over the fire. Vicente would carry what he could back to his community and we would take as much as we could manage, too.

The incident reinforced my belief that we were right not to walk with firearms. I didn't want this expedition to turn into a Victorian hunting farce.

We weren't too far from the Colombian border but there were no paths in sight. Every which way we turned was a wall of thick, dark forest that stretched for miles and miles and we weren't following a river either. I entered the coordinates of where I could see the river crossing the Colombian border into my GPS and got a compass bearing to walk on. Then we just blasted through the jungle in a straight line, opening a path as we went. The terrain was hilly but with all the trees we still never got any view. It was almost as if we were driving a car in the pouring rain with broken windscreen wipers so that we couldn't see out of the windscreen. We were reliant on our compass and had to have faith that the bearing was good and that in a few days we would hit the border post. What we would find there – armed military, drugs traffickers, razor wire, passport control, a gift shop, information centre – I had no idea.

Then, just as we were in a position in which we were fairly reliant on the GPS, it decided to die. It had moisture inside it and none of the controls worked. So we headed on the compass bearing to a point where we all thought the community, and the Colombian border, would be. We could judge distance only really on a feeling or hunch that it had been a seven-kilometre day, or perhaps an eight.

Sometimes you need a bit of luck, but our accuracy was extraordinary. At 4 p.m. on our fourth day from Platanal we heard music and before long stumbled out into a party that was being held in Tierra Amarillo. The village was a cleared area of forest on the banks of the River Loreto Yacu. Tatty thatched huts housed friendly, drunken, indigenous people who offered us *masato* to drink. We were in Colombia.

The Peruvian part of the expedition was now over. It had taken us 11 months and 2 days, only four weeks short of my original estimation for the entire journey. Cho and I were shattered and needed a rest and time to dry out our sores and parasite infections. We'd been walking without a real break for over two months in the relentless rain and I was drained of enthusiasm, energy and life. I had raw sores on my hips from my pack, my feet felt bruised and my muscles weak and empty. I dreamed of a hotel room with a real bed, fresh white sheets, and air conditioning. I didn't want to see any people – if I'd been on my own I could have cried from exhaustion. I just wanted to sleep.

Diary entry from 4 March 2009 – Tierra Amarillo:

Pull your socks up, Staffs – you sound like a right pathetic twat. Two days in Leticia and you'll be right as rain. Well maybe five days anyway.

As was always the case when we broke free of the jungle, my mind turned to our desperate money situation. I was living well beyond my means and accruing debts that I had no ability to pay off. This feeling of being out of control financially continued to keep me awake at night and seemed to take the fun out of everything.

There was no passport control at the point at the border where we had arrived so we had to take a boat down the Loreto Yacu and then another to the Colombian city of Leticia. There we could leave Peru officially, get our passports stamped, try to source some maps of Colombia, then return to the border to walk the short (three-week) Colombian stretch to Brazil.

It was this type of journey, external to the expedition, which cost me valuable time and money. Moneywise, I couldn't keep the four men on for this period time and as Boruga had dual Colombian/Peruvian citizenship I had to send Juan home. The big man was sad to go; I could tell his pride was hurt that Boruga had been chosen over him and that the team would continue without him. But I had to be logical rather than sentimental and Juan didn't have a passport to travel outside Peru. So home he went.

We spent six days in Leticia in the end and my diary tells me I spent about 80 per cent of my waking time in front of a computer doing neglected accounts and sorting the running of the expedition. We couldn't afford nice hotels or air-con so we slummed it in a cheap place and I would wake up with my face stuck with sweat to the old mattress. An old school friend of mine, Sam Dyson, had said that he would come out and walk with us for a while and I organised his entry. The vast majority of this time was spent trying to chase the Brazilian fixers so that we would have permits to enter the indigenous reserve on the Brazilian side of the border.

We had been put in contact with two Brazilian men, Kavos and Dwight, who were reported to be the best at sorting logistics problems for foreign film crews. Despite not being a film crew I had met the two men in Brazil on the way out in 2008 and they agreed to help me with my visas and permits for Brazil, but for a not insignificant fee. Without these papers I couldn't continue and by April 2009 I was getting very irritated with their attitude and the complete lack of progress. This was quite stressful at the time and meant that I couldn't relax with Cho and Boruga because, unless I was working hard to move things forward, the expedition couldn't continue without us having to backtrack or detour several weeks north into Colombia. Permits from Kavos were vital if we were to avoid this vast detour.

Everyone told us that the southern spit of Colombia we were about to go through was a big drugs-trafficking route and very dangerous. The bottom line was that we had no option if we wanted to complete the expedition. Back at the border once more with a Colombian Ticuna guide from Nariño, we quietly re-entered Colombia on foot and unnoticed.

Ticunas are the indigenous people of the south of Colombia and western Brazil. Senou, our guide, was quiet and clearly didn't know the jungle at all. I ended up putting Boruga at the front with Senou following lamely behind. With no GPS to map the river, we were still walking fairly blind, unable to be too close to the river due to the floods, but we soon hit a series of Ticuna settlements interspersed with small trails.

The remarkable thing about the Ticuna communities was that they were welcoming and friendly. We met nothing but broad smiles and waves as we came through and it was such a refreshing change from the looks of dazed confusion we'd encountered in much of Peru. The trails between the communities were all severely flooded and whenever the water got above head height we had to inflate the rafts and paddle through the *varzea*.

We'd managed to convince a local man from the last Colombian village to show us where the 'path' went, but all the other people had said the *only* way to go was by river in a boat. We had explained, as we always did, that we couldn't go by river because the aim of the expedition was to walk. The usual laughter and telling us we were mad ensued.

Four hours in and I could see their point. In places the 'path' was perhaps 10 metres below the surface of the jet-black floodwater. I was deep in concentration trying to guide my inflatable raft through spaces, seemingly far too small to pass, that were covered in spines as sharp as needles. The raft was made from very thin rubber, specifically so that it packed up small and could be carried in a rucksack. Every part of my brain was focused on steering and stopping; the worry of a puncture wasn't just swimming – it was swimming and trying to save the 35-kilogram rucksack that I was sitting on.

Boruga was paddling the other raft and both our paddles kept getting caught in the vines all around us, knocking biting ants down the backs of our necks. It was near 100 per cent humidity and the mosquitoes were constantly whining in our ears. Conditions don't get much more unpleasant and yet I was loving it. It was that odd type of enjoyment that's so hard to explain. I suppose the task was enthralling because everything was focused on the present;

there was no room for reflections or worries about the future because every action had an immediate effect. I couldn't help but be entirely infected by the thrill of the challenge.

Luckily we were right; we could and did follow the path through the flooded forest until we eventually reached a Ticuna village mid-afternoon.

We were progressing well but my moods were erratic, to say the least, and my diary at the time reads as a string of curses at guides who I had hired and who didn't know the way. I had not yet learned not to get upset by things that could not be remedied. The problem was that the locals weren't prepared to walk further than the next village, which might only be two hours away, and I was having to pay them as much as I was paying Cho for an entire day. Embarrassingly, I stopped asking some of them their names at this point. It was as if they were all the same annoying man constantly reinvented in a slightly different body but retaining the same essential characteristic of being indecisive and navigationally retarded. I was unreasonable at this time, I know, but there was the germ of a reason for my irritation.

On 2 April, Cho, Boruga, Jaime (a seventeen-year-old Ticuna boy), and I spilled into a small village called Santa Sofia. It was the first anniversary of the expedition and so I bought the guys some beers and we had a nice time sitting in a circle on plastic chairs talking rubbish. Cho and Boruga got drunk enough to keep telling me what a good leader I was. It was nice but surprising to hear as I felt far from a good leader at the time.

Two more days and we walked down an asphalt road into Leticia. Leticia is in Colombia on the border with Brazil's city of Tabatinga.

It had taken just over a year to reach Brazil and, despite being exhausted, we were all elated to have Colombia and Peru both behind us. In the past twelve months I had crossed the entire Andes mountain range; found the furthest source of the Amazon and descended the deepest canyon in the world. I had walked through the heart of the Red Zone; passed through countless defensive indigenous tribes; been detained at arrow point and accused of murder. I had met Cho, walked through flooded forest for weeks on end and crossed the infamous southern tip of Colombia – although we hadn't seen any sign of drugs traffickers in the last month.

We knew that we had to wait a couple of weeks for my mate Sam to arrive from the UK. That was fine by me, and by Cho, too; we felt that at this key point we deserved the rest. It was essential to recharge physically and mentally before setting out again. Boruga went back to Peru after spending all his wages on nights out in Leticia. I felt sorry for his wife and kids who would have had been waiting for his wealthy homecoming.

Despite the epic saga behind us, Cho and I knew we were about to set out on the hardest part of the expedition: reportedly fierce tribes, a new language, worse maps, bigger floods and unfathomable distances between communities across stretches of rainforest where nobody was known to have ever walked. We were both more than a little intimidated by the 3,000 kilometres of Brazil that we still had to cross on foot.

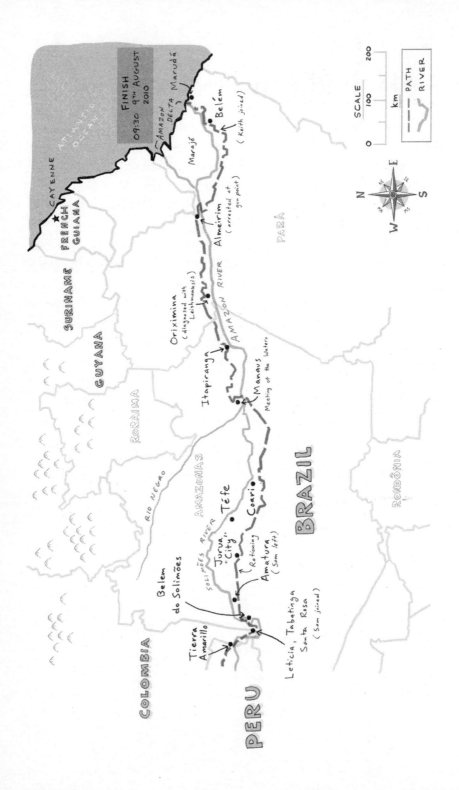

PART 4: BRAZIL

Chapter Eleven

Entering Brazil

Visas and permits are boring, I know. The problem is that they were also crucial to whether the expedition was successful or ended prematurely in embarrassment and shame. Kavos had had more than a year to sort out three things: a valid visa to enable me to enter Brazil and stay there for the duration of the expedition; permits to enter the indigenous reserves; and topographical maps of the Brazilian jungle. I had now arrived at the Brazilian border and it appeared as if he'd not actually started on any of them. He came highly recommended but I found dealing with him torturous. Despite being infuriated that these things weren't ready (I had hoped they would be prepared a year ago, before I even left England), I was in a predicament with this man as I'd paid him a grand and a half and, because I'd opted to use him to sort the visas, I'd ended up snubbing the Brazilian Consulate in London which was no longer answering my emails. Without maps, visas or permits our journey would be over.

Cho and I checked into a hotel and waited. The two towns of Tabatinga (Brazil) and Leticia (Colombia) merged into one and the border was open for people to come and go. On the other side of the river was Santa Rosa (Peru) and together the area was referred to as the triple frontier. Motorbikers from the stricter Colombia would cross the border and remove their helmets with one hand in the distinctly more relaxed Brazil. The towns received tourists, mostly backpackers, but had very little to offer us really. We turned down several opportunities from persistent touts to go on daytrips to see the jungle.

On 9 April, to his credit, Kavos came good. He wrote to me saying that on 11 April the Ticuna tribal leaders would be gathering in a nearby town called Benjamin Constant and he had organised for my request to walk through the Ticuna reserves to be heard. He said that they had asked if I would film the event so that their opinions on public policy relating to indigenous people could be aired.

This was a big step forward – if the tribal chiefs said I could pass that would be amazing. The meeting would allow them all to know me by face, too, before I arrived at their communities on foot. I was happy to film them but at the time I had no links with broadcasters who could publicise their plight.

This was exactly the sort of thing that I'd paid Kavos to sort and for this I was grateful. I was apprehensive about the meeting and was told it would last all day. My Portuguese was very basic at the time as I had been speaking Spanish for the past year and so I hired a tourist guide from Tabatinga to act as a translator. Kavos himself and Dwight, his sidekick, had warned me that these tribes were fierce, 'the fiercest in the whole Amazon,' Dwight had said. I was very nervous.

I genuinely believed that FUNAI, the organisation that oversees indigenous people in Brazil, had granted us permission at this stage but it turns out that Kavos had not gone through any official process with FUNAI, claiming it was far too difficult.

The translator, Cho, Ursula (who had come to visit me from Peru) and I went to meet the tribal chiefs. We took the fast boat from Tabatinga to Benjamin Constant and in my naivety I envisaged a traditional Ticuna community with everyone wearing traditional indigenous dress.

We arrived in the modern town and were shown to a concrete village hall where about a hundred Ticuna chiefs and members from various other communities had gathered on red plastic bucket seats.

'As we all know,' said the Ticuna chief of chiefs, 'white men have different minds to us, but they no longer come here to kill us.'

'A relatively positive start,' I thought, as I looked out across the crowd. The chiefs, although in Western clothing, still had jaguar and caiman teeth strung around their necks. One chief had augmented this decoration with a USB pen-drive. Behind me a Ticuna scribe was entering the minutes into a Ticuna laptop.

The meeting was not just for my benefit. The leaders from all the neighbouring reserves had come to talk about their various issues and plights. The Ticunas were very aware of past atrocities and so sensitivity as to how I presented myself seemed to be key.

The main chief continued, recounting stories and reminding people about their history. I understood some of what he said and made an effort to look unthreatening, polite and interested. I glanced to my right and saw that Cho, who had been out drinking the night before, had his head slumped to one side. He was fast asleep.

At two in the afternoon things came to a head and I was told that if I could help the communities then they would help me. I was still concerned that their ideas about what I could offer them would be beyond my relatively humble means. I addressed the crowd in broken Portuguese as they didn't seem to like me talking through a translator. As the vast majority of this was in Ticuna dialect anyway, the translator hadn't a clue what was going on.

'We will let you pass through,' said the main chief finally after long discussions with the community chiefs, 'if you can pay for the cost of today's lunch for everyone.'

It came to about US$25 and the feeling of sheer elation that soared up through my body made my eyes water as I strode towards him, beaming from ear to ear, to shake his hand.

I hadn't realised quite how worked up I'd been about these permits until that point. Suddenly everything felt possible again and the meeting injected me with a new confidence.

Kavos emailed three days later saying that I didn't have official permission from FUNAI but that if the Ticuna chiefs were happy then that was all I needed. I knew this was a bit under the radar and that these reserves required entry permits, and that all entrants had to have medical screening prior to entry, but it was the best I could do at the moment and the chiefs would let me physically pass so we had a functional plan.

The goal was now very simple: to make as much progress into Brazil as possible. Finances and time were big stresses and I needed to cut out the distractions and get some serious miles under the belt.

On 6 May 2009 the CEO of my main sponsors sent me this email:

Ed

I hope this finds you well.

Since we last spoke JBS Associates has been hit by the downturn in the global markets. We have encountered a number of clients not paying or unable to pay us for work completed.

The upshot is that we are unable to make the payment to you this month.

I hope to be able to rectify the situation in the coming weeks and will keep you posted on any changes from our side.

I am sorry to be the bearer of bad news. We remain committed and appreciate this is a long-term investment for us. When we next speak I hope to have better news.

If you have any questions or want to talk then give me a call on the mobile.

Take care and all the best.

Jonathan Stokes

This was our only monthly income at the time and the news was catastrophic. The amount that they had been paying hadn't covered all the costs and so I was at the limit of my £10,000 credit card and absolutely dependent on their £1,000 a month. The waiting in town was costing a small fortune and we just had to leave and get into the jungle where things were cheaper. Hopefully they would be OK to pay the following month.

Just over a year into the expedition I still felt that the journey would be more fun if I had a friend join me. Keith had been great and had lifted me out of a dark couple of months of depression and so when my old school friend Sam Dyson offered to join me I had taken him up on it.

The visas weren't ready by the time Sam arrived but soon after we were granted three-month tourist visas that we could have organised ourselves. This meant that after three months in Brazil we would have to return by boat to Colombia to renew the visas. Far from ideal.

I'd seen Sam three times in the fourteen years since leaving school, two of those in the months before departure. He'd spent much of his time since school training to be a martial artist and was in fact an ordained Shaolin 'warrior' monk. His keenness to come, our old friendship and his commitment to martial arts were all contributing factors to him coming out. He had never been to the jungle before but I thought he had the transferable skills to make it work. He'd told me stories about being trained to run up stone steps up a mountain behind the Shaolin temple in China until he passed out. That was the sort of strength of mind (and body) I wanted in a new partner.

Sam is exactly the same height as me at six foot one. He arrived with his eighties flat-top haircut and an erect warrior stance, which made him look considerably taller than the hunched, weary explorer that I'd become. On his arrival, we talked incessantly about old times and what lay ahead in the jungle. It was good to have a friend around again.

The first leg that Sam, Cho and I embarked on together was an eight-day crossing from Tabatinga to the town of Belém do Solimões. Upon entry to Brazil the Amazon's name had changed to the Solimões and we would not be next to the river that went by that name again until Manaus – some 2,000 kilometres downstream. In return for Sam giving a self-defence class to the Indian Police Service we secured two Ticunan Indian Police Service guides who, despite not knowing the jungle, were happy to walk with us. Before we left, the chief, who had been at the meeting in Benjamin Constant and agreed to let me pass, said that we could do so only if we bought him a gas cooker for his house. We had no option, of course, and the chief knew it, so we paid the chief the money to buy a brand-new cooker.

It was now May, pretty much as high as the floods would ever be, and so we had to head inland. Unlike Peru, there were no hills to speak of and we only just managed to find routes that were above the flood line. Antonio and Sanderley, the two Indian guides, were young and polite and happy to be out walking. Despite them not knowing a route (thus we were navigating off my compass bearing and the new GPS that Sam had brought out) I thought it was prudent to take the guides. According to advice it was an exceptionally dangerous reserve, and the Ticunan Indians might well be able to talk us out of trouble.

One Saturday morning I woke up slightly groggy after a typically broken night's sleep in my hammock. I wandered over to where the two guides were busily gutting fish. I smiled widely as I saw the size of the catch. We had two fish each and they were making a fish broth on the fire. They'd brought the fishing net back in and packed it away neatly. The camp was functioning automatically without me having to ask; it made me smile. Scents of garlic and onion hung in the air and everyone was eager to eat.

I don't know why but none of the locals ever liked dishing up so I lifted the pan with the shiny new metal handle we'd picked up in Tabatinga. In slow motion I then watched the pan fall into the side of the fire, having slipped clean off the handle. I saw the faces of the guides and they could not hide their disappointment – the fish was scraped up but the tasty broth was gone. Food takes on far greater significance in these circumstances and I felt furious about my clumsiness.

Later that day, deep in the jungle and a good distance from the main channel of the river, we approached a community. Antonio and Sanderley suggested that Sam and I wait outside while they went in and asked the chief for permission for us to enter. The more remote settlements lived defensively and we had been told they would kill a white man on sight if surprised. We decided not to surprise them and nervously sat on a log in a yucca field, wondering how fierce these Ticuna would be. Would they be wearing Western clothing? Would they let us through?

The guys returned with the good news that the community, Nosa

Senora Parisida, had accepted us and would allow us to enter. Our first sight of the elderly chief was as he wobbled towards us from some thatched huts on a spanking-new Honda moped that he obviously did not know how to ride. The village had no roads and was about 200 metres long but the moped was clearly his status symbol as chief. He was warm and kind and allowed us to string up hammocks in his own wooden house.

Cho, Antonio and Sanderley played football with the locals and Sam and I wearily dozed in our hammocks, relieved that everything had gone smoothly. I started to wonder just how dangerous this reserve really was. Could it be that Kavos and Dwight had been overplaying the dangers to discourage us? Perhaps they too were just regurgitating unsubstantiated myths. These people were friendly and welcoming.

For most of the 80 kilometres we had to cut our own path through the jungle following a compass bearing and using the GPS. For Sam it was quite a shock to the system. He'd not imagined it to be so physically exhausting and, as a big man, he tired quickly. Much of each day was spent chest-deep in swamps following the leading man as he hacked his way through the branches avoiding snakes and large ants' nests. The swamps were actually cool and refreshing to walk through and made a pleasant change from constant sweating on hard ground. Despite the fact that we were averaging less than a kilometre an hour in the floods, we reached a village called Piranha in eight days by mid-May and hired a boat to take us out to Belém do Solimões.

Sam and I chatted about his introduction to the jungle and he identified a few things that I'd overlooked. It was good to have a fresh pair of eyes on our methodologies and an example of something we changed was upping the anti-venom to forty-eight hours' worth so that we could stay in one place and self-administer. This was due to the fact that we knew that we were going to be many days away from medical help and so, if one of us was bitten, unless we had enough anti-venom to treat him until the toxins had worn off there was no point in carrying any at all.

Filming was important to me in order to have a record of the journey but both our video cameras decided to die. We had no option but to return to the border to receive new units. Humidity in the jungle was such that the average lifespan of an HD video camera being used every day was about three months. We went through ten during the whole expedition. Ignoring the inconvenient truth that customs would be a nightmare, I requested two more to be sent out by DHL. I elected to have the cameras sent into Colombia as the border was open and we didn't have a safe place to receive the cameras in Brazil. Rather than just signing for the cameras as in any normal country, I had to employ a Colombian solicitor draw up a power of attorney, a public notary to authenticate passport copies and a translator to write begging letters to customs explaining what we are doing. The process was mind-numbingly exasperating and took over a week. We used the week to brainstorm some ideas and, thanks largely to Sam's advice, I decided to set up an account with a new social networking site I'd never heard of – Twitter. It would be a pain to have to get the satellite phone out on a daily basis, find a fallen tree (and a break in the canopy to get reception), but it suited perfectly the spirit of broadcasting the expedition live since we could now 'tweet' live from the jungle each day.

He also suggested that I blog weekly and set a day and a time so that followers would know when to look for a new post. Each blog would have a video that I edited myself so that it was timely and relevant to the week's entry. I have no doubt that this increased our online following greatly, which would have huge repercussions in future months when we came to call on our followers.

It was the beginning of June by the time we were back in Belém do Solimões with new cameras. The dilapidated town didn't look much like an indigenous settlement, with houses built from sawn timber with tin roofs, but the inhabitants were 100 per cent Ticuna.

The chief was called Vilmar Luis Geraldo and he was clearly not happy with his lot.

Belém had 5,320 inhabitants living in 772 thatched and tin-roofed houses. The two schools in the community held 545 and

1,320 pupils and were both very overcrowded. Class sizes rarely dropped below forty students. Like many Ticuna communities, Belém had had a lot of problems with violence. There had been seventy-two deaths related to domestic violence, alcohol and drugs in recent years. Chemical abuse has become so bad that Vilmar told me of kids even snorting petrol.

Alcohol is prohibited in Indian reserves for a very good reason. It is well documented and understood that indigenous people have a low tolerance to drink. But the thing is, they don't just get drunk and vomit or fall asleep – to quote Vilmar, they 'go mad'. When people in these communities are left to drink uncontrolled they can become aggressive and aggression can escalate to a stabbing or shooting very rapidly.

Vilmar had a stern, sad face when he was recounting this. He was a religious man and clearly wanted to rise out of this spiral of social decay. He felt that the problem was twofold.

Firstly, there was not enough money for education. Not everyone could get a good schooling and virtually no one could go to university. Vilmar wanted the government to build a university in Belém; he explained to me that no one had the money to travel to Tabatinga and pay for accommodation to continue their education there.

Secondly, there were no jobs. This was because the community stood in the middle of an Indian reserve and, as far as I knew, non-indigenous companies could not set up in the reserve. This was a law established to give the locals their own land and autonomy but it now meant that even if they got an education there was not a single paid job available in Belém for them to take up.

The people earned what little money they could by selling crops – yucca, rice and bananas in the main – but Vilmar explained that a year of hard work brought in about $R560 (less than £200) per capita. To exacerbate this problem even further, extreme flooding had destroyed many of the year's crops. So the trickle of money for many had stopped completely.

All the village's water came straight from the Amazon. We were only 120 kilometres or so downstream from two big cities that pumped sewage directly into the river. The water was filthy.

There was no doctor or hospital in Belém and the one nurse-manned clinic was sadly depleted of medical stock.

The situation wasn't good. It wasn't difficult to see why so many Ticuna people saw their future as bleak and turned to drugs or alcohol to get their kicks. While we were there the local FUNAI representative had to leave to go and see four men who were practising what was described as black magic. In a Christian community this was considered desperate behaviour that had to be stopped. The story of a recent sacrifice of a child in such a ceremony was chilling to hear.

The Indian Police Service did a good job controlling violence but the policemen were all volunteers and clearly they could not grow crops while they were working for the police.

According to Vilmar, Belém do Solimões was in a downward spiral that had become impossible to get out of. Poor education, lack of jobs and extreme poverty were compounded by the regulations of the reserves. The people we interacted with showed great warmth and generosity and the young children were happy and smiley. These people were surviving but it seemed clear that they felt that they were being neglected.

I had no background knowledge of how many grants the indigenous people actually received from the Brazilian government and whether these claims were overstated or not. But the one clear, undeniable truth appeared to be that there was an incompatibility between a reserve, intended to protect a subsistence, indigenous way of life, and these people who lived in a medium-sized town where money was necessary to survive. If the people dispersed and went back to their historical way of life they wouldn't need money as they would live hand to mouth, as we had seen numerous times in Peru. But here in Brazil the Ticunas wanted electricity, TVs, convenience food and 10-megapixel digital cameras and so they had to trade with the rest of Brazil to earn money. Vilmar's crime statistics offered uncomfortable evidence that things were not working under the current system.

The poverty and despair reminded me of Peru. This was, I would learn, atypical of Brazil, a country that had recently invested huge sums in education across the Amazon. Under President Lula, parents were now given grants if their children attended school and, as a result, the young population of Brazil was educated and open-minded – even in the remotest settlements. But there were still serious issues that Lula didn't want or seem able to confront with regard to the rainforest.

From reading an article on Mongabay.com at this time I knew that a change had started to come about in the way companies and the World Bank dealt with the cattle industry in Brazil. Cattle ranching accounted for 79.9 per cent of deforestation and the World Bank withdrew a $90 million loan to the Brazilian cattle giant Bertin. I was stunned that the loan had been agreed in the first place but the withdrawal was a positive step towards stopping global support of this devastating industry.

At the same time the three biggest supermarket chains in Brazil – Carrefour, Wal-Mart and Pão de Açúcar – said they would suspend all trade in cattle products from farms involved in deforestation in a key area of the Amazon.

President Lula was still passing laws that privatised huge areas of the Amazon – the Brazilian government didn't seem to feel the need to hide its close relationship with the agribusiness. Barack Obama was to describe him as 'the most popular politician on earth' but with regard to the environment Lula appeared weak to me. He was talking the talk about climate change, and taking offence when foreign countries wanted to stick their noses into Brazil's affairs, and yet in June 2009 he passed legislation that was originally intended to legalise the landholdings of small settlers, but was changed to include provisions that benefited large land grabbers and business interests. The law would privatise ownership of up to sixty-seven million hectares of the Amazon rainforest, land that had been occupied illegally. This was an area bigger than Norway and Germany combined and the legislation flew in the face of Lula's talk of conservation.

We bade Vilmar goodbye and headed back to Piranha where we had left off walking. As the narrow motor boat turned into the smaller Calderón tributary from the vast Solimões, the sudden immersion in lush green jungle gave me the same excited tingling in my stomach as if I had just caught sight of a girl I liked but hadn't seen in ages. The tangled gallery forest sagged over the river's edges, a heavy fringe of lianas and bromeliads. A smile played on my lips and, as Cho and I exchanged glances, it felt as if we were back where we belonged. I was in love with the jungle again.

From the village of Piranha we plunged back into walking. The first few hours after a significant break were always uncomfortable and these were a real effort. Our bodies and minds had grown flabby and complained at the exertion we were imposing on them.

We were now moving through flooded forest perhaps 40 per cent of the walking day. We would attempt to push away from the river and hop from one patch of high ground to another but we no longer had maps with contour lines on them, so we were having to rely on local advice and guesswork. Progress was slow, on average five kilometres a day at this stage, but Cho and I had been through worse and so we were comfortable enough.

Sam, like Luke before him, had bought boots that were fractionally too small and as a result his toes rubbed and all his toenails became infected in the constant wet. This made his experience much more painful, and he found himself in an environment that was unpleasant and exhausting.

Sam's toes were bad and I suggested that he take a break from the expedition and return to Tabatinga, a suggestion he took with both hands. Sitting it out for a few days with some strong antibiotics in him would do him no harm – he was covered with hundreds of bites, cuts and bruises and his ankles were swollen like an old woman's.

It was interesting to me that neither Cho nor I had a single blemish on our bodies at this time. It was clearly a sign that we were adapting the way we were walking so that we didn't fall, we didn't get scratched, and we'd long ago stopped reacting to bites. I felt a stronger bond with Cho than ever before and we continued on our own with a feeling of calm, quiet efficiency.

We'd all left Tabatinga fat. All of us had been overeating in the way you do when food has been scarce before. But now we were facing a serious calorie deficit. One of Sam's toys had been a heart-rate monitor and it was telling him that he was burning 6,000 calories during the walking day. As that didn't include evenings, nights and mornings, you could have conservatively estimated that he and I were burning 7,000 calories a day as we were about the same weight. Cho would be burning slightly less as he was lighter, but our 3,000-calorie-a-day diet certainly left a huge deficit for all of us.

Cho and I left Vendeval, from where Sam had taken the boat, with Enrique and Paulo, our two new guides. They had an intelligent sparkle in their eyes that relaxed me from the outset and they turned out to be great companions. Like so many of our transient team, they knew the jungle because they were hunters and they used to walk deep into the forest with their shotguns looking for tapirs, large rodents such as agouti, or the skunk-like kinkajou.

Sam rejoined us on 16 June in a colonial town called Santa Rita. We'd not realised it but we'd spilled out of the other side of the first indigenous reserve. It angered me how fearful I'd been about entering that reserve based solely on the horror stories I'd been told. It meant that Cho and I were increasingly fearless of these reserves from this point on. We'd wasted so much energy on worrying, that we stopped bothering to listen when people told us about the dangers to come.

To say the route ahead looked ominous was an understatement. This region of Brazil holds the largest extent of *varzea* in the world. It was June and the waters were now at their highest in this part of the river; the highest water level months alter significantly as the river flows into Brazil. We looked ahead at the floods and at the seemingly impossible task of following the river and making any progress at all. The floods posed two main problems: there was nowhere to camp, put up hammocks or light a fire, and also the speed at which we could walk was slowed dramatically. The lack of speed meant that each leg took longer and therefore we needed more food and so our packs were heavier.

The nice thing was that I knew where most of the floods were. The

NASA imagery and Google Earth both highlighted clearly that if we wanted to stay anywhere near the Amazon we had to cross over to the south side at this point. Enter these coordinates into Google Earth [−3.564115°, −69.366513°] to try to plan a route on the northern bank. The curved scars that you can see are cut by the water and show clearly the extent of the *varzea*. The north side was almost out of the question and would have involved cutting over 20 kilometres or more into the forest and handrailing the river at that distance around the outside of a meander.

We all agreed we had to cross the main channel of the river and as Cho and I hadn't done this for months we were apprehensive about the paddling distance involved. We had three pack rafts at the time but the risk was that we could get separated and arrive at points on the other side that were too far apart for us to see each other in order to meet up. The waves were huge, as big as those found at sea, the river was stuffed with caiman and our rafts comprised just one chamber of air and a very thin lightweight PVC material. The prospect of crossing and having problems in the centre of the river was daunting. The solution was that we hired a wooden boat from Santa Rita, and paddled it like a Canadian canoe, all of us in one boat, to the other side. This worked perfectly and it took us a mere fifteen minutes to cover the kilometre and a half.

The community of Ticuna people on the far side of the river was very surprised to see us but the people weren't at all aggressive. Some of the women were noticeably timid of us; the village was set back behind the floods on the high ground and therefore they had less contact with the main river's traffic.

Their main artery of transport for the community was a small, straight 10-metre-wide river heading 40 kilometres north-east to the town of São Paulo de Olivença. Our plan was simple: we would stay on the higher ground to the east of this river all the way to São Paulo, which was back on the main channel of the Solimões. From here, as far as we could see, the south side of the Solimões looked walkable – although we had some huge tributaries to cross along the way that would have their associated flooded forest adjacent to them. The problem with navigation was that, although the Brazilians had great topographical 1:100,000 maps of the country, they would not give them to us. We had tried the military, we had tried private companies in the USA, but all we could get were navigational charts of the river. These were indeed 1:100,000, so that scale was navigable, but they had no elevation markings. The only thing we wanted to do was to stick to high ground to avoid the floods but the one thing we didn't have on any of our maps or images was any sort of contour lines. Our ability to see high ground on the maps was therefore somewhat limited.

From the Ticuna village we made São Paulo in eight days. On the eighth day we heard music, which Cho advised knowingly was six kilometres away. After a kilometre, we came out by an out-of-town bar that served beer and where a giant oil-drum barbecue was churning out spicy chicken legs for the clients. We drank beer and ate huge plates of chicken and then Sam and I went swimming with some local children in the natural pool at the rear of the bar.

From the town the 100 kilometres eastwards towards Amatura looked relatively easy. The majority of the terrain was high and we picked our way along the raised ground, often following old cattle trails or hunters' paths, passing small farms and cattle ranches.

My method of navigating with Cho was simple. We'd rotate every half an hour and whatever decision one of us made in our half-hour at the front, the other would follow to the letter. There were always several options and the truth was that it didn't matter which one we took. So Cho and I had this unwritten rule that to avoid wasting energy, the navigator's decision was final.

I don't think Sam could help it but he couldn't stop questioning our navigational decisions. 'Is there a reason we've come through here?' he would ask me. I would justify my decision and if he disagreed he would tell me. The thing was, by this stage Cho and I were on autopilot and we never verbalised our decisions, so to be challenged was the equivalent of being insulted. Worse, when Cho was navigating (and he never once got us lost), Sam would insist that I translate to Cho his queries about Cho's navigation. This was doubly worse because it was coming through me, annoying me that

I was having to translate unnecessary provocations and pissing Cho off that his decisions were being repeatedly challenged.

Two things were concerning me now: one (as usual) was money (or the lack of it) and the other was the time the expedition was taking. Our three-month Brazilian visas were shortly to expire and we had no option but to go all the way back to Leticia, in Colombia, to renew them. I was irritated by this wasted time and money and the fact that I'd put these logistics in the hands of a man (Kavos) who seemed not to care.

The positive side to this enforced break was that by now everyone was shattered. Tempers were fraying and even the legendary patience of Cho was faltering. One day he walked 150 metres behind Sam and me, refusing to speak. He was at the end of his tether and really not enjoying the dynamics of the team.

Back in Tabatinga, on the Brazilian side, when we re-entered Brazil with our new three-month visas the Federal Police told us that the only way we would be able to get a third three-month visa was to go back to the UK. We could not get one in Colombia again. I relayed this news to Kavos who told me he would try to sort something in Manaus when we next needed to renew. It wasn't very reassuring and it still meant that in three months' time we would have to stop the expedition yet again and this time travel ahead of ourselves to Manaus.

Then I received an email from Kavos which sparked a feud that never died. He wrote to me with a suggested filming schedule for my time in Manaus. It involved filming in the opera house and other stuff irrelevant to me and, as I was stressed about money and visas at the time, I wrote the following stroppy reply:

OK Kavos,

I think you misunderstand the expedition. I do not have filming schedules or a crew. I am a one-man band who is essentially recording the hardships of walking for two years for a gritty documentary. I have no need to film Manaus. I'm not Bruce Parry! I still have no commission from any broadcaster and therefore no money.

The visas are my concern and are the ONLY thing that I need you to help me on . . .

The short-term 3 months is not useful as we will be in the middle of the jungle when we need to renew them. Also, when I entered Brazil the man said that after I had renewed once I would not be able to do so again as I can only be in Brazil for 6 months of the year! I really need the full-length visa to be in the country the whole of the expedition. I expect to arrive in Manaus by Christmas and Belém do Para in July 2010. I cannot afford for the expedition to fall apart because of the visas not being sorted. I have paid you $1,500 for this – and need you to sort it once and for all.

Getting through FUNAI areas was done in a fairly underhand way and I never had proper authorisation from FUNAI. But we got through by paying people bribes and buying chiefs cookers! This is not good enough really, Kavos. We hoped that by using a professional like you we could be completely legitimate.

What I need from you is the visas sorting properly once and for all. I have no more FUNAI areas to pass so they are not a problem any more. Just the visas for Gadiel [Cho] and for me.

Thanks,

Ed

On 4 July I got this reply from Kavos:

Ed,

The email was for not for you. I'm working on another production and the person is also Ed.

Please stop treating me as dog and anti occupation. I trigger my lawyer against you.

Kavos

The threat of legal action made me despair of Kavos. The expedition had become so stagnant because of this toing and froing to renew visas and he wasn't helping in the way I had hoped he could. The vast stretches of jungle looming ahead of us before we reached Manaus were daunting and I didn't want this negativity any more.

Back at the border and with access to airports, Sam received the news that his martial arts schools were suffering at the hands of the people he had left them in charge of. He'd spent a few years building them up and so felt obligated to return to England to sort them out. We both also recognised that a three-man team was one man too many and that Cho and I would progress better by ourselves from now on. My Spanish had improved enough for Cho and me to be able to chat freely about any subject, which meant the need for a friend from outside had diminished. Although Sam and I talked of him returning at some future point, I think I knew this wouldn't happen.

No discredit to Sam though – he had come in with new ideas and energy at a time when I had still been struggling to hold everything together. He had done his bit and the expedition had evolved accordingly.

Somehow Cho and I had a system that worked but it was a delicate one, easily upset by a new member. From then on I never looked further than Cho for a jungle companion – he completely understood my cause. We didn't celebrate Sam's departure at all, but we were quietly content with the far simpler dynamic provided by the two of us on our own.

Chapter Twelve

Starvation

In Peru local Amazonians who hadn't had much access to education or the outside world thought I was a *pela cara* and that we were human body organ traffickers. They would indicate this as we came through by running an index finger around their startled faces. In Brazil there appeared to be another myth attached to gringos – they feared I was a '*corta cabeza*' (literally 'head cutter'), and the Ticunan people had started making the throat-slitting sign with their index finger across the front of the throat.

The stories varied but many included people telling of bright lights in the sky and unaccountable deaths involving heads being removed. There was an ingrained fear and distrust of white men that made the walk more unsettling again.

For the first time on the expedition I almost lost my temper at an indigenous woman when she started shouting at us, saying that we shouldn't be there and that I was a *corta cabeza*. I think it was the horrid recognition that we were going to have to go through another period of having people fear us until we proved otherwise – coupled with the lack of patience for such ignorance because of experiencing so much of it in Peru – that almost made me snap. The months of paranoia in Peru were a dark memory that I wanted to forget.

It broke Cho and my newfound positivity for a day or so. It's hard to explain how happy we had been to wave goodbye to such ignorant fear in Peru. To be welcomed in Colombia with warm smiles was nothing short of wonderful. To see the problems recurring punched us both hard in the stomachs. We could deal with it – and it was no doubt somewhat linked to the way indigenous peoples have been treated in the past by colonial setters – but it was sad that such fear still existed in these people's lives.

In early August 2009 Cho and I reached Amatura on foot and the remarkable thing was how much the water had dropped. The town sat aloft huge mudflats with many moored boats now stranded above the waterline. Cho and I grinned at the evidence of our first Amazonian flood season being behind us – and what an exceptional flood season it had been, one of the worst in years. The ground would now be harder, the rivers lower, and we had to take advantage of these advantageous conditions while we had them. We just needed to make as much ground as possible before the waters started rising again in November and December.

Cho and I went for a very quiet beer, spread the map out over the table and calmly considered the route ahead. There was a huge, sweeping meander in the Solimões River ahead of us that curved north from Amatura up to Fonte Boa like a giant rollercoaster and then curved back down south to the town of Tefé. The problem was that this route passed many populated areas and we now had no money at all. We could not afford food, lodging or local guides. As Cho and I were alone again and we had renewed confidence in each other's abilities, we made the bold decision that had been playing on my mind for a while. My idea was to cut straight across the meander from Amatura to Tefé. It would be some 350 kilometres as the crow flies and I estimated we could do the leg in two months. That would be two whole months until we saw the main channel of the river again. It meant a number of things: we would be avoiding the towns and villages to the north that flanked the river, and we would be pretty much alone in the jungle for the next two months which was – importantly – dirt cheap.

It actually meant so much more than that: we would be starting a whole different level of expedition. Rather than merely passing from settlement to settlement with the safety of the main river just a stone's throw away as an evacuation route, we would be completely isolated in the middle of the rainforest and we would just have to cope by ourselves. There were no boat or helicopter rescue or medic teams here. There is no emergency call-out number to the jungle. We did have our insurance package that had four Ex-Med medics in Hereford on sixteen hours' notice to move, to fly out to wherever we had sent the distress message from, but the insurance was about to lapse (because of the time we had taken) and we had no money to renew it.

If we got into trouble we just had to deal with it. There was no other way round it. The plan was simple: an evacuation would be to walk or carry the casualty to the nearest big river that was navigable in our little inflatable rafts and paddle downstream, towing the casualty's raft if necessary, until we came to a community with a boat and a motor. We would then pay whatever was necessary to get us to the nearest hospital, possibly upgrading to a faster boat as we went. Once in a hospital, the Brazilians would treat us for free. We'd tested this. So as long as we could get ourselves there we were fine.

The danger was in the remoteness, however. At times we would be five days' walk from the last navigable river and five days from the next. If one of us was seriously ill or injured then that five days could take much longer. If one of us couldn't walk, it could be impossible. We deliberately spoke about this. If we needed medical treatment urgently when we were remote we would die. Were we prepared to take that seemingly unacceptable risk? 'Of course,' said Cho without flinching. 'Me, too,' I smiled.

The idea was to carry huge amounts of food but ration it strictly. Limit ourselves to a specific quantity of farine per day and we could push the distances that we could cover. We would stop carrying tins of tuna, cured meat or sardines and we would save yet more weight. We simply had to catch fish if we wanted animal protein.

We kept hearing stories of the fierce tribes that lived further away from the river and we weren't sure what to expect if we came across communities. Would they be civilised like those tribes next to the river? Would they let us pass? By this point Cho and I had a lot of confidence in people who had been less contacted. We'd heard so many exaggerated stories that we were sure we would cope; we had to.

We were entering territory where encounters with the big Amazonian creatures became far more of a possibility: the bushmaster – the largest pit viper in the world; the black caiman – the largest carnivorous reptile in South America; herds of hundreds of fierce, defensive peccaries with their dangerous tusks; elusive pumas and certainly majestic jaguars.

A surge of adrenaline shot through me as I fantasised about what we were about to attempt. We would have to draw upon all our knowledge and experience to date and we would soon see if we were as competent in the jungle as we now thought we were.

We sourced permits from a local FUNAI outpost to enter the local Ticuna reserve. We then hired a canoe and travelled into the reserve to the village of Bon Pastur to look for a guide. Our gift to the chief was our old dry-cell motorcycle battery. This might seem an odd present but we knew it would be handy for running electric lights at night when the generator was turned off and no gift ever seemed to be patronising. I had often seen Cho give a half-bottle of warm Inca Kola as a present to tribal chiefs in Peru. Two Ticuna men from the community, Wilson and Valdir, agreed to walk with us all the way to Tefé. Wilson was chubbier and more Westernised, with a kind smile and a chatty manner. Valdir looked every bit the wild, indigenous Amazonian man. He was stern, with much darker skin and a lean, uncompromising body without a gram of fat on him. Valdir rarely spoke to us, but I was pleased to have such a tough-looking individual walking with us. The two of them agreed to meet us the following day in Amatura, and Cho and I went back to the town to get ready.

The battery was the one we'd been using to charge the laptop. The system was inefficient and just too heavy so we gave the battery away and put the solar rolls and the inverter in our spares bag that we left back in Tabatinga. This meant that we were now reliant on generators in communities to charge everything and, in between, we just had to make the batteries last by being very prudent with use of all electronic kit.

In an expedition through the jungle when you are on the move every day I would advise against solar charging. We had four six-foot solar rolls resembling silver foil scrolls that we would lay out in the all-too-rare clearings. But the few patches of direct sunlight made us chase them round the forest floor as the day progressed and the shadows shifted. As a result things charged at a painfully slow speed – if we could get them to power up at all. With hindsight, I would have chosen a computer less power-hungry and lighter than my two-kilogram Macbook. With the advances in technology since I'd set off, the expedition now could be blogged, including edited videos, with palm-held devices that ran direct from 12v – but our planning had been done in pre-iPad days.

Cho and I chatted about the cost of the two Ticuna guides. If they walked with us all the way to Tefé we would have to pay for their boat journeys home. We couldn't afford this and so we asked them if they could just accompany us for the first ten days to the village of Porto Seguro. It was not ideal but, anyway, there was something about attempting the most remote section of the expedition without local guides that appealed to us. We were beginning to find a working relationship that was very complementary and anyone who came in might upset that.

Cho bought supplies for us but this time only after a very thorough list was drawn up and analysed meticulously by both of us. We calculated everything to reduce weight and keep us walking longer. We couldn't afford any luxury food (chocolate, oats, peanuts etc.) and we couldn't afford to take any boat trips ahead to conduct reconnaissance – even if we found tributaries.

Cho and I didn't feel sorry for ourselves; our financial situation simply meant that we were going to experience one hell of an adventure. Clearly, I had the worry of my house being taken away if my mortgage payments weren't met but, as far as the expedition was concerned, we would make it work. We would have to be permanently based in our hammocks for the foreseeable future and rely far more on fishing and foraging to stay healthy. If, in the next two months, we came across settlements big enough to have basic hostels we would have to move straight on; we couldn't afford to stay in them.

Before we set out I had to do something to rectify the financial situation. Even though we had enough to cover the next two months I had to recognise that JBS Associates might never be able to pay again – and, quite apart from the effects of the recession on them, they had already been more than generous, expending £35,000 in total. I needed to find alternative sponsors or donors to help the expedition otherwise in Tefé we would probably have to admit defeat and go home due to lack of funds.

I put out a plea online asking people to ask their companies if they would sponsor us. I put a PayPal donate button on the website and asked readers if they could possibly donate to keep the expedition going. My lifelong friend from school, George, and my mum, Ba, did huge amounts of work behind the scenes talking to people and writing letters to try to bring in some much-needed funds. Every family friend was asked and as many grants/sponsorships as they could think of were applied for.

I left Amatura with Cho and the Ticunas on 7 August thinking I'd done as much as I could to set right our financial difficulties. I just had to hope things worked and recognised that I needed to focus on the 350 kilometres of jungle that lay ahead until we saw the main river again.

Wilson and Valdir, the Ticuna men from Bon Pastur, settled into a pace and we progressed well, although I could tell the guys weren't enjoying it that much.

Our first target, Porto Seguro, was about 80 kilometres from Amatura, but it wasn't marked on our 1:1 million aeronautical map. We found it on somebody else's map in the FUNAI office in Amatura and so we drew it on our white featureless chart in pencil. Then we found it somewhere else on another map in a school, so we drew that on to our map, too. The two pencil points for Porto Seguro on our map were, comically, 30 kilometres (three or four days' jungle walking) apart and we hoped that one of them would be correct.

We were walking through the Amazon with no idea where the next river would come, with water in our camera bags (deliberately) acting as a reserve, looking for a community that might be anywhere within an area the size of central London.

Of far greater concern was an email from an old sergeant major of mine, Mark Hale, by this time commissioned, who told me that my old regiment (now 2nd Battalion The Rifles) was only halfway through its tour of Afghanistan and had had thirteen men killed and ninety injured. They still had three months of their tour to push. This was a huge loss for any unit to absorb and continue fighting, and it made me realise that my journey was child's play in comparison.

On 20 August, after walking about nine kilometres a day, we broke out into an old agricultural field. Our eyes jolted at the shock of being able to focus at distance and our pupils contracted in the blaze of sunlight. We'd not seen any signs of human life for seven days – no paths, no cut foliage, nothing, so when we saw a huge clump of sugar cane we sat down on the baked earth and, in my rush to chew the sweet sticks, I snapped off my false tooth. I sat considering how far away from a dentist I was with sugary dribble running down my stubbly chin.

While replenishing the glycogen stores in our muscles with the sugar cane, we heard the vibration of small motor boat and knew we were close to humanity. Wiping our mouths, we searched for the exit from this cleared plot of land and soon found a wide path heading east. The path became wider as we followed it with the Ticuna men up front so that they would be the first to meet anyone we encountered. We crossed a small log bridge and in the distance I could see a thatched house. We walked straight into a community smiling and offering '*Boa tarde!*' to the surprised villagers. Their surprise didn't last long and their welcome was universally accepting and kind. These people weren't Ticunas; they were *caboclos* – mixed-race Brazilians – who were living a very simple life away from the Solimões in a fishing village deep in the forest on a small river. They told us we were in Porto Seguro.

I plotted our position on the map and chuckled at our blind luck. We had headed east, sometimes using a compass and sometimes just the sun, and we had, after eight days, walked straight into the settlement that we'd been aiming for. The funny bit was that the two pencil marks on my map were still 20 and 26 kilometres away in opposite directions. The chance of being this accurate if we'd known where we were going would have been slight – but to walk straight in down the main path without having any idea that the community was here was astonishing. As on many other occasions I felt as if we were being looked after and, even though I'm not religious, I could not help but ponder on our continuing incredible fortune.

Valdir and Wilson hadn't enjoyed the walking, however. They were exhausted, found the weight too much and wanted to go home. This suited us anyway as we couldn't afford to keep them on and so we organised to hire a boat from the village to take them back. I'm not sure why Cho and I then asked around the village for more guides – perhaps it was habit – but no one wanted to walk. These were fishermen and didn't ever enter the jungle at all. I was surprised at this as they lived in a more remote location than Cho or I had visited to date and yet they never went into the trees. It worked for us, anyway, and made the acceptance of the fact that from here we were walking on our own easier to accept.

Porto Seguro was good to us and we were shown the school, given food and talked through what little the inhabitants knew about what lay ahead for us. After eight days' walking we were tired and decided to take the following day off. I lazed in my hammock and sewed a hem into my cut-off shorts while Cho was invited to go fishing.

The Porto Seguro villagers waved us off with friendly jibes that we would be eaten by jaguars. Our next target was the Riozinho, a smaller tributary that we expected to be six days' walk away. We knew there were settlements on the river but had no idea where.

The forest floor as we left Porto Seguro was saturated mud that

With Keith Ducatel (photographer), sharing a rare crate of beer.

With Ursula (centre) and family in Iquitos.

Spider monkey view of me walking.
© KEITH DUCATEL

My favourite time of the day – getting
clean again. © KEITH DUCATEL

Aerial view of camp. © KEITH DUCATEL

Crossing a slippery log bridge. © KEITH DUCATEL

Cho fishing with an improvised rod made from a sapling.

Cho and me smoking fish above the fire. © PETE CASEY

Camp life. Warm, clean, dry clothes every morning from above the fire.

The concrete jungle: checking the map and having a quick sit down.

The final river crossing to Belem at dawn – a final reminder of how small and weak we really were. © KEITH DUCATEL

The road to Belem – Crocs and socks – what trendsetters. © KEITH DUCATEL

The final road stretch with a tight schedule meant long days and very little sleep.
© KEITH DUCATEL

The sprint into the Atlantic – the happiest day of my life to date. © KEITH DUCATEL

Cho and me in the Atlantic Ocean – godzillaesque drama. © KEITH DUCATEL

The champagne celebration – it was the first time Cho had ever seen the sea.

The sponsorship flag – everyone who sponsored us and helped us out were on it.

had very recently been underwater. Imagine a place that has twisted, gnarled roots, thick, razor wire-like thorns and mud that sucks you down into it, weighing - every - laboured - step - down. Then imagine not having any idea when it will end. In an hour? Four hours? Four days?

I had what could almost be described as a panic attack on day two of this leg. I had an intense feeling of claustrophobia; not only could I not get out from the dark walls of green vegetation that closed in all around us but I had no idea when the terrain would change. It was the closest, most difficult and unpleasant forest to cut through that we'd encountered so far. We found patches of high ground, islands really, to camp on at night but fishing was impossible as there were no rivers, just mud, thorns, mosquitoes and horseflies.

It took five days to leave the area that the river flooded during the wet season. That's not five days to the next river and community; it was five days just to leave the riverine jungle that surrounded Porto Seguro.

Cho and I were getting on better than ever before. I would give him basic English lessons and we would chat in Spanish far longer and in more depth than we had done to date. After having spoken to Cho solely in Spanish for 11 months, his first official lesson made me smile: 'Ed, when there is more than one of something, add an "s".' We'd seen so many people come and go – guides, photographers, journalists, friends – but the one constant and reliable presence we had was each other, and we started to appreciate that.

Cho and I feigned nonchalance but we were both shocked by the weight we were now carrying as a two-man team. My pack at this stage was up to about 38 kilograms and Cho's just under, at about 35 kilograms; when working hard with a machete through the dense jungle those were considerable weights to deal with. Cho weighed only 60 kilograms himself and so he was carrying well over 50 per cent of his bodyweight, but we needed to ensure we had enough food to last us until we found another settlement.

The weight ultimately proved too much for Cho and he sprained his ankle quite badly, a nuisance in most circumstances, potentially life-threatening in ours. I took some of the weight off him and he was brave about carrying on; but the shock of just how serious an injury could be to both of us at this point made us much more careful about how we walked and jumped down from huge fallen trees. If either of us could not walk we were in big trouble. Neither of us had ever been so remote.

We passed the next river, the Riozinho, on 27 August and again we were unbelievably lucky and walked straight into a village. Despite having no shop, the confused villagers sold us eight kilos of farine, two of salt and three heads of garlic. The total cost was seventeen *reais* (under £4) and we hoped it would last us eight days. That was all we needed to keep going – carbohydrates and salt. As long as we could find some big enough rivers to fish, Cho and I were OK. We stopped for only twenty minutes on the Riozinho; neither of us wanted to stay any longer. More than ever we felt part of the jungle now and increasingly we shied away from people.

One day beyond the Riozinho we found an oxbow lake and decided to have an admin day. We could fish, Cho could rest his ankle and we would both benefit from not walking for a day.

The lake was stunning, a completely isolated bean shape that was curtained on all sides by lianas and vines hanging down into the brown water. Our camp was comfortably above the water level and, as the water was dropping, the fish were highly concentrated in the lake. Cho took one of the rafts out with a hook and line and peacefully caught one fish after another. I took the other boat and set the gill net close to the bank among the shaded shallow areas. These nets are so efficient that they are illegal in the UK; the fish swim into the holes and get stuck – it is that simple. Even before leaving the net I retrieved several piranhas and it was clear that the lake was abundant enough to mean we would have more fish than we could eat in one day. I made a drying rack above the fire; nothing complicated, just four 'Y'-shaped uprights, a couple of crossbars and then lots of thin green sticks to act as the grill. It was about a metre high so that the fish would be smoked rather than cooked. I was experimenting really, having watched this process before in different places, but never having had to rely on it for our sole source of protein. I then spent the afternoon in a factory-like process of retrieving fish from the net, taking the ones that Cho had caught, too, scaling, gutting, salting and generally kippering them. My hands stung where the scratches had salt rubbed into them and my shorts were plastered in fish scales and blood.

As the day wore on the sun set on the far side of the lake, casting a warm, orange glow upon me as I stood in my shorts and Crocs preparing fish. Cho stopped after a while as we had so many fish we weren't sure we could carry any more. Once they were on the green-stick grill we covered the kippered fish with fresh leaves to keep the heat and smoke circling around them as they cured.

We cooked on the fire below the rack and ate a hearty fish broth with farine. It had been an important day for us in terms of resting and building up our protein stock but, probably more importantly, it showed that we were so far surviving very well without indigenous guides. As we went to bed we checked the smoked piranhas and tasted them. They were just fantastic, really salty and dry like beef jerky. They would make fantastic snacks over the next few days.

In the morning I carefully lifted off the foliage that was now dry and crisp to reveal thirty of the best-looking kippered fish I had ever seen. It would have been such a boost for morale but for one accident. My boat, which I had left tied up but inflated in the water overnight, had an eight-inch tear in it. I never discovered the culprit but I suspected a caiman. We had eight to ten days' walk to the next river that we thought might have settlements on it and my boat was completely unserviceable. These boats were not just for crossing rivers; with only two of us we could ferry each other across the rivers using just one of them. More dramatically and to the point, they were our emergency evacuation mode of transport, and now, with no medical insurance and just one boat, we were walking a tightrope.

After a week of walking and living well on kippered fish and plentiful farine, Cho and I had started to run out of luck. We reached the river that had been our next target, the Minerazinho, on 3 September. This time, however, we'd not come out at a settlement and so we had to go searching.

We patched the boat using thirteen bicycle inner tube patches from our boat repair kit so that they slightly overlapped each other. These held enough for me to paddle gently but I had to top up the air by mouth every ten minutes or so. As we paddled downstream at one point I heard what I thought was barking, only to see two giant river otters perched on a log. They soon plunged into the water but I could see there were more. I counted six in total; we had split the group, some above us and some downriver, and they were calling angrily to each other, rising high out of the water as they barked. The fact that they were not running away made me doubt there were any settlements around this area. The otters seemed to be completely undeterred by our presence.

After two days of paddling, we had made only 9.32 kilometres' direct line of sight and my boat had started leaking badly again. We had no idea if there were further communities downriver and we were 150 kilometres from the mouth of this river where it joined the Solimões as the crow flies. There could be a month of paddling at this speed.

There was only one thing for it. We had to deflate the boats, walk back to where we had arrived on foot two days before, and push on without resupplying. The boat search had added three days to our journey already and I checked our farine supply to reveal that we had four cups left – 1,800 grams. I looked at the map and found a settlement marked: this was Maruá, 65 kilometres to our east. I estimated we could reach Maruá in eight days and we split the *farine* into eight portions so that we wouldn't run out. That left us 225 grams a day between the two of us – some 450 calories per man per day – not much more calories than a single bagel each all day for eight days.

We had another admin day and tried to catch as many fish as possible but unlike the oxbow lake, the river wasn't as easy to harvest. We had lost our wire leaders that were necessary to stop the piranhas biting the hooks clean off the line. Never one to admit defeat, Cho ingeniously forged a daisy chain of sewing needles together in the fire using my Leatherman, and now he could fish again for piranhas with a hook and line. We ate river rushes for lunch and Cho managed to get quite badly bitten by a piranha in the afternoon; it took a good flap of skin off his index finger. He'd been too casual and, rather than carefully grabbing the fish from behind the head, he had somehow managed to allow his finger to be in the vicinity of the piranha's mouth. You don't make that mistake twice and the razor-sharp teeth had sliced clean through the tip of his finger. Cho wasn't bothered by the bite; we were already far more worried about our stomachs. Even before we set off we were both really low on energy and we'd simply not got enough food in us to continue operating in the same way.

We left the Minerazinho with perhaps twelve kippered piranhas and our now seven days of rationed farine. We were constantly on the lookout for fruit and nuts on the forest floor. Occasionally we would find nutrient-dense Brazil nuts and spend ten minutes eating them and then pocket the remainder for supper and move on. On the best foraging days I would say we got our daily calorie count up to 2,000 a day with seasonal fruit and nuts, but we knew we were burning in excess of 5,000 calories a day. Most days we had the ration of a quarter of a cup of farine and nothing else.

Weight was dropping off us both fast and neither of us could think for long about anything other than food. I couldn't sleep at night, lying in my hammock dreaming of Mr Kipling French Fancies and stodgy flapjack. We would get up in the morning like zombies and laugh at our withering bodies. When it came to eating the small ration of farine we treated it with reverence; our meal became almost a ceremony and the most important part of the day. In texture farine is quite similar to soy protein; it's a yellow, grainy, pellet-like substance. Each one of these small pellets became a nugget of gold to us. We savoured every spoonful with a bit of salt.

On day five of this extreme rationing we came across a beautiful small brook at about two in the afternoon and we both saw the opportunity to try to fish, despite it not being the end of the walking day. I laid the gill net across the three-metre-wide stream and within seconds I had caught six decent-sized fish. We could not pass up this dream river and so decided to stop for the day and make camp. Cho used a rod and line while I just harvested with the net. Both of us brought in big catches that were all for the pot. We had eaten three pots of fish broth by the time we were full. The sensation was phenomenal; the fats in the fish floated on the surface of the broth and as the food entered our stomachs they started to groan, as if they were coming back to life. The fats were absorbed immediately and our brains started to function again. We had highs purely from eating food. We were so hungry that we didn't even consider smoking any of these fish; we just wanted a full recharge. That said, we did save some fish for the morning and slept soundly with full bellies.

On the eighth and last day of rationing we ate all our farine at breakfast knowing that we needed to walk a long twelve-kilometre day to reach Maruá. The jungle had become swampy and gnarled again as it was the flooded forest of the upcoming River Juruá. This meant the going should have been slow but as we had no food in our packs now, and because the end was in sight, we crashed through the stunted black trees at a phenomenal pace.

At 7 p.m. we'd gone straight through the coordinates that the map had given us and we were a full kilometre beyond. Our heads dropped as we realised there was no settlement, and we'd punished ourselves all day to arrive before nightfall. It was now completely dark and we hadn't seen water for hours so we just decided to put up our hammocks and sleep. Without even clearing a space in the undergrowth we each found two trees quickly and hung our hammocks. Unfed and unwashed, we went to bed. The grimy layer of sweat and dirt on our skin made the night unpleasant as well as dispiriting. We took tiny sips from our almost empty water bottles and tried to sleep.

In the morning, with sleep our mood had lifted and nearby we found some aguaje fruits, a nut with a soft, orange flesh with a vague smell of vomit, to complement the last of a single dried piranha. We sipped the dregs of our water, which was brown as it had come from a puddle rather than a river, and had no option but to continue. All we had by way of edible provisions was a half-kilo of salt.

To us, unwashed, exhausted and starving, that morning represented everything that, deep down, I wanted from the expedition. We were 150 kilometres from the main channel of the Solimões (Amazon), about 25 kilometres away from the next big tributary, the Juruá. We had had a deficit of over 3,000 calories a day for the past eight days and we had no option but to put the facts to one side and continue as normal. No words would make any difference, no blame, no analysis. We just had to go on and deep down we expected to be OK.

There were no rivers so we ate only palm hearts all day. Our first trial at sourcing all our carbohydrates from the jungle worked but you have to eat a lot of these salad vegetables to fill you up. *Palmitos*, or heart of palm, in fact became our salvation. Normally we wouldn't have cut these down because, in order to get to the soft, white palm heart in the centre at the top of the tree, you cannot avoid killing the whole palm. In our feeble state, each palm was quite an effort to fell with our machetes but the white flesh inside was the best salad vegetable I have ever tasted. These patches of *palmitos* were sporadic at best, however, and so we kept our eyes peeled for the tops of the trees, looking for the distinctive red stems.

Cho looked like a featherweight boxer now and I, too, had never lost so much weight. My normal weight is about 92 kilograms. I had dropped to about 88 kilograms before I set out on this leg of the expedition and by the time I arrived at the banks of the Solimões again I would be 81 kilograms. As we walked we stumbled frequently and snapped in and out of blood sugar crashes as we impaled ourselves on spiky vegetation in our half-aware state.

The following day everything came good. Cho walked straight into a huge tortoise weighing in at around 10 kilograms. It was morning and so we couldn't lose time by stopping and preparing the animal. We would just have to carry it. We took turns to pack the lead-weight live animal into the tops of our packs.

Eventually we came to a large river, the first we'd seen in a week or so, and I set about cutting up the tortoise. I'd watched Boruga and the Asheninka men do this before and so I knew how to do it; but I never expected it to be quite such a horrific task. If you are not used to killing animals a tortoise is not the best to start with. You have to turn it on its back, hack at the exoskeleton shell between the foot holes until the bottom is loose and then peel it back like the lid of a tin of beans. Except that the bottom is clearly attached to the tortoise still inside and needs to be sliced off with the machete. The underside of the shell has to be off before you can kill the animal and so I grabbed the now defenceless head and cut it off to kill the creature as quickly as I could. The body then kept twitching for the whole time that it took to cut out the rest of the meat and remove the intestines. I washed everything and used the upturned shell as a bowl and cut the tortoise up into small strips which I then salted. Cho made a drying rack and we had a huge amount of meat cured and smoking over the fire. Our morale was flooding back and we were elated by the prospect of food.

I realise that some people might be shocked and distressed about the killing of tortoises, but I think it has to be put into the context of where we were and how long we had travelled with so little food. In our natural state we humans are designed to be omnivores and the jungle is a place where we could survive if we took advantage of what nature had to offer. Although the physical process of killing the animal was quite an ordeal I won't pretend I was sad – this was a natural way of living and the tortoise was part of our food chain. I had begun to see animals in the forest as the locals did – rather than exotic beasts that needed to be preserved, I saw food.

In the morning we crossed the river simply by walking through it. It was perhaps 40 metres wide, but it was shallow and the small part that we had to cross was easy. We strode out on the far side and could immediately tell that people had been in the area. Small paths turned into what appeared to be a dirt logging road which we followed in the hope that it would lead us to people. We ate only our tortoise-meat jerky throughout the morning and had not eaten any carbohydrates, save the limp palm hearts, for over three days.

At about 1 p.m. we saw a wooden shack with a tin roof on top of a hill and made straight for it. As we approached, a woman came to the door and I explained what we were doing. I have no idea what we must have looked like after thirty-seven straight days of jungle from Amatura. The woman called her husband who had been making farine and he came and spoke to us. They were amazed when we told them where we had come from; they said that, to their knowledge, no one had ever made that journey before. They were about to have lunch and invited us to eat.

We dumped our packs outside in the blistering dry heat of the cleared hill and climbed a ladder to enter the cooler wooden hut on stilts. Inside there was no furniture, just a huge pan of fish broth in the middle of the floor, a plastic tub of fresh farine that was still warm, having just been made, and a stack of glass plates. The woman dished us out a plate of soup each as we sat on the floor among the family's children. They watched us wolf down the first plate, then the second, then the third. I know we had eaten tortoise jerky earlier that morning, but the cumulative carbohydrate rationing and overall calorie deficit meant that our bodies had still felt starved and we ate and ate this glut of farine. Looking back, I doubt the farine was any different from farine elsewhere in Brazil, but at the time Cho and I could not stop eating it. It had the most wonderful warm texture and when eaten with the broth it was the best meal I had ever tasted. It is certainly true that the best way to appreciate food is to be truly hungry before you eat. I will never forget that meal as long as I live.

The family waved goodbye to us at about 3 p.m. and pointed us in the direction of Juruá. We had 30 kilometres to cover and expected it to take four days. We bought farine from the family to last us over this time and we also bought coffee, milk powder and sugar, luxuries we hadn't had for weeks.

The next few days saw the worst jungle of the entire expedition: low, tangled rainforest, with a canopy no higher than six metres, with gnarled, black branches blocking our path. Every soggy step gave way and sank our feet up to our thighs; every branch we clung to was covered either in spines or ants. It was the height of dry season now and I dreaded to think what the forest would have been like at any other time of year; completely impassable I suspect. It bore out my decision to cut across the meander from Amaturá to Tefé.

Our progress was painfully slow. One morning we advanced no more that 400 metres. After the false dawn of a house on the hill, I had thought we were home and dry and had pretty much reached Juruá City. I couldn't have been more wrong.

That distance took us six of the toughest days I could remember. I hated every step of it. I was no longer thriving on the thrill of adventure and no longer in survival mode. I had had enough and I just allowed myself to be miserable and pissed off all day long.

Eventually, after hearing motor boats for two days, we could see daylight ahead. The Juruá River itself was vast compared to anything we'd seen since leaving the Solimões and carved out an impressive gorge through the forest, ripping palms and hardwoods from the ground ruthlessly as it constantly altered its course.

Despite our lack of money, I asked for the best hotel in Juruá City. It wasn't luxurious by Western standards but the fact that Cho and I had a double bed each and air conditioning meant that we were in a palace after more than forty days of walking through what must have been some of the most difficult rainforest anywhere in the world.

The Juruá River marked the halfway point to Tefé. Juruá 'City' was a humid, sweaty jungle town with wood-built shops that sat perched on a rare mound of high ground overlooking the low, green sprawl of the Amazon Basin. If a man in a Stetson with low-slung six-shooters had trotted into town on a horse named Silver he would have fitted in perfectly. As long as he spoke a bit of Portuguese.

The contrast between stepping out of the famine of our expedition into the excess of civilisation was remarkable. I spotted one local girl who was not overweight but the rest of the town seemed like personifications of sloth and greed.

We indulged in both those sins. My inbuilt regulator that should have stopped me eating had broken down. I was riding a rollercoaster that was flipping me back and forth between hunger and sickening overeating. Our bodies wanted to build up some fat stores again as we ploughed through cream cakes and egg sandwiches as if we had just been let out of a concentration camp.

Chapter Thirteen

'Cuando hay – hay. Cuando no hay – no hay'

I made a little hole in the mosquito net in my room in Juruá and fed the LAN cable through it. Outside I balanced the plastic BGAN on a nearby wall and pointed it at the invisible geostationary Inmarsat satellite in the sky to my west. Once connected up, I had the fastest Internet in the whole of the Amazon in a town that had never heard of Google. I decided as I was in a town that I could afford a few precious megabytes of bandwidth to check the news and brought up the BBC website. I trawled through the last month of news.

'Soldiers died helping colleague' I read. Then I went cold. No way. Mark Hale, my first sergeant major in the army, who had written to me about the casualties that the regiment had taken in Afghanistan, had been killed. Just four days after his email on 9 August he had been caught in an explosion while helping an injured soldier to safety near Sangin.

I knew he had a wife, Brenda, and two daughters, although I'd never met them, and I just sat on my bed absorbing the sad truth. Like most blokes, we hadn't kept in contact but I'd sponsored him online for a charity event he'd done recently and we'd exchanged a couple of emails since.

I had been happy to be back in contact with Mark. He was an inspirational man who was looked up to by many and he had a big influence on me as a young officer after my dad died. He was a very fit and strong man, a rugby player, and he had gained a masters degree in psychology while serving in the army and eventually became a captain. When I struggled to hold it together in the jungle at times, I thought of Mark and how he would deal with situations with composure, humour and wisdom. I couldn't believe he was dead; then, as it sank in, I felt honoured to have had that small bit of contact with him before he died.

Death does seem to be amazing at cutting through what does and doesn't matter. Suddenly being a bit low on food and having some scratches on my body from thorny bushes seemed the most trivial thing in the world. As I stared at his photo on the screen I took a long, deep breath, held it, and then slowly let it out. I was going to take strength from Mark; I was going to make sure that the exemplary impact he had had on me lasted even beyond his death.

On 24 September Cho and I struggled even to put our packs on as we clomped out of Juruá City. With nine kilograms of food each – enough to last us two weeks – my pack was an absurd 40 kilograms and Cho's close behind at 36 kilograms. We had not carried this much since Luke and I left Camaná in April 2008 but our map ahead was blank – there was nowhere to resupply.

The immediate jungle was a mess. Tangled thorns grew where old agricultural fields had been and in three hours we were scratched, frustrated and had barely gone three kilometres. It was 3.30 p.m.

Concurrently we found water and a wide path that led back to Juruá. In theory we should have made camp but the mosquitoes were bad and we were fed up with the pathetic start we had made.

Then a cheeky idea came into my head. 'Why don't we hide our packs here, Cho, and nip back to Juruá for one last night in a bed?' I said. I wanted a good sleep but I certainly didn't fancy carrying this huge weight all the way back to the town. The plan was hatched and we buried our packs under lots of foliage and used the wide path to reach the town again in a mere forty minutes. We took with us nothing more than our water bottles and my wallet.

A few hours later, back in the same hotel room, Cho called through the closed door: 'Ed, the police are here and would like to speak to you.' I went outside to where two policemen were sitting in a shiny new police car. I smiled and asked the officers if there was a problem.

'We've had reports that you and your friend have been acting suspiciously on the outskirts of the town and we need to see your passports,' said the police chief in Portuguese.

'Of course, no problem,' I replied. 'The only slight hiccup is that we've hidden our passports in the bushes three kilometres out of town.'

Not surprisingly, that didn't go down as unsuspicious behaviour and they arrested us on suspicion of drugs running.

The police chief was not a nice man and he took great pleasure in locking us up. There was no space in the single male cell that had about six men living on top of each other in hammocks, so we were told to sleep on the concrete floor in the corridor between the male and female cells.

There was no bed, let alone bedding, and the iron door was locked on us from the outside. Through the letterbox window we could look out at the policemen sitting around a table playing cards and laughing. We might have been in a spaghetti western.

The next morning we were accompanied by four armed police to the place where we'd hidden the packs and then ordered to carry them back to the police station in town. At the station we first showed our passports and then had to empty all the contents of our packs and explain every item. It was funny how these policemen were as suspicious of us as the Asheninka tribe in Peru had been more than a year ago and that we were now being asked to do the same thing. On this occasion, though, I reckoned the police were offended that we hadn't presented ourselves to them on arrival and explained ourselves. They seemed to me to be demonstrating their power.

By mid-afternoon, proceedings were over and we checked into the hotel once again. Cho and I went to get something to eat as we were starving and we met a family – American husband, Brazilian wife – who worked for IBAMA, the agency that looks after Brazil's national parks. When we explained what we were doing, the wife announced that the area we were about to walk through was a reserve and that we didn't have permits to do so.

Ever conscious of wasting time and therefore money, I kept calm and polite on the outside while I considered the additional bureaucracy that we would need to overcome to get permits. She arranged a meeting at her offices and said we would need to apply through her for a permit. We would also have to hire a trusted guide from her department to ensure that we complied with the rules of the reserve. Obviously I was fine with that but it was frustrating to be delayed by yet another problem.

In the meantime, one positive was that we had received quite a few donations through PayPal so that we had money for the next leg after Tefé.

Soon we were off again, permit in hand and very expensive obligatory guide in tow. We scooted down the clearly defined network of paths and cleared the reserve in two easy days. We said goodbye to the guide who, in the short time he was with us, considerably enhanced our fishing skills, and headed into a part of the country which there seemed to be no record of anyone having entered before.

Imagine a forest designed for the training of soldiers to fight trench warfare. Mazes of tunnels under logs and channels running off in every direction. Each trench is four foot deep, dry as a bone, and is barricaded with fallen trees, thorns the size of four-inch nails and brambles that cut your skin like a cheese grater.

This was the jungle we had entered. I had never seen anything like it. The dry ditches were clearly natural drainage channels in the wet season but now they were nothing but obstacles in our path. The fact that they reminded me of military training meant that the whole thing seemed like some elaborate test of our bottle. We shared the machete work – half an hour each up front – our hands increasingly wounded on the spines. We slid down the mud into the ditches full of matted thorns and hauled ourselves up and out the far side on our muddy knees. After finding a log bridge to cross one trench, Cho turned to me. 'In life there are many obstacles, Ed, you must learn to find solutions.' 'What a golden nugget of wisdom, Cho. Christ,' I thought silently, rolling my eyes.

Over the days my hopes of being strengthened by Mark Hale's splendid example faded and I found it hard to stop feeling sorry for myself. Every step was tiring and slow, and after falling through a rotten log into a trench and slicing a chunk out of my calf I could see the pity on Cho's face. I was also annoyed with myself for failing to raise my game.

In Cho's look I caught a glimpse of what it was like to view myself from the outside. So, after we made camp and had a reinvigorating sweet coffee and the last of the fried salted beef, I fell to thinking. I concluded that all my weakness was in my head and that I would turn things into a game. I did just that and, for now at least, it worked.

I would start the day positive and upbeat and then, as each negative experience cropped up, I would set myself the challenge of laughing at it and not allowing it to bring me down. Each time I succeeded I would give myself a pat on the back and it boosted my morale further to think I was gaining control over the way I reacted to external influences. Each cut, fall or sting became an excuse to reaffirm how in control I was – and I started thoroughly to enjoy walking again and we began to flow through the jungle. The slog became a thrill – our speed increased and it was almost like playing a computer game as snakes, wasps' nests or log bridges became hurdles to be overcome efficiently and nonchalantly as we cruised along. I felt like Keanu Reeves in *The Matrix* – the point at which he becomes so powerful that he can fight with just one arm working at super-speed while the rest of his body is still and relaxed.

The unexpected trenches had slowed us down, however, and so in early October we had to halve our farine rations again so that we didn't run out. If we didn't catch fish we were on a thousand calories a day; we soon got used to what seemed a luxury compared to the 450 daily calories before Juruá.

On 5 October we left the small puddle in which we'd camped and set out with our muddy two litres of sodium-hydroxide-treated water. The bizarre trench forest now looked hurricane-damaged, with every large tree splintered and horizontal. As the sunlight poured in, the undergrowth spread over it as if it had been put on a course of anabolic steroids. Our progress slowed to two kilometres in the whole eight-hour day. We had to take our packs off to hack through the dense wall, one cutting, the resting man bringing both packs forward.

The combination of the ripped-up jungle and start of the dry season meant that at 5 p.m. we were very dehydrated and still sipping the brown water dregs from the previous night's puddle. The water table was too low here, so no point in digging a well, and we started to become concerned that we wouldn't find water. We would have nothing to drink or cook with, and an unpleasant night of grimy, unwashed sleep lay ahead.

As if on cue, thunder started to rumble, deep and long over the canopy. The light dimmed markedly and Cho and I exchanged a knowing look through the deepening gloom.

Quick as a flash, we changed our plan. Cho smashed ahead without his pack to look for trees that were still upright so that we could erect our flysheets. I dragged the two rucksacks up from behind, getting caught up on every thorny branch.

As the first spots of rain filtered through the branches, we were tying the last truckers' hitch to our canopies, a waterproof camera bag under one side of my tarpaulin and my backpack liner under the other. As the cloud properly burst the fresh water flowed from our flysheets into our makeshift reservoirs like garden hoses filling kids' paddling pools.

The tropical downpour lasted only six minutes but we collected thirty-five litres of water: thirty-five pure, clear litres that needed no chemical treatment.

We bathed, drank coffee by the bucket-load, Cho said a quick thank you to God, and then we retired to our hammocks, and slept like the fallen logs that lay around us.

By mid-October we were again even more remote than I'd ever been in my life. Granted, this was not in terms of distance; it was in terms of the number of days it would take us to get back to civilisation. My second GPS broke and so we had to convert to using map and compass bearings. I had two maps with me, the 1:1 million navigational chart for aeroplanes and a 1:4 million Stanfords map of the whole of the top half of South America. Neither had contours, neither was designed for navigating at this micro scale. I was estimating the distance that we'd travelled since the last time the GPS had worked and I was trying to keep us walking in as straight a line as possible through the dense trees. Each day, though, the margin for error grew and there was no way of crosschecking where we really were.

We would often have to redraw the rivers on the navigational chart in pencil because it was so inaccurate and the rivers were only rough indications of where there might be a watercourse on the ground. In fact, we started using the more accurate but less detailed 1:4 million map instead. I had only brought it along to show interested locals the walk in its entirety; it covered *nine* countries. One millimetre on this Stanfords map represented four whole kilometres on the ground. We would rarely move position by more than three millimetres a day and to take bearings when distances were so small left massive scope for inaccuracies. It was a navigational joke; if it hadn't been life-threatening it would have been hilarious.

We were carrying an EPIRB but, as our medical insurance had long since lapsed, if we had pulled the plug then nothing would have happened. No evacuation would have been initiated. We were on our own.

The remoteness from mankind was reflected in the wildlife here, too. For the first time ever we'd caught two baby caiman in the fishing net. Babies weren't our worry, however; it was the adults that we were more concerned about as we retrieved the fish.

There was something reassuring about the fact that the pair of us seldom got ill. Cho had been sick once but on the whole we seemed to have strong constitutions and perhaps a lot of luck. We took pride in it and so, when Cho started to complain of headaches and dark, obscured vision, it was a serious concern.

Cho was in severe pain and was being sick as well. I had no real idea what it was and gave him painkillers. The battery on our thermometer had run out and I remembered the conversation with Luke in Hereford during our medical training when we had both agreed we needed to carry a mercury one.

By evening, after agreeing that Cho struggle through the walking day until we at least found water, we came upon a shallow puddle that I knew I could excavate and allowed Cho to collapse. He did just that. The man who took huge pride in his strength of mind and spirit simply allowed his pack to fall to the floor and he immediately followed it.

I decided that a hot, sweet cup of coffee and a good meal would do Cho good and so set about making camp while he lay motionless. I dug out the puddle so that I could get a plastic Lock & Lock container (lunchbox) in it to bail water into the reservoir I had made from my rucksack liner. I collected firewood, lit a fire and put water on to make coffee. While the water was heating, I put up Cho's hammock and instructed him firmly to use the water reservoir to wash and put on his dry evening clothes. He then got into his hammock and fell fast asleep while I put up my own hammock and made coffee and supper.

I became aware just how we reliant we were on each other that night. The evening was a busy one as I had to do all the jobs that the two of us normally shared. I woke Cho up just as it was getting dark and gave him supper. He was looking better already and ate his food and kept it down. The moment he finished it, he went straight back to sleep while I washed by torchlight.

There is a purity of mind that only really comes about when you forget about yourself and have to go into overdrive to help someone else. One of us getting seriously ill here would be fatal. There was no evacuation apart from me dragging or carrying Cho. If he couldn't walk he was dead and he knew it.

In the morning, though, he was better. This was partly due to his mental strength and I could tell he felt he'd let himself down the day before. He got up that morning in a state of mind that said he would be better.

I posted a video blog of the day online and, ironically, the diagnosis of Cho's illness came from one of the blog readers. A number of people told me it sounded like severe migraine and that seemed to make sense.

While online, I read that Sir Ranulph Fiennes's expedition trust had come good again and given us yet more money. This time I got two emails, too, one from Sir Ranulph himself, the other from Anton, a trustee of the Transglobe Expedition Trust.

Dear Ed [wrote Sir Ranulph]

Congratulations on your progress to date.

I think things will get increasingly difficult for you. Over forty years I must have been involved with over thirty big journeys, at least half of which have failed. It is always a matter for the traveller to decide in his/her own head when to turn back and when to continue.

Sometimes to continue is plain daft and irresponsible, at other times there is a chance that pushing on over a particular obstacle or series of obstacles may make things look a whole lot better in which case it's well worth fighting off 'weak thoughts' which occur when the morale is down. Only you can be your own final arbiter.

Whatever you may decide over the weeks/months ahead, know that you have already done fantastically well and we at the Transglobe Expedition Trust are proud of you.

Very best wishes,

Ran

I was over the moon just to receive the email but surprised by the 'get out clause' that he seemed to be offering. I had too much time to think while walking and I began to wonder about the dangers he was referring to. Was I cracking up? Was it obvious from my blogs? *Was* I being irresponsible?

Cho and I sat down and talked it through. As Sir Ranulph said, '*only you can be your own final arbiter*'. Were we going to give up?

Were we fuck.

Anton's email was a more straightforward morale booster:

Dear Ed,

I have seen a copy of Ran's email to you and it has prompted me to join in!

At the Transglobe Expedition Trust, we get many applications for funding. One of our criteria for offering support is that the project should be sufficiently ambitious to make a significant impact in the evolution of human achievement. We get hardly any applications that fully meet these terms. We aim to support expeditions that match our 'mad but marvellous' criteria. When we asked one of Britain's leading authorities on the Amazon region for his view of your proposed expedition, he thought it was an impossible journey. However, he pointed out that although it was a 'mad' idea, it would be truly 'marvellous' if you succeeded. It was therefore, the perfect expedition for us to support. As Ran says, not all expeditions succeed and we, at the Transglobe Expedition Trust, fully understand when the going gets too tough. However, if you press on and confound the pundits by travelling where no one else thought it possible, you will be in the very front line of human achievement.

You have a growing audience in the UK and further afield who are gunning for you all the way. None of us can fully appreciate how grim it must get for you. Good luck in these difficult times. If you can hack it, you both will have done something truly amazing and worthwhile which has already gained you enormous admiration from far and wide.

With very best wishes,

Anton

That was the one that brought tears to my eyes. What an amazing email to receive in the middle of the jungle. I did indeed have some incredible support behind me and I used it to bolster my determination.

It was now late October and the dry season was sucking every drop of moisture from the jungle. Dried-up riverbeds had Cho and me pathetically waiting under the puniest of jungle vines for a few drops of life-giving liquid. We resorted to digging down in the dried-up beds trying to hit the water table, often to no effect.

Thankfully, the dry season did not mean no rain – just lower water levels – so we were saved by an evening deluge on more than one occasion and were now slick operators with our improvised reservoirs.

As fish live in rivers, our parched state was exacerbated by grumbling stomachs. For several weeks we didn't catch enough fish to smoke and carry with us. We lived hand to mouth – a catch of fish would be wolfed down in seconds and neither of us wanted to think ahead and save food for the days that followed. We were content to eat as well as we could when we could and then use all our wits to ensure we found food again.

Cho would always quote what seemed to me a blindingly obvious statement: '*Cuando hay – hay. Cuando no hay – no hay.*' It translates pretty literally as 'When you have – you have. When you don't – you don't.'

This used to wind me up, a worthless homily that rubbed salt into an angry wound. But after hearing his tales of living in hiding in the mountainous forests of Peru at the height of the infamous Shining Path's terrorist activities, I started to put his words into context.

It was a way of saying that there is no point grumbling if there is no food – no point in dwelling on it either. If you accept that it is outside your control and move on regardless, you will learn to be content with less.

As we reached the River Bauaná, which led down to Lago Tefé and then to Tefé itself, we finished off the last of our rations. With another 40 kilometres or so until the next big river that also ran down to Lago Tefé, we made the prudent decision to mark the spot and head downstream looking for people. We were still 100 kilometres from Tefé but we'd already made the decision to turn south so that we would never actually pass through Tefé on foot. There was just no need to take ourselves so close to the main Solimões River and there were huge lakes that we could avoid if we stayed about 100 kilometres from the main channel.

I tied coloured plastic bags to the bow of a tree to mark the spot and we inflated the rafts so that we could set off to find food. In my head the similarity between this and the wasted time on the Minerazinho in September was haunting me but the difference was that we knew this led to Tefé, and so we suspected that this river might actually be populated.

At 4 p.m. we decided to stop paddling and set up camp. With no food, we needed a couple of hours of fishing if we were to eat anything at all. I set the nets in the mouth of a small stream flowing into the river and Cho went digging for worms to use as bait. Half an hour passed – nothing in the net. Cho hadn't managed to find any bait either. Another half an hour and still nothing. As I was checking the net I heard what I thought were voices coming from upriver.

'*Cho, hay personas!*' I called to him. We both listened intently and decided it must have been monkeys. I peered further and thought I could make out a blue tarpaulin covering part of a boat.

'*Hay gente pe,*' I confirmed. 'There *are* people.' Cho and I quickly forgot our failed fishing attempts and decided to go and introduce ourselves. Fishermen and hunters usually had loads of food and our stomachs groaned as we paddled towards the boat that was perhaps 100 metres away. As I was filming with one hand, Cho got there well before me and he introduced himself to the two men. Then he called out to me that they had invited us to eat with them. They had a fish broth made and a big white bucket full of farine.

Our luck was once again unbelievable. We were still well over 100 kilometres from the city of Tefé, and only about eight hours after finishing the last of our supplies we'd found fishermen with food in abundance. We poured a generous pile of the golden farine pellets into our soup and took large, appreciative mouthfuls. It was amazing how deeply ingrained hospitality was in this part of the Amazon. The first thing people would often say to us was 'Would you like some food? You must be hungry!' Questions about where we were from came later.

The men had finished fishing and were heading back downriver. If we wanted we could accompany them to the nearest village a few kilometres away. We jumped at the chance as we needed to buy food and we all piled into the small boat and chugged downriver to a small cluster of thatched buildings on a patch of high ground. The village actually comprised just a single family and they gave us an abandoned outhouse in which to string up our hammocks in the dark. The family then fed us as well again and we went to bed with stretched bellies and gurgling sounds coming from our bowels.

The owner of the house, Antonio, didn't have spare food for us to buy but he was going downriver to the shop the next day. If we didn't mind waiting, he would take us there and back. Cho and I took the opportunity to have a rest day. We lazed about and helped the family make farine. Huge three-metre-diameter pans were perched on top of mud-oven walls that surrounded large, hot wood fires. The farine was being toasted and tossed around the bath-sized pans with a wooden canoe paddle. The smell of new farine was just wonderful, like morning wafts from a traditional bakery.

Once we'd bought food the following day Antonio agreed to take us back to where I'd tied the plastic bags to the branch. We put our hammocks up and reflected on the luckiest, most efficient break and resupply imaginable. Forty-eight hours not walking and we'd got a complete stock of food: farine, salt, coffee, sugar, milk powder and a couple of heads of garlic and we'd rested and relaxed, too, having spent very little money.

The BGAN, our Internet and telephone link to the outside world, then chose to die. It just wouldn't power up. Aside from emergencies, it was essential so that we could continue our mission of broadcasting videos and blogs from the expedition live. When we got to Tefé, and Internet access, I would have to ask Marlene in Lima to send our spare unit to Iquitos. I would then send Cho back to

Peru to get it. It sounded extravagant but when you start trying to mail things across international borders in South America you soon learn that it's far safer just to go yourself and transport the thing as part of your luggage. Otherwise the paperwork takes weeks. Cho liked the idea anyway as he would have to fly from Tefé to Tabatinga. He'd never been on an aeroplane before.

The response to my plea for financial help had been so resounding that by now we had enough money to reinsure the expedition and so I arranged that with our previous insurers, THB Clowes. Our kit was no longer insured but at least we had medical cover again. In hindsight, I'm not sure I would have bothered taking out such a specialist (and expensive) insurance as we'd pretty much accepted that we would have to self-evacuate anyway. The problem was that, because the journey was already under way and we couldn't get standard British Mountaineering Council (BMC) insurance, we were forced to pay well over a thousand pounds again. At the same time I ordered a new GPS online and had it sent to one of our new sponsors, Pete Casey, who I had agreed could come and walk with us for three weeks in return for his generous donations. He would bring in any new items of kit we needed with him and so his visit would be really valuable to us at a time when everything seemed to be falling apart.

In hindsight, the period of time spent navigating with just an inaccurate map and a cheap compass from the UK that wasn't even balanced for South America made the journey far more exciting. We simply had to make do and revert to methodologies used hundreds of years ago. We were still moving forward; we just had to be that much more switched on and aware of our speed and our route planning: *'Cuando hay – hay. Cuando no hay – no hay.'*

Cho and I arrived at a large inland lake and made camp. The lake level was low and we had to walk through ankle-deep mud to get to the water's edge, but there was a great area of higher woodland overlooking the lake in which we could camp. In desperate need of protein, we waded into the lake with a gill net and two long poles each and set them across the thigh-deep water.

Before we'd finished attaching the other ends of the nets to the poles we started catching fish. The presence of fish in the lake was so concentrated that the catch was abundant and we extracted one fish after another for the pot. None of the fish appeared to be piranhas here so we made the decision to leave the nets in overnight so that we would have a bumper catch in the morning. (Piranhas would have eaten the trapped fish and destroyed the nets in the process.)

As the sun started to set, our camp felt homely and beautiful. The open space around the lake felt relaxing after so long in dense vegetation and we bumbled down to the water for a wash. When the sun set, we used our head torches in the gloom, and as we stripped off at the side of the lake, balancing on pieces of wood laid on the mud so as to keep our feet clean, I caught a glimpse of what looked like reflective dots all over the surface of the lake.

'*Concha su madre!*' I said to Cho. 'Crikey. Look at the number of caiman in this lake!' At first Cho didn't think they were caiman, then he looked more closely and saw that I was right. The lake was stuffed, and the number of eyes reflected in our torchlight, just above the level of the water, confirmed our fears. The black caiman, a species of alligator, could grow to five metres. Due to their size they could attack and kill an adult human being in the water with ease. Any idea of retrieving a final catch from the nets vanished and we giggled like kids at the thought of how vulnerable we were standing on the edge of this lake washing ourselves in the presence of perhaps fifteen of these huge predators.

As we walked up the hill the thrashing started and we realised that the caiman were feeding off fish that had been caught in our nets. The thrashing went on all night. I hardly slept a wink.

The next morning I found my net detached from the poles and floating on the other side of the lake. Cho's was tangled up in some bushes on our side of the bank. Both nets were seriously damaged and had large holes in them, yet another thing that we now needed to replace, yet another lesson learned.

Within 200 metres of setting out we hit the River Tefé. This led down to Tefé itself and we had already decided that we were going to break here and travel the 90 kilometres downriver to the town as that was where we were meeting Pete, the sponsor. The lake was an obvious marker to return to and so we paddled downriver looking for a boat to hire to take us to Tefé.

We soon found a community that allowed us to stay, that fed us and organised us to go on one of the canoes that was travelling to Tefé the following day. As usual in Brazil we were fed well, entertained impeccably and watched Brazilian soap operas on their satellite television in the evening.

Tefé, formerly known as Ega, is the town in which the Leicester-born naturalist and explorer Henry Walter Bates based himself in the 1800s. During his time in the Amazon he sent home 14,000 species (mostly insects) of which 8,000 were new to science. His tales of exploration with indigenous Indians as guides were recorded in his book *The Naturalist on the River Amazons*, regarded as one of the finest reports of natural history travels.

Tefé, like many towns on the Amazon, has no roads running into it. It is situated at the northern end of Lago Tefé, an enormous lake formed at the mouth of the River Tefé. Arriving from across the lake, Cho told me that, although he had never seen the sea, he now knew what it must look like. Large waves crashed over the bows of the small canoe and you could see 30 kilometres in both directions from the mid-point.

The hotel we stayed in was the first since Juruá, forty-three days earlier, and, even though we knew people in the town, Cho and I hid away in our hotel for three whole days and slept. We surfaced for meals, but that was about it. We had about as much desire to socialise as an autistic maths professor.

Slowly, we began to return to normality and I sent Cho off to Iquitos. This was really cutting things fine as our Brazilian visas were now good for only a few more days. If Cho was delayed there was a chance he wouldn't be let back into the country. But we needed communication with the outside world and so back Cho went.

As much as we wanted to stay legal in Brazil, we'd given up on that now. Kavos had told us that we could fly to Venezuela and try to re-enter through there but that he couldn't guarantee us entry back into Brazil. Clearly, being stuck outside Brazil and not being allowed back in was a far worse prospect than staying in Brazil and risking being asked to leave. We still had nine and a half months left to walk and we had to avoid the Federal Police at all costs from this point, as we were now illegal immigrants.

Cho returned with the spare BGAN and Pete arrived with a mountain of replacement kit, the most important of which was a GPS but also included a new Macpac rucksack for Cho and some new Altberg boots for us both.

It was early November when we hired another small boat to take us back to the caiman-infested lake. After a long day's travel we arrived and, as it was dark, the boat stayed with us and we all camped the night. I plugged the BGAN in to update the map with our new position now that we had a GPS. To my disgust the new BGAN didn't work. I could make voice calls but the Internet wasn't working. I spent a good two hours, and all the battery power that we had, on the phone to AST Satellite Communications in the UK and they couldn't fix the problem without me being connected to the Internet. Apparently Inmarsat's network had had a 'critical satellite alteration' and we needed to download new software for our unit that had been inactive for months sitting in Marlene's flat in Lima. As frustrating as it was, we had no option but to continue without Internet access. The next three weeks of blogs would have to be phoned through on the satellite phone to Chloë, my ex-girlfriend, whose number was the only one in the world I knew off by heart, and she would post the blog from England using library images ripped from Google.

We set out carrying more weight than ever before. I had estimated that this leg was twenty-four days without a single community and so we needed to have enough food. As Pete was walking with us I splashed out on cereal bars for lunch so that we could keep our energy levels up throughout the day. We bought 432 cereal bars, wiping out the entire stock in about five Tefé shops, and our bags were now phenomenally heavy. Cho had about 40 kilograms, I was up to 44 kilograms and Pete, who'd never walked in the jungle before, was on about 35 kilograms, more than Cho and I had been carrying for the vast majority of the expedition.

The going was abominable. The first day we hit a field thick with razor grass but had no option but to push through. A paper cut doesn't compare to the wounds you get from razor grass; it is like paper that has been dipped in glue and then finely crushed glass. Our hands became bloody and our clothes got ripped up. We managed only four hours that day before collapsing and deciding that we would have to camp.

Pete was a builder from Crawley in the south of England. He was physically strong but had no idea what he had let himself in for.

This is definitely the hardest thing I've ever done, I didn't realise it would be this tough. You have to experience this to believe it; words could not do it justice [said Pete after the first day].

He had twenty-three more ahead of him.

Pete immediately became covered in mosquito and sand-fly bites and I felt sorry for him. He reacted badly to everything and we had to give him large doses of antihistamines each night to allow him to get any sleep at all. I was used to washing in excavated holes in the mud now and eating dry farine and nothing else for supper when there was no river to fish in, but suddenly I saw what a basic, animalistic life we'd been living. Pete was visibly shocked by what was being expected of him physically and mentally, but luckily he had a fierce desire not to let himself or us down and so he just put up with the horrible conditions and brutally long days. He rarely complained.

On 12 November 2009, while cutting at the front, machete in hand, I unknowingly stepped straight over a muscular, coiled pit viper. Pete saw a flicker of movement on the floor as the viper prepared to strike. The colouring of the brown and black snake was so similar to that of the forest floor that it was a miracle he saw it at all and he jerked back to avoid it.

This wasn't an uncommon incident. It happened to Cho and me regularly, but that one probably remains with me because I was seeing it through the eyes of an outsider for the first time. It was a reminder of how alone we were there; we had forty-eight hours of anti-venom with us and so could keep one of us alive for that long. Evacuation through the vegetation we were covering was an absurd thought, and would have taken a week, absolute minimum, had it been possible to carry a stretcher through the tangled forest.

It was sobering to think that, had Pete been bitten and envenomated, all we could have done was to make camp, immobilise his leg in a hammock and administer injections of anti-venom for the next two days. If after that the venom was still in his system, he would, of course, die. Even if he didn't die, he would then have to walk out of there himself. It had been that way all along but seeing it through the eyes of a novice made me readdress the risks we were taking to complete this world-first expedition.

Our insurance may have been valid again but, realistically, how quickly was our four-man team from Ex-Med in Hereford going to arrive? By the time they arrived incountry, procured maps, transport and local guides and then set out from the nearest navigable river to our location on foot, it would have been a minimum of several days.

A week later Cho, Pete and I descended a muddy, forested slope. The horizon, normally obscured by the trees, appeared, signalling that a river was ahead. At the bottom of the slope we were confronted by the most depressing wall of tight bamboo cane interwoven with razor grass. Cho slumped noticeably and we cringed at the hours of effort we would have to put in to haul ourselves through the dense bamboo. We knew we would advance at snail's pace; our knuckles would be raw and bleeding from the close machete work.

Our maps had no detail on them for small-scale navigation but, for the first time in months, I remembered that Google Earth could help us. We still had no Internet connection but the images were cached in the memory and, as we'd not been using the Macbook, it still had plenty of battery power.

I took out the computer and entered our latitude and longitude from the new GPS into Google Earth. Immediately I could see where we were and I could see the exact shape of the river ahead. I could see, too, that the apex of one of the huge meanders of the river came close to us if we walked off to our right and so I took that point on the meander from Google Earth, entered the coordinates into our GPS, retrieved a bearing from it that we all three entered into our compasses, and suddenly we had a new direction and the shortest possible distance to the river.

The direction was hard right and we never once had to enter the bamboo. It was a combination of technologies that enabled me to plot the new course and I was quite chuffed with how it worked. Just over a kilometre later we broke out on to the wide river and congratulated ourselves. Almost zero effort and we'd avoided a hellish afternoon. From that point on Google Earth, rather than the inaccurate, large-scale maps, became my primary aid for navigating. For the remainder of this leg we would use it directly on the Macbook, but when we set off from the next big town we would print off screenshots of the route ahead with the grid overlaid. That's how we navigated for the nine months and more than 2,000 kilometres that lay ahead.

Even Google had its limitations, however. I misinterpreted a white line that I was adamant was a road that would help our advance to the town of Coari. The line was indeed a man-made cutting through the trees but it was not a road, it was an oil pipeline. This was a double knock-back: we were not only losing out on what I thought would be a few days of easy walking by road – but the jungle in the area was recent grow-back from cutting in the pipeline. Our progress was gruellingly slow in the burning equatorial sunlight, and, with no upper canopy to control regeneration, vegetation had grown furiously to fill the void.

We nervously approached a camp full of men wearing orange overalls, as we were fairly sure that the oil company wouldn't be too happy that we were passing through their area without permission. We needn't have worried; the pipeline workers force-fed us pork, coffee and ice-cold juice and then, incredibly, gave us a standing ovation as we left their camp. Touches of human kindness like this after three weeks non-stop in the jungle were impossible not to get emotional about. It meant so much to us that people understood what we were doing and showed their support. As in many places in Brazil, the workers wouldn't accept a penny in return for their food. They just wanted us to leave them happy.

In Coari we said goodbye to Pete who'd lost six kilograms in three weeks but had stuck with it and done himself credit. Despite his dogged toughness, it was his humility and kindness to Cho that made his visit work for me.

I hung out of hotel windows with my BGAN and eventually was remotely talked through a 'remote factory reset' to get it running by the techies at AST. Easy when you know how but it took forty-eight hours of trying everything until the AST techies at last came up with the simple solution.

Cho and I used the kitchen at the hotel to make 'dog biscuits', a calorie-packed energy snack made from flour, sugar, oats, butter and *dulce de leche*, a South American variant on golden syrup. With cinnamon and ginger to flavour them, these were gorgeously delicious; they cost a fraction of the price of the cereal bars. Finally, we bought two cheap Santa hats from the market and set off into the trees once again.

Chapter Fourteen

'Dedication'

On 10 December 2009, having walked for twenty-one months, but still with seven months left to push, I sat down on my pack and said to Cho that I was bored. Not exhausted, shattered or fatigued – just bored.

I could see by the look on Cho's face that he understood me completely. We were only three days into a nine-day leg and we had rested well. Our current hurdle wasn't physical – it was mental.

We knew that ahead of us we'd another Christmas away from our families. We knew that it would be spent in the jungle eating farine with salt. We knew that we would try to make over seven kilometres that day and would then look for a place to put the fishing net if the river was big enough. Everything was frighteningly familiar.

It wasn't a question of would we give up – that never entered our heads. Melodramatic or not: we would both have died before coming home as failures. What we were trying to look for now was a way to reinvigorate the walk which had become, at times, something close to a self-inflicted prison sentence.

Blog entry from 17 December 2009:

Ten years ago yesterday I was sleeping in the spare room at my mum and dad's house in the small rural village of Mowsley in Leicestershire. I had recently graduated from the Royal Military Academy Sandhurst and, as a young second lieutenant without a place of my own, was staying with my parents whilst on military leave until my first reporting date with the Devonshire and Dorset Regiment.

It was still dark and I was half asleep when Mum burst into the room and, failing to keep the earth-shattering grief out of her voice, said, 'Your father's dead.'

Mum and I had driven him to the Royal Infirmary the night before. A place he hated and did not want to go to. A place where the drugs that they put him on made him hallucinate and ask me whether I really did love him at all. A place where we left him alone that night and drove home via the pub.

Mum and I sat on the floor at the top of the stairs hugging each other with tears streaming down our faces and I could not stop saying out loud, 'I love you Dad, I love you Dad, I love you Dad.' I needed him to know – I needed the message to get to through to him somehow.

The last time I ever saw him was a few hours later when we went to the hospital. Unmade up, and with his mouth hanging half open, his body lay there with no life in it. The strongest part of our family – the strength that held us all together – had gone. I asked one of the nurses to take the gold signet ring off his finger and I put it on. I wore it from that day on until it attracted too much attention with the Ashaninka Indians in Peru and I had to ask Marlene to look after it in Lima where it is now.

Dad was tall for his generation at six foot three inches; he was a man of few words and had a dry sense of humour. He had fought off cancer twice previously and was physically in pretty poor shape for much of his adult life as a result of the chemotherapy and archaic radiotherapy that he'd received since his early twenties. Mentally and morally he was one of the strongest men I have ever known and the love he had for my mum, my sister and me was unquestionable.

Whatever the weather he would always show up and stand on the touchline with a drip on the end of his nose in his flat cap, Barber and wellies to watch me play rugby. Even when he was very ill and his blood platelet count was so low that had he been hit by the ball he would have died – would have haemorrhaged uncontrollably to death – he still came and watched. That's not a show of support a son forgets.

While I wrote that I had tears pouring down my face. It was a channel that allowed me to release so much tension, worry and loneliness. It wasn't that I hadn't dealt with Dad's death; it was that I needed to get in touch with my emotions again after months of suppressing fear and anxiety. While I couldn't go on without allowing myself this short period of weakness, it enabled me to move on and be stronger, with a calmer, more balanced outlook.

The Amazon is not a normal river, like the Thames, for instance – it is the focal point of a huge sheet of water that surges through the forest when the waters are high. This deluge of water can be more than 100 kilometres wide in places; it is the same distance as London to Paris at its mouth where it gushes out at over 200,000 cubic metres per second into the Atlantic Ocean. It is not where two rather small, insignificant and helpless ramblers wanted to get caught. Overnight flash floods would reportedly sweep away complete camps, killing everybody and leaving no trace.

The rains had begun. Cho and I hadn't lit a fire with dry wood in days but luckily we knew how to start one with wet wood – we'd had rather a lot of practice by now. We ate our food naked after having washed – there was no point putting on our dry clothes (they would just get wet again) – and we were long past the embarrassment stage by now.

On Christmas Eve we were too close to the main channel of the Solimões to be safe from the flooded forests. We were in annually flooded forest now and the muddy forest floor was getting soggier and harder to walk on by the day.

We needed to escape from the *varzea* and a search for high ground before the floods came for real. High ground would be the best Christmas present we could wish for.

On Christmas Day it hardly stopped raining. We had a wet day walking and then recorded some silly video messages for the website and posed as two men in Santa hats in a hammock for a daft photo for the website. As we set up camp, the heavy rain was relentless. I made a fire from sodden wood and Cho went to see if he could catch fish in a river. I was sure he would have no luck.

Cho was ages and I sat in the rain thinking about the lonely, isolated Christmas I was having; but then, just as it was getting dark, Cho returned with a catch of seven or eight fish speared through the gills on a stick to carry them.

'Nice one, Cho!' I beamed and helped him scale and gut them in the stream nearby. We fried some garlic in oil, and added the fish chunks and water. It was a perfect bumper catch and a great Christmas present. We laughed and joked and Cho practised saying 'Happy Christmas' in English. 'This time next year, Cho, we'll be at home with our families,' I said. We sat gazing into the orange flames and dreaming of the outside world.

Each day Cho and I walked with our clothes painted to our bodies with sweat. We broke for ten minutes every hour and habitually wrung out our tops – that was as dry as they got all day. They were then used as rags to wipe the jungle grit and grime from the back of our necks and the crooks of our elbows. For those precious ten minutes we would sit on our packs and exchange exhausted glances.

Raindrops were refreshing in the high humidity but the regular precipitation also meant that the rivers were now swollen and bloated. Their discharge was steadily seeping into the lower-lying *varzea* – but only so much as to give us wet boots at the moment. We were still making good progress.

By 31 December we had just cut through a thick patch of thorny bamboo to get to a river's edge and, up to our waists in water, were clearing the rushes to make space to inflate the pack rafts. We only had to cross the river at this point, but it was New Year's Eve, we were tired, and we were inflating the rafts anyway . . .

'Cho,' I ventured, 'we could just head downriver in the rafts to the fishing village of Paricatuba rather than spending the night in the jungle on our own . . .' He smiled, acknowledged that he'd just been thinking the very same thing, and we had a new plan to bring in the New Year.

We marked the spot with the GPS to return to the next day (or the day after, depending on how good our night was). Four hours later we were sitting on a wooden deck of a floating house at the front of the pretty village with a beer each. The cleared ground stretched up from the river behind us with a big, pink, concrete church at the top of the hill. The hot evening sun scorched my gringo neck as we toasted our new circumstances.

The evening was comprised mostly of sitting in a circle watching a five-inch screen on which was playing Brazilian pop music in Portuguese. I had thought I was getting good at Portuguese – with its nasal words all running into each other – but trying to understand slurred, drunken Portuguese was seriously difficult. The night ended in a slight blur of very sincere old men hugging us and telling us we were their friends.

Cho was keen for a rest day when we woke up and so I checked emails and did my accounts. We'd spent about £12 on New Year's Eve between the two of us so I didn't feel too guilty about the indulgence. The beer had had that cold, thirst-quenching quality that just made you smile with pleasure. It had been worth it.

On 2 January we had to go back to where we'd left off walking so we hired a wooden boat and Amaral, a short, plump man with a big smile, steered us back upriver, his engine putt-putt-putting behind us. We had to return to exactly where we'd left off, and as we closed in on the GPS waypoint, I started to inflate the pack raft we'd used to travel downstream to Paricatuba. I was standing up in the bows of the narrow boat, puffing the last few breaths into the raft to make it as taut as a drum, when a gust of wind took the rubber canoe and me clean overboard. Unfazed by my premature dip, I turned round, grinning goofily, ready for a ribbing from Cho, when I saw that I'd overturned the entire canoe and the two slightly panicky crew were grabbing loose items of kit as the boat and its heavy engine disappeared below the murky surface.

Cho grabbed the dry bag with my wallet and GPS in it while Amaral tried to free the outboard from the reeds on the riverbed three metres below. I dragged the submerged wooden boat to shallow water and managed to tip the water out quickly so that I could return to the still rather panic-stricken Amaral who then, still out of his depth, showed Hulk-like strength to haul the motor up the side and into the boat. We regrouped and realised, much to our relief, that our only loss had been the single machete that we'd brought for the day. It could have been so much worse.

Cho and I apologised for my clumsiness – and for the fact that Amaral would now have to paddle back because his engine had water in it. We crossed the river and had the most pleasant day walking through surprisingly dry, open, *varzea* without needing the now drowned machete once. We walked into Paricatuba at two in the afternoon to the news that the boat hadn't returned and I had to hire another canoe to go on a search and rescue mission to find poor old Amaral.

With a new boat driver, Alvaro, who looked amusingly similar to the actor who plays Chris Finch in *The Office* (British version), we covered the whole stretch of water searching thoroughly. Time drew on. No Amaral and no boat. Finchy and I exchanged silent glances. We were both coming to the conclusion that Amaral must have drowned in the perilous, choppy waves when we checked in the one floating house that we'd not passed en route to find a smiling Amaral sipping coffee and drying his engine out in the sun.

The great thing about being in Paricatuba for real on foot was that at the top of the cleared riverbank behind the pink church was high ground all the way to the broad highway that led to Manaus. We'd escaped the floods, for now, and estimated we would arrive at the road in just ten days.

Everything is relative and, when you've been walking for 639 days, a ten-day leg through unknown jungle that no one in the village could remember being walked in living history seemed nothing. We set off in search of Highway BR-319 with fresh supplies and high morale. We knew that in Manaus we would take a proper break and it felt like the holiday had started already after our warm welcome by the Paricatubans.

But after four days of nasty jungle, Cho flatly told me, 'Not many people in the world would follow you through this.'

He had a point. There was nothing pleasurable about those ten days. No beautiful rivers, hardly any wildlife, just kilometres of secondary messy bush that required a lot of machete work to make any progress. Maybe because Manaus was in spitting distance we were counting the minutes in each hour and our brains often spiralled into near maddening despair. We'd let our guard down before the end of the fight and the negatives of how hard and slow this leg was had got to us.

We had to change our approach and revert to working on taking back control of our minds. My solutions varied daily but I can remember singing 'Dedication', the theme tune to the old BBC children's programme *Record Breakers*, sung, and trumpeted, by the late Roy Castle. I had not heard it in years – it was Cho's behaviour that made it stick in my head.

One morning he fell off a slippery log and, feeling the machete leave his hand, he instinctively grabbed it as he landed, pulling his fingers down the blade. I watched in slow motion as the panicked look on his face said it all and I prayed he'd not lost any fingers. Clutching his hand, he scrambled out of the far side and I ripped out the medical kit in seconds. The wound had seriously cut all four fingers on his left hand and the cut on the little finger was very deep. After washing and adding iodine, we tightly bound his hand with duct tape to stop the bleeding. Brave as ever, Cho made to continue walking but I told him we were making camp where we were. Sometimes, pushing on was just not necessary and certainly not to anyone's benefit. The river would make a great camp anyway.

Cho was still in pain when he started fishing at 2.30 that afternoon. He was keen not to be hampered by his wound and so, when I made the fire, he found a slow pool in the meandering river and threw in his hook and line.

I made supper, our small ration of rice and beans with black coffee, and called him to come but he asked me to put in his Lock & Lock box as he would eat it later. I went to bed when it got dark around 6.20, having eaten alone. I read in my cosy, dry hammock den. At eight o'clock I had just finished my book when I saw Cho's head torch bobbing through the trees back towards the embers of the fading fire.

'We have supper!' he proclaimed and slapped down a big catfish with a grin that I could not see in the dark but I knew was there. It had taken him five and a half hours to land his prize. I got up and gutted and cooked the catfish while Cho bathed.

As we ate I complimented Cho on his remarkable patience. It had given us both an injection of protein we had needed for several days. He brushed it off in his usual way. For him, fishing was a distraction from the monotony of the walk but this time I suspected such perseverance was his way of gaining control again over the jungle after his machete accident.

I thought back to how Luke and I had clashed and how different my relationship with Cho was. With mutual respect and complementary skills, a two-man team could work very well indeed. I was so lucky to have Cho with me. So it was that his dedication set that song going round and round in my head. Cho learned the words and would sing 'Dedication is what you need!' at the top of his voice in English while walking.

The BR-319 is a dead-straight, open wound across the face of the Amazon. It was mid-January 2010 by the time we broke out on to the crumbling road that marked the end of the vast stretch of jungle that we had crossed since Tabatinga. Once paved, it cut a scar through the Amazon rainforest from Manaus to Porto Velho in the south-west. The total traffic it saw was about two 4×4 trucks a day.

We used the road to advance north-east towards the vast city of Manaus. The first few days we walked in direct, blistering sunlight. I wore my silk sleeping-bag liner under my cap to protect my neck and face from the burning sun. With the increased distances that we had to put in on the road our bodies complained and we became scorched walking corpses. Cho was struggling more – there was something wrong with him and at the end of a long day we stopped in a disused road construction camp and he went straight to sleep. The next day at midday he could hardly walk. We had to stop in a house and ask for water for Cho. I think he had thought that, because he had dark skin, he couldn't get sunstroke, but that was what it looked like to me. He'd not covered up at all and he was taking doxycycline as an anti-malarial so he would be hyper-sensitive to light anyway.

For the first time in months I decided to leave Cho and continue alone. I was not worried about him. Cho could rest up and then catch up with me when he was well by getting a lift on the family's motorbike. I felt very liberated walking alone for the first time and sang songs to myself. It rained hard for two hours and yet I felt strong and free. I spent a night in an abandoned *palapa* by the side of the road and was very aware that I was truly on my own for the first time in months.

By the next day Cho was feeling better and met up with me a little further north and we continued walking together. The people we spoke to told us that the area adjacent to the road was in fact a forestry reserve and that you even had to have a permit to cut trees to build your house. This was good to hear but the same people said that the BR-319 would be completely resurfaced by 2014 and I couldn't help but worry that the increased traffic to the area couldn't be good for conservation of the area as a whole.

I then had the idea to walk at night. We could clock up cool night-time kilometres without the oppressive heat of the day. We set off at 5 p.m. and after two hours – just after dark – it started raining.

Rain in the jungle is refreshing and cools you down. Rain in the pitch dark on an open road with a fierce wind ripping at our sodden T-shirts was another matter. With no warm or waterproof clothes to put on, by ten o'clock we were gibbering wrecks with a real risk of hypothermia.

We were forced now to look for shelter but we could not find two trees close enough for us to erect our tarps. The adjacent forest had been cleared, there was no moon and, to top it all, there were floods on both sides of the road. The telegraph poles that carried an absurdly modern fibre-optic cable through the wilderness teased us as they were the only vertical columns to be seen – but clearly spaced far too far apart for us to make use of.

We tried knocking on houses to ask for shelter as the rain bit into our faces. We didn't need to have swallowed an *English–Portuguese Collins Gem* to understand when someone was telling us to piss off. Loud and clear, the same message came from inside their warm, safe houses.

At 11.45 p.m. Cho was a walking zombie – he was prone to reacting badly to the cold, as we knew from the Peru floods – but he was colder than he had ever been.

With no Plan B, we shivered on. A light a few hundred metres ahead of us attracted our attention and so we made for it. A man's silhouette could be seen from a distance in his open-sided house and I somehow knew immediately that he would be different from the others. I marched ahead of Cho (who had by now lost the will to live) and forced a grin as I asked if we could use his surrounding trees to put up our tarpaulins.

'Of course,' smiled the man with unquestioning warmth. 'And, please, have some fried fish and rice.'

Our slightly biblical tale ended when, in dry clothes with a mouth full of succulent fish, I asked the man his name.

'Messiah,' he responded. I smiled and shook my head.

For 95 per cent of the past seven or eight months in Brazil, Cho and I hadn't seen roads. We hadn't even seen many paths either. Our normal routine had had us enclosed by dense jungle, not able to see more than a few metres in any direction, rotating half-hour shifts at the front with machete in hand cutting openings through the line of least resistance in the trees.

Most locals travel through the remote Amazon areas by boat – the vast network of rivers makes it the obvious choice of travel. Unfortunately, that didn't work for our slightly absurd commitment to walk the entire river's length. So, like the village hunters, but with twenty times as much weight on our backs, we had headed into the dense rainforest. Since the border with Colombia in May 2009 we had averaged seven kilometres a day like this.

But the Amazon was changing as we drew closer to the mouth. For the next two weeks the lines of least resistance for Cho and me were the roads running in and out of Manaus. It felt odd walking in

Crocs on smooth tarmac while we could still hear troops of howler monkeys roaring from the wild jungle roadsides.

Some days we made 40 or 45 kilometres. The advantage of this surreal strip of civilisation was that we would make great progress towards the Atlantic – and home.

On 16 February 2010 we arrived at the south side of the Solimões River and needed to cross over to the north side to Manaus to continue. From this point we knew we had around 1,800 kilometres to go until we reached the Atlantic. The worry was that there was a Federal Police checkpoint where the ferries departed from. We were now illegal and if the Feds checked our passports we were likely to be detained, locked up and possibly deported. The Feds had the power to stop anyone who entered Manaus and my heart was pounding as we walked past the stern-faced, uniformed men. They didn't bat an eyelid.

In front of us was the vast confluence of the River Solimões, which we had been following loosely since Colombia, and the River Negro, a huge black-water river that came down from the north from the Guiana Shield Mountains. The fast-flowing Solimões picks up sediment, which makes it muddy and brown, whereas the Negro is a black-water river which means it is slower and, because of the tannins leaching out of the vegetation at this slower speed, it is both acidic and as dark as tea. The Negro is noticeably warmer, too. Where the rivers meet their waters remain separate for several kilometres before mixing, and the two very distinct colours create a striking visual effect. Together the two rivers become the Amazon once more.

Cho and I paddled without incident across to the northern side of the river where Manaus is situated. We proceeded to walk from the Kawasaki factory on the river through the busy backstreets of Manaus. As we dodged thunderous buses and gambled at amber pedestrian crossings, a long-forgotten world wrenched itself from my unconsciousness.

Another part of my world to reopen was that of love. In Manaus my ex-girlfriend Chloë came from England to visit. We'd been in contact via Skype and email and despite the clear risks to both of us, we had decided it would be fun if she came over and we spent some time together. It was.

When her visit was drawing to a close, however, I instinctively knew that I couldn't commit to her as I felt she wanted me to. I still had six months of jungle walking ahead of me and I didn't want the distraction of having someone outside who was expecting a phone call or worrying about me. I had to be selfish if I was to complete the journey – it invariably involved some sacrifice – so we both remained single when she went home.

Chloë still remains the single most supportive person to me throughout the entire journey, apart, perhaps, from the ever-present Cho or my ever-loving mother. Chloë understood me completely and deserves a mention as being the person I could turn to most readily in my darkest moments. She also did a great deal of work sourcing and posting environmental issues to the website and keeping that side of our mission afloat when I was shattered and unable to do so. We are still, and I hope we will remain, the closest of friends.

Chloë now gone, Cho and I went to acquire some supplies before setting out and we went to one of Manaus's huge shopping malls. We mounted an escalator and Cho struggled to stay on his feet. As he looked around him in amazement at the stairs that were moving uphill all by themselves I realised he'd never seen such a thing before.

In late February 2010 we left the city behind us and pushed on towards Itapiranga on the AM-010, and at kilometre 134 we stopped for the night in a dirty roadside village. Had we been hungry and tired this place would have been a welcome site: electricity to charge the laptop, running water and a lady to cook us a stodgy meal. But we weren't particularly hungry, nor particularly tired; we'd come from the luxury of a break in Manaus so we saw things as they really were.

The weathered, litter-strewn village looked as if no one there was particularly bothered about personal happiness. We spent the night in a shed that smelled like the outbuilding, just away from school, where boys used to go to smoke and urinate. When I turned on the tap I had a lifetime first of recoiling from the stench of the water I was about to wash in. Torn pages from a pornographic magazine were trodden into the scum under my hammock and, even after my 'wash', I felt distinctly grotty. I had the posh room – in Cho's there was a pile of human shit in the corner.

We had four walls and a roof and so I shouldn't have grumbled, even to myself. But I did. Give us horrendous natural conditions in the jungle and we would make good and normally end up loving it. But there was something soul-destroying about that dump whose name, I have to admit, I never got round to asking.

The one consolation was that just after we'd gone to bed I heard a smack as Cho's hammock came undone and he hit the ground hard. Even though he was winded and in pain I couldn't stop tears of laughter rolling down my face for minutes as curses, gasps and groans came from his room.

Chapter Fifteen

'He doesn't talk much, the gringo'

In early March I was distracted by a small ulcer-like sore on my left biceps that wouldn't go away. It came from a mere sand-fly bite on New Year's Day and left a small, open lesion that had been wet (weepy) for nine weeks by this point. The 'crater' was only the size of a pea and the whole 'volcano' would fit on a ten-pence piece. It wasn't painful but it had a defined, inflamed, circular edge and just wouldn't heal.

I thought it was a tropical ulcer and I treated it with an antiseptic powder and took courses of ampicillin and metronidazole antibiotics sequentially as flucloxacillin was impossible to get hold of. They had absolutely no effect and a small bit of me was annoyed that I hadn't managed to shrug this off despite a full month out of the moist jungle and on dry, sterile roads.

Public response from blogging, in particular from two doctors, John James and Caroline Baugh, let me know I most probably had leishmaniasis. In its present form I had nothing to worry about, but I had a 6 per cent chance of it mutating into mucocutaneous leishmaniasis which could be disfiguring, possibly eating away my soft palate (mouth and nose), leaving a permanent hole in my face. I was resigned to living with it for a few months as I wanted us to keep moving forward and didn't want to stop the expedition.

The end of the road network from Manaus was the town of

Itapiranga where we took a break for one day before heading into the jungle again. From there we crossed low marshland that fortunately had once had a road running through it and the remaining embankment kept us out of most of the floods.

Cho was walking up front when I saw him raise his machete to his shoulder, like a rifle, and mimic firing a shot at something he had seen ahead. I peered round him and thought I saw a two-metre-plus anaconda.

Quick as a flash my pack was off and my camera out and I ran forward to film it. Rather than dart away from me, the brave snake seemed interested, spread its neck wide almost like a cobra, and headed towards me. I stopped and stepped back a pace. The snake stopped, too.

The confusing thing was that I wasn't quite sure whether it was dangerous or not. Although I'd initially thought it was a small anaconda (harmless to a human being), I was now confused by the lack of markings and the shape of its head.

I sent some pictures to my mate Ash Holland in Guyana; it turned out to be a large false water cobra (*Hydrodynastes gigas*). Neither Cho nor I had ever seen a 'hydro' before. There are no real cobras in the Americas so the name came from their general similarity in appearance to Asian cobras and from their defensive shows of bravado, which include an expansion of the throat and neck – exactly what I'd seen.

After a few seconds it disappeared into the undergrowth and we never saw one again. The new sighting made me take stock of all the incredible things around me that I didn't yet know about. Retaining interest in what we were seeing daily was harder than you might think when we were exhausted. I realised that actively forcing myself to learn more would be a way of keeping my mind healthy.

Even if I didn't know what things were I could make the effort to look up and actually think about the rainforest again. I'd long ago switched off and treated the jungle like an obstacle course to be overcome. I rarely appreciated the beauty of the shafts of piercing light that cut down through the high, dark canopy. I seldom stopped to take in the sheer size of the trees or the beauty of their moss-covered buttress roots. I ignored the birds and I didn't bother photographing troops of monkeys that screamed and shook branches overhead. Around me the wonders of nature might as well have been whitewashed walls and I recognised that I was being both ignorant and stupid. My mind could do with this sort of stimulation to stop it becoming bored and destructive.

All I needed to do was to give my brain positive stimulus and the expedition was easy. All my problems now came from an isolated, bored, stagnant brain. A lazy, bored brain latches on to negativity and problems and exaggerates them until they become out of perspective and all-consuming. That happened to me a lot if I didn't actively make the effort to keep myself positive.

To enter São Sebastiao we had to cross a large tributary; the town looked pretty from the water with a steepled church and pastel-coloured houses. We were watched by about thirty men and women in the port as we paddled up, disembarked, deflated the boats and strapped them on to our packs, and walked up into the town to the nearest hotel. I felt like Sean Connery as James Bond in *Goldfinger*, when he peels off his wetsuit to reveal his tuxedo and red carnation. We then skirted 14 kilometres round to Urucará, always finding ground that was just firm enough to walk on. Occasionally we had small dips or swims but we were fortunate to be able to cross the lowland at some pace. From Urucará we headed north into the mountains behind. From here we knew that we had 100 kilometres to reach the River Nhamundá where we would next find settlements and people.

My boots finally fell apart and I bought a pair of wellies from Urucará that were one full size too small. There weren't many size 46 feet in the Amazon, it would seem. It was an interesting buy to live with over the following weeks. We bought fifteen days' of food and set off with packs that weighed around 45 kilograms. I was aware that the last 800 kilometres had been on the road and that heading back into the trees with that weight was going to be a shock to our bodies. But because of the hills we didn't expect to be able to fish and we had to carry as much as possible. As it was, 2,000 calories per man per day was all we could take with us.

This far into the expedition I was also surprised at how mountainous the jungle could be, and we faced climbs that required us to haul ourselves up slopes through tangled thorns that just went up and up and up. Without contours on our Google Earth printouts, and unable to see more than 15 to 20 metres around us, it was like navigating in whiteout, polar conditions that make it impossible to determine your direction, and there was no chance of sensible route planning.

At the top of a slope, with calves exploding and lungs burning, when all we wanted to see was a flat ridge that we could follow to maintain altitude, a crevasse-like chasm would loom below us that we had to throw ourselves down. Time after time after time.

The trees were quite well spaced apart so the going would have been fast but for the hills. We barely used our machetes as we clambered up and down them. The first day we made three kilometres and stopped after five hours. We hardly had the spirit to collect firewood that day. But as the days went on the packs lightened and our calves hardened.

Both of my little toes had large blisters on them, as did the balls of both feet. No amount of tape could disguise the fact that the cheap boots were too small and the treads were hard and uncushioned. I could live with them, but every step made me wince and I had to clench my toes to stop them touching the ends of the boots.

On 14 March, after five and a half hours' walking, I stopped at a stream to fill up with water. Both Cho and I dumped our packs down and I filled up, added chlorine and put my pack back on. Cho had taken his pack and shirt off and was standing astride the stream bucketing water over his head with his water bottle.

'Don't you want to bathe?' Cho asked me.

'No, mate. I want to get to a camp and bath later,' I replied.

'I didn't realise we were in a rush.'

'We're not, Cho, I'm just tired and I want to get there.'

Cho took offence at me hurrying him and as it was his turn up front he decided he would teach me a lesson.

He set off at rocket pace up the steep, forested slope. He would show me how fast we could walk if we were in a hurry. Rather than telling him to slow down and not be stupid, I decided to join in the childish game and beat him at it.

Up and up through the trees we climbed. Five minutes, ten minutes, fifteen minutes. Every time Cho turned round there I was right on his shoulder, trying to look as nonchalant and composed as I could. Sweat poured off both of us as neither wanted to slow down or give up. We went faster and faster up the hill until, after twenty-five minutes and at the summit, it was time for our hourly break. We took our packs off and Cho was clearly annoyed that he hadn't left me for dead. When we'd started walking together in Peru he could easily have done so. I was breathing out of my arse but I'd stayed with him without too many problems.

We were simmering at each other, but as yet nothing had been said.

'How old are you, Cho?'

'Thirty.'

'More like thirteen,' I jabbed.

'I thought you were in a rush,' he countered.

We glared at each other. This was the closest we'd ever come to actually having an argument and we held each other's furious stares.

'Are you all right, Ed?'

'Fine. You, Cho?' And then it broke. I can't explain why but at the same time we both saw our folly and started laughing at ourselves. The tension lifted instantly and it was almost like a high from the exertion of the hardest twenty-five minutes of walking we ever did in the expedition. Veins still throbbing, leg muscles pumped, we shook hands and that was that.

The incident was unusual because, although we both occasionally slipped into bad moods, normally we just ignored each other, said nothing and waited for it to pass. This had been the first time ever that we'd taken on each other head-to-head and it was lucky that it was manifested in a hill climb rather than a fist fight, but a battle it was nonetheless. No one had lost so neither of us had a problem with it. It was just us learning even more about each other and how we could walk together.

The day was topped off by Cho finding four wildfowl eggs at the base of a palm and we celebrated by having fried eggs and coffee for supper.

We tracked our progress on the A4 Google Earth printouts each evening by plotting the GPS coordinates. Slowly we edged east.

At 10 a.m. on 18 March we rested at the top of a huge hill that Cho had led us up. After our regimented ten minutes it was my turn to lead and, rather than descend the steep slope in our desired direction, I decided to gamble and veered to our right and continued up the ridge line. The trouble with such speculative navigation was that I couldn't see further than 15 metres because of the trees and I didn't know if the speculative direction would help us or not. I had a hunch that the valley was in fact amphitheatre-shaped and that the spur would start to veer back towards our direction of travel. Walking up the ridge, the light flowed in much more and, where we walked, the ground was almost flat, falling off sharply to our left. Sure enough, after a while the drop off to our left started to change and we were bending round in our desired direction again. The leaves underfoot might have come straight out of an autumnal English woodland and instead of a hellish descent and then a further climb we had just skirted around and were maintaining altitude in the most pleasant forest.

I started to smile as, below us, we could see the huge valley that we'd avoided, but all the time I was sure our luck would change and that the spur would start to descend. For a whole hour we maintained this height along the most elegant of ridges that soared through the roof of the rainforest. A fresh breeze blew in from the open side and cooled our left cheeks.

Troops of squirrel monkeys sprang through the trees overhead and we knew that very few people ever came through here. We were five days' walk in any direction from a navigable river and hunters just wouldn't walk this far. The combination of my hunch paying off and the beautiful forest made it the most pleasurable section of walking of the journey for me. I dreamed of milk biscuits.

Our camp routine was by now so slick that the evenings were luxury. Chloë had brought out new Hex Flies (lightweight hexagonal rain tarpaulins) for our hammocks (and paid for them, bless her) and so we were using Cho's old one as the fire shelter. To have perhaps nine square metres of dry space to cook, eat, store firewood and dry clothes was a luxury that made carrying one extra fly easily worth it. We attached a cord that hung lengthways under the fly and that was our washing line to hang our day clothes that we'd just washed in the river. Every morning we had dry, clean clothes. That wasn't just good for hygiene, it was amazing for morale. They were even warm as if they'd just come out of the airing cupboard.

We would cut long 'Y' poles that would lift the fly high from the fire while we were cooking and eating so that the smoke didn't get in our eyes. Even if it was raining when we set up camp, and continued raining overnight, we would always have dry clothes in the morning and dry wood to start the fire.

My cheap Casio watchstrap broke and I replaced it with an ice-axe strap from my pack. It wasn't pretty but it worked fine right to the finish.

Then the jungle got closer and slower. I allowed my painful feet to get to me. I cut through four wasps' nests in one day and at the last two I roared out loud with anger pathetically. It was an ugly day; I was out of control mentally. I wanted to go home.

Two days short of the River Nhamundá I woke to my phone alarm at 0545 and 0555 and ignored them both. When I woke again naturally at 0640, I looked out of my hammock to the pleasant sight of Cho having got the fire ready and breakfast on. We set off in good time and walked well together for six hours but then I faltered again and Cho, seeing the onset of a crash from me, suggested that we stop and make camp.

It was nice to hear. Usually I made most of the decisions but Cho and I understood each other so well now that we could tell how far to push each other and when we needed to rest.

We supped on half a kilo of rice and two Lock & Lock boxes of hot, sweet milk made from powder. It was like nectar to drink and I could feel the sugar running into my muscles and brain, recharging the depleted batteries. We had three days' of food left to last two days and so were on luxury rationing and were very appreciative of it.

Diary entry from 22 March 2010:

I will miss this life. I know I have low days and it's not easy all the time, but I will miss the nights of just Cho and me in the trees cooking basic food and feeling in control of our walk and relaxed.

We dug out the Stanfords map tonight and it looks like we will finish in mid-August. We'll have to cross the 'neck' of the Amazon delta in mid-June (peak flood season) but we need some excitement to keep us going.

This astronaut pen is amazing as it writes upside-down. Great for hammock diary writing – and for astronauts I suppose.

Our time pressure across this stretch of forest was a liaison with a reporter from ABC News in the States. The GPS wouldn't turn on and I had trouble knowing how far from the river we still were. Luckily he cancelled and the pressure was off – we would have stood him up anyway. Following ridges to maintain height meant that it was harder to be sure if we'd stayed on our bearing and we could only estimate how far we had walked.

March 24 was our final day and we made nine and a half kilometres, finally reaching the Rio Nhamundá. I had never been as thin as I was at this point of the journey and as Cho and I wandered down the sandy river beach looking out across the striking black-water river, I had to hold my shorts up with my hand the whole way.

We had to find people in order to resupply so we paddled

upstream which was surprisingly easy as the black-water river flowed so slowly. We arrived at a house where a family immediately invited us in for lunch. The husband was called Ciro and he grew watermelons in his fields behind the house. We ate one after another, the fresh, sweet juices dribbling down our smiling faces. The family were heading downriver to Nhamundá City the following day and we saw this as a great opportunity to (a) buy a new GPS, (b) charge all our electrical kit, (c) buy food, (d) buy new boots to avoid the blisters, and (e) rest.

It was now the end of March and it had taken eleven months to walk from the Colombian border to where Cho and I were now. We had crossed over 2,000 kilometres of rainforest that nobody in history had ever before crossed on foot. The river was two kilometres wide, almost lake-like, and the boat chugged over the flat surface like an ocean liner. The river represented the border between the Brazilian states of Amazonas and Pará and I decided we could to do the entire state of Pará, to finish the expedition, in a little under five months.

The two things we couldn't procure were larger boots and a GPS. We were told we would have to go to Manaus to find the latter and I wasn't prepared to do that. After spending so much time trying to fix the BGAN in Coari I now knew the unit really well and knew it had a very crude GPS inside. It gave degrees and whole minutes only, meaning that we couldn't pinpoint exactly where we were but we were able to say we were somewhere within a circle two kilometres in diameter. That was accurate enough for me – we would push on with the BGAN as our main form of navigational aid and my feet crammed into the same small rubber boots.

We headed back upriver and were dropped off on the west side where we had last finished walking. We inflated the little rafts and slowly paddled across the vast black mirror. We unknowingly arrived straight into a small village that had been hidden from the water by an island and I was at first worried about how welcome we would be.

I needn't have been. Within an hour we were sitting with the entire village outside their church playing bingo in Portuguese. I won a big bunch of *pifayos* (savoury orange fruits) and a young couple cooked them for Cho and me for supper.

From the village I had identified some mines 50 kilometres away on a bearing of 62° magnetic through the jungle. They were huge scars that were easily visible on Google Earth and from them led a road that could help us. The 50 kilometres were, according to the village, unwalkable, but we set off with eight days' of food, quite content in our madness.

On 29 March, after our first day walking, I plotted our first two-kilometre circle on the map using data from the BGAN and determined that we had walked between 8 and 12 kilometres. This was amazing news: as we'd been wading through swamps, floods and thick bramble bushes all day, if we really had made around 10 kilometres that was outstanding.

We'd been cutting all day long and had no momentum. At one point I almost fainted with dehydration. I made a conscious effort to stop cleaning my leishmaniasis wound with my tongue as I thought that would increase the likelihood of it mutating or migrating to my mouth.

As the BGAN was out for navigating I also checked emails. Incredibly, an individual whom I had never heard of, Barry McCarthy, had donated £6,000 to the expedition. Cho and I actually danced around at this news – it was an incredible bit of generosity to receive.

The one new ingredient that Cho and I had decided to carry this time round was flour. We'd always had a few spices and we'd always carried some salt and cooking oil, and we decided the addition of a little flour would liven up mealtimes. As I write this I can tell this would actually be of interest only to Cho and to me but suffice it to say that Cho's sardines *en croute* were made with such attention to detail and so much care taken over kneading the dough that I swear I have never enjoyed pastry more anywhere. Evenings were so much more fun as a result of this silly addition and it really did lift us both.

The terrain was less hilly than on the Amazonas side of the Rio Nhamundá but there were lots of fallen trees that kept the pace slower. On day four we hit a dirt road that had been built recently and decided to follow it despite it not going our way. In the end it led us to a house whose occupants took us in for the night and fed us steaming plates of cow's liver stew.

When we talked to the middle-aged couple they advised us that we should present our passports to the Federal Police in Trombetas when we arrived. I was surprised to hear that Trombetas had an outpost and Cho and I looked at each other without speaking; we both knew we would not be going anywhere near the place.

The family told us about the new road and informed us that it led all the way to the mine. They didn't mention that the road was private and we didn't ask. It was just an unpaved road.

So we changed our plan. We would walk along the road, past the mining area, but before we reached Trombetas we would leave the road (avoiding the Feds) and head through the jungle. It was just as well that we weren't meeting the ABC reporter any more because Trombetas had been our rendezvous. It would have been a complete farce if we'd arrived to meet him and promptly been arrested.

On 2 April we left early and made good progress on the road. Mid-morning we passed an IBAMA outpost and, as we were illegal, we waved from a distance, shouted, 'Nice monkey!' in a jokey way at the park warden's monkey, and walked on on the far side of the road without stopping. He hadn't stopped us. We had successfully entered the protected national forest south of the mining area.

As it grew dark we decided that, as we were illegals and we were going to camp in a protected forest without permits, we needed to be a safe distance from the road. We went perhaps 100 metres into the trees along a stream and made camp with minimum cutting and noise, ensuring that our smoke would not drift on to the road.

The next morning we approached the mining area from the south. It was an amazing sight: an open-cast bauxite mine that was removing the rainforest completely, in huge areas, and digging out the aluminium bauxite in vast quantities. There were enormous industrial conveyor belts and the mining company had its own train track to ship out the trailers of unprocessed earth. I had not seen an example of such dramatic change to the rainforest apart from the city of Manaus itself. The scars are very visible on Google Earth; search for Trombetas and look to the south.

I have since learned that the mine has a 100 per cent replanting scheme and that they replant 100 different indigenous species. It was still a completely different forest afterwards but at least it wasn't then cleared into cattle ranches.

We were almost out of the other side of the mine when a man in a booth hailed us. We went over to him and he told us firmly to wait where we were while he called his boss. Did we know we were on private land? Apparently the IBAMA outpost with the pet monkey had called through and they had waited two days to detain us further up the road.

The company was called Mineracão Rio do Norte (MRN) and they flatly refused us permission to walk through their land. The manager of this area of mine came in a shiny black pick-up truck with blacked-out windows and told us immediately that we could not walk down this road as it was private and that he was personally going to drive us to the Federal Police in Trombetas. This was one of those moments when you feel like you are in serious trouble and there is no escape. Then I decided upon a whopping lie to get us out of the situation. I explained our journey and I pretended that in addition to walking every step of the way (true) that we had never set foot in a motor vehicle for the entire journey (completely untrue) and that if he made us go in his vehicle we would have walked for over two years for nothing.

As self-important as he was, he was not heartless and I promised that Cho and I would walk all the way back along the road the way we had come and we would cross the Amazon and we would walk on the other side. It would take us weeks longer but we had to do it right – we could not get in a car.

The man accepted this, his sidekick took a photo of us and they let us go. They warned us to be careful of jaguars and we both laughed. 'I am deadly serious,' he called after us. 'They are abundant here and often walk out on to the roads.' I did believe that the place was teeming with jaguars. We'd seen two red-rumped agoutis and a peccary already that day and howler monkeys seemed to be calling constantly all around us. Despite the mining, the wildlife was varied and abundant.

As soon as we were out of sight we slipped straight into the trees, on to their private property and headed east as we'd originally planned. No time lost, no backtracking, and they would never find us in the jungle. Out of sight, out of mind and yet again we'd narrowly avoided the Feds. After that I received a couple of warnings from Brazilians online that the people I would meet in Pará were more dangerous than any of the indigenous people that I'd encountered so far. Agribusiness, logging and mining were huge here and people who got in the way didn't last long. I was determined not to be worried by such threats.

Due east from here to the River Trombetas was 46 kilometres and we had five days' of food. The problem was that we were further south than we'd wanted to be and therefore closer to the main channel of the Amazon.

The inevitable happened the very next morning. We hit floods that were knee-height, then waist-, then chest-, and we were hopping from one piece of dry land to another. Progress, as always in the flooded forest, dropped right down to a couple of hundred metres an hour and we knew if it continued that our food wouldn't last until the River Trombetas.

Then I had an idea. It had just started to rain and we were on an island of land perhaps three metres by four but I needed to use the computer, so we erected my flysheet over the island. I needed to know if the flooding would continue and so I got out the laptop and dug out the old flooded forest data image from NASA that I'd been sent prior to the expedition starting. It was a large eight megabyte jpeg image without any form of grid laid over it. I then got a two-kilometre-diameter circle from the BGAN and plotted it on the Google Earth printout that had a latitude and longitude grid, and looked at the two maps side by side. I could use the shape of the river to roughly transpose the circle that denoted our approximate position on to the computer-screen jpeg image of the floods. I instantly saw that there was a slender hairline of the colour that represented flooding going straight through the area. This meant that the area was generally dry and that, if we kept going, we should be out of the narrow band of floods in less than a couple of hours.

We packed away the electronics and tarpaulin and pushed on through the floods. Within the hour the water levels started to drop and we were back to our waists, then to our knees and then we were back on hard ground. It was another example of ridiculous navigation techniques working and it had saved us from the need to turn back for days until we could have bought more food or chosen another route. The only map or chart in the world that could have given us the information we needed was that jpeg image from NASA.

I sat down, took my wellies off and poured out the water, twigs and leaves from the floods and wrung out my socks. From here to the River Trombetas was all dry ground. I was sure of it and we could escape this unfriendly mining area without being noticed.

Cho put some sugar in the pastry that night and the height of the ecstasy bar was raised again. I would not have swapped this pastry for kobe beef or Peking duck – it was extraordinary.

On 8 April we hit a hunters' trail that led down to the River Trombetas. We stayed with a mixed-race *caboclo* family who told us that there was an IBAMA path that led the whole way to the town of Oriximina and we could then just paddle straight across the River Trombetas into the town. It didn't quite work out like that, however.

The path soon ran out and I have to admit I had reached a stage of tiredness where I was very short with Cho. We were both exhausted and needed to rest but we desperately wanted to reach Oriximina on foot to avoid having to come back to complete any walking. I was thoroughly unreasonable and it's a credit to Cho that he put up with me on this leg. He, too, was tired but he didn't have the worries that I had – about money, time pressures, clashes with members of the production company back home who were changing the goalposts, and just keeping the wheels from falling off this increasingly complex expedition. Cho just had to walk and I envied him the luxury. I felt as if I was running a business, and from a mobile Internet unit in a swamp. With no money for an operations manager in the UK, I dealt with every email and I was the person coordinating most aspects of the journey. All on a strict ration of battery hours and limited bandwidth per month. It was hard to feel in control of it all but I recognised it was rarely Cho's fault and that I needed to stop taking frustrations out on him.

Walking along the edge of the river involved passing lots of agricultural fields and isolated houses with workers living in them. We would stay with families and I would often struggle with Portuguese in the evenings and feel like a social leper when I'd eaten because all I could think about was crawling into my hammock and falling asleep. Cho was fantastic in that he picked up Portuguese quicker than me and he had a real interest in these people. He would pick one of three subjects – religion, forestry or agriculture – and talk for hours. His laugh was ever-present and it was great to hear and made the peasant families relax in his company. I have to say I could not always see that things he laughed at were remotely funny but laugh he did and I am sure he played a huge part in making the people we met make us feel so welcome.

I would sometimes cringe when I heard the families say, 'He doesn't talk much, the gringo', and I would think how hard it was to explain to them what an ordeal this whole journey had been for me and that I was struggling to hold it together at times, and that evenings were the worst because I couldn't see people's mouths in the dark and my brain was too tired to translate the Portugese.

In the mornings I would always make a special effort to chat to the families, with more energy and a night's sleep behind me. But I would never advise anyone to travel as I did if they want to meet people and learn about different cultures. I was almost always too tired to care.

I booked my flight home on 13 April 2010. It was important to get this booked to keep the cost down but it was nerve-racking to put my cards down on the table with four and a half months to push. So much could still happen but the fact that we now had to get this expedition done in a finite time was good for our morale. I predicted I would arrive into Heathrow on 29 August.

On 22 April a pure white flash exploded before our eyes and an almighty snap ripped down through the warm, wet air. A telegraph pole, three metres from where Cho and I were standing in the driving tropical rain, had been struck by lightning. We could not stop smiling and laughing, completely charged with the adrenaline our bodies had pumped into us to deal with what they interpreted as a crisis. We almost floated down the street through the rain grinning and shouting, 'No WAY, man!', like Bill and Ted.

When confronted with an incident that was serious and had an element of danger to it, like most people we clicked into overdrive to deal with the problem. Our senses heightened and our perception of time slowed down. We all have a survival instinct and our bodies are programmed to give us all the help they can in dealing with an emergency. We became incredibly focused and capable whenever we were in this crisis stage.

People often asked how we dealt with the dangers: wading through waters inhabited by huge black caiman, stepping close to deadly pit vipers, or encountering fierce tribes. The honest answer was that these times were thrilling and exciting – time flew. They helped distract us from the far more destructive phenomena – monotony and boredom.

Increasingly now, Cho and I were not recovering when we rested. The day after breaking for two days we would be walking zombies again, showing no sign of having recovered at all.

The expedition was by now a prison sentence of repetitive activity. No matter what people said, it was *impossible* to stay positive all the time. Our minds screamed for new stimulus and were revolting against the placid, polite conversations we had daily with local people about how bonkers we were. There were times when I couldn't give a toss about the fate of the Amazon – all I wanted was to see my friends, watch some sport, go to the pub. Chop the whole rainforest down – I just wanted to be at the birth of my first nephew. Chronic tiredness can sap one's passion for anything and at times we passed majestic trees covered in orchids, walls of interwoven lianas and vines and sandy-bottomed streams of the purest crystal-clear water and paid them no attention whatsoever. Would it help us get through the day? No? Sod it then.

Deep down the passion, the drive, the belief were all still there. Cho and I laughed at people who asked us if we thought of giving up because it was just an absurd concept after all this time. Of course we wouldn't – we hadn't walked two years to give up – we both had a fierce determination to succeed that came from very deep within us.

It was the fickle, easily tired brain that gave us our problems, and my aim was to try to master it. Danger was easy – it was the mundane that we were finding hard to combat.

I tested positive for cutaneous leishmaniasis in Oriximina and convinced the doctor to give me the entire course of intravenous injections as I had a walk to get on with. He reluctantly agreed and for the next twenty days I had to find veins to get a needle into. I had done this in practice before but never for real (and never on myself) and it was somewhat of an ordeal to get a needle into my veins. Some days it was easy, others I made a bloody mess of my arms and left myself feeling sick.

From Oriximina, Cho and I broke into a whole different type of Amazon. Here was the culture of the gaucho, and the cattle ranches stretched as far as the eye could see. Long, dusty roads connected all the small towns down this stretch of the northern shore of the Amazon and most of the rainforest had long since been removed.

Each town was more like a Texas backwater than the Amazon and there were next to no indigenous-looking people. This was the land of the colonial settler and it would appear that the whiter you were the more land and money you acquired. I recognised traits from Argentina here, too: the style of gaucho clothing was similar and the drinking of *mate* (pronounced mat-ay). *Mate* is a drink of hot water poured over dried leaves of *yerba mate* served with a metal straw from a shared hollowed-out gourd. I struggled to connect the wonderful relaxed Argentine culture with this agribusiness. Argentina's cattle business made sense; they had thousands of hectares of pampas or natural grassland that produced the finest beef. Here every scrap of meat was from an area that had once been lush, diverse rainforest and as much as I warmed to the farmers' generosity and Latin cowboy style, I knew that this was an industry I was opposed to.

Logistically, it was a dream for us: lots of places to buy food, and a big fat dusty road to walk down in our Crocs. We could have used this as a sort of dusty walking break from the jungle but neither of us wanted to hang about and so we put in long distances each day to get the barren agricultural section done and to get back into the jungle and closer to the finish.

At this time Vikki, my publicist, organised for ABC News to come out and film us for a couple of days. The cameraman/producer was a New Zealander called Bart Price and he had tried to hire a speedboat to come to meet us. I offered to organise this for him and he concurrently tried to organise it through a fixer in Manaus. I had no idea what luck he had had with his fixer but, as I was walking on dusty roads and didn't need Cho at the time, I sent him to the city of Santarém to source the best fast boat he could for the Americans. Cho loved the task and having to talk to as many people as possible to find the best boat. It took him three days but eventually he found a perfect craft that would suit the news team down to the ground.

I reported back to Bart that we had found a boat and he told us to go ahead and book it. I was happy for Cho as he'd come up with the goods and Bart was happy.

When Bart arrived in the early hours of the morning we immediately went for beers with him and, from the start, enjoyed his war-torn humour and cynical outlook. He was a big man, taller than me and overweight by quite a few kilograms and he had spent a lot of his time reporting on stories in various war zones across the world. He had lots of stories to tell but the conversation eventually came back to the boat and he told me that the fixer he had spoken to in Manaus was 'a useless wanker' who had said that finding a fast boat in Santarém was 'impossible'. I smiled widely. I knew at once who he had spoken to. 'Was he by any chance called Kavos?' I asked, proud of the fact that Cho had managed to source the classiest of boats when Kavos hadn't even bothered to try.

The filming with them worked well and Bart was joined by the ABC News presenter, Bill Weir, a couple of days later and we spent some time in the jungle together filming. It was time out from our schedule but I thought that the walk would be worth much less if no one knew about it and this was going to be made into news pieces for several different programmes on their network. The break from the norm was nice, too, and the two men went away happy.

Archie, my first nephew, was born soon after and it was yet another reminder of the life I was missing back at home. We walked on.

Diary entry from 14 May 2010:

Whenever I write the date I feel like I'm in the future. Are we really in 2010? Christ.

We finished the road section by mid-May and were ready to head back into the jungle. But as the road on our map finished the roads on the ground continued. Fresh logging roads had extended east within the last three years and Cho and I were told that they continued all the way to Almeirim, which is where we wanted to cross the Amazon for one last time. Ever conscious of not making our life harder than it needed to be, we decided to cache our heavy kit – boots, boats, paddles and fishing gear, everything that we didn't need for the road – and we went light through the hills on the brand-new road. We would come back for the heavy gear by boat when we got to Almeirim and it meant our packs dropped from around 40 kilos each to around 10. Perfect.

Then, of course, the inevitable happened. The new road ran out at the Paru River and we had to walk through the jungle with our reduced road kit. It was nice to be under the canopy again after so many weeks of dust and cowshit but we were totally unprepared.

With Cho in Jesus sandals and me in Crocs we headed into the trees feeling somewhat naked and vulnerable. I would never advise anyone to enter the jungle in such footwear – we fell lots of times and got large thorns in our feet. Any river crossing would have to be swum now using our packs as flotation devices if there was nobody to borrow a canoe from. We had to make our two days' of rations last for five days as our speed had dropped and as we had no means of catching fish.

Our half-ration suppers consisted of a shared Ramen noodle soup packet and one sardine. We were low on batteries and enthusiasm and felt as if we had been caught off guard somewhat.

The agricultural areas brought a new treat for us – ticks. We were covered in them and they were so small that if you didn't look hard you could be mistaken in thinking you just had an itch. We both had throat infections, too, at this point and as Cho picked ticks off my back I managed to squeeze out a thick black thorn from my knee. Very satisfying.

Squatting in our small square of cleared earth under my rain fly, we were surrounded by walls of jungle on all sides. The high drone of insects pulsed like the heart of the rainforest. Thin shafts of evening light pierced the tall canopy, highlighting the bright green leaves against the darkness beyond.

The cumulative nature of the walk and the fact that we still had two months to go meant we were both slightly depressed. We were away from people we cared about and doing a repetitive task that we no longer enjoyed.

We emerged from the jungle and picked up a track that headed south down to the town of Almeirim and the Amazon River banks. As we crested the last hill and could see down across the rear of the town and the huge expanse of river in front of us, a police motorcycle with two men on it came towards us up the hill. It stopped and the man on the back stepped off, drew his pistol, and shouted, 'Put your hands up!'

'This is it,' I thought. The Federal Police have caught up with us. We've been tracked down and we are about to be imprisoned and charged with being illegally in Brazil. We were ordered into a police car and as I went to pick up my bag the policeman with the pistol screamed at me to stay away from it.

Adrenaline was flowing and my mind was going through the options. We would just answer questions, be polite and try to downplay our illegality as much as possible. These police were local men rather than Feds – they might not know.

In the station we were searched – again. We were asked to remove everything in our packs – again. Then after our passports were scrutinised they were handed back to us and we were told we could leave the station. Confused, I asked them what we had been arrested for. It turned out that there had been a report that we were approaching the town from the north carrying weapons. Once they had established that we had no weapons they let us go and recommended a good hotel. I think it must have been the microphone boom on the video camera that the person had seen. Either way, the local police had completely missed the expired visas in our passports and yet again we were breathing huge sighs of relief.

From a hotel balcony in Almeirim I decided that I needed to professionalise how I dealt with the expedition mentally. Everyone who had carried out an expedition had advised me that it was the mental side of the expedition that would be the hardest but, strangely, this was the one thing that I'd never bothered to learn about or train in. I'd cobbled together things that worked for periods of time but I'd always lapsed into states of mind that were undesirable and negative. I wanted to learn more about the human brain and did some Internet research into basic human needs so that I could put my mental state in context in relation to the stress I was undergoing.

I was also given the number of an NLP (neuro linguistic programming) guru called Phil Parker to see if he could assist me in getting a better handle on my state of mind. I spoke to Phil three times for about half an hour on each occasion and he told me some remarkably simple tricks to help me to regain a perspective on my problems and to lift me out of the claustrophobic intensity that I had created by focusing so hard on one single task.

There was no magic solution but speaking to someone who understood the brain as well as Phil did was reassuring. I think the main thing I took from the conversations was that I was free to choose my reaction to any event. I was able to become far less reactive and to elect the state of mind that was best suited for the job in hand.

From Almeirim we would cross the main channel of the Amazon for the last time. It was 28 kilometres to the far side, about twice the width it was when we crossed at Manaus, and Cho and I were sufficiently cocky to do it in our little rubber pack rafts.

Chapter 16

The Sprint Finish

With the Amazon in front of us, our self-imposed rule that if we paddled across any river then we had to walk back to a point on the far bank perpendicular to where we had set out was taking on a whole new scale. I predicted that we could end up 50 kilometres downriver by the time we reached the far side and so we had to counter that distance advanced using the river's flow by walking those 50 kilometres. The south side (walking back) was a non-starter due to the fact it was all low-lying, so I told Cho that, before we set out, we had to walk 50 kilometres further downriver on the northern bank.

Google *Maps* said there was a road, which would have meant two days of easy strolling. Despite Google *Earth* suggesting that there was no road, there was in fact a dirt track overhung with tall trees that was hidden from Google's satellites. The road headed inland, away from the river, and past a huge old rice plantation called San Raimundo, where the track stopped. San Raimundo was a colonial settlement that had been started when an American came in and decided to grow rice in the flooded forest. He brought in local workers from all around, paying them a half-decent wage and housing them in a nearby village called Pesquisa. The experiment had failed but during its operations they cleared a massive area of rainforest still visible today on Google Earth.

San Raimundo is on a high escarpment that towers over the rice plantations looking out over the entire Amazon delta. It's the last high ground of note before the sea and it was worrying to talk to the old man who seemed to be looking after the deserted buildings when he said that our chosen route was impossible. There just wasn't enough hard ground between here and the sea, he said, to walk. The only way was in a boat. He'd lived and worked in this area for twenty years and laughed at us openly as being naive. I hope he reads this book one day.

Not wanting to stay with the prophet of doom in San Raimundo we made our way down the escarpment to the small workers' village of Pesquisa. The inhabitants were the remnants of the rice plantation workers who had stayed on and were trying to survive by fishing and growing the usual manioc crops.

The welcome was one of the friendliest, not least because the entire village seemed to be half drunk in a happy way. We shuffled down a shabby street littered with rubbish and merry, semi-clad Brazilians. Within ten minutes the president told us we were 'at home' and a lady called Nazareth with a very suggestive smile was cooking us fried chicken.

From here logistically the plan was very easy but everyone told us it would be flooded. We just had to handrail a small river that bordered the old plantation and it would lead us all the way out to the Amazon main channel and we would have done our 50-kilometre correction.

The following morning we started by following an embankment that must have been an old road above the flooded rice fields and we made good progress for about five kilometres with the flooded plantation on each side. Soon we were forced off the embankment into the water by thick brambles and razor grass and as we entered the reeds we were enveloped by clouds of blood-sucking mosquitoes. We pulled our way through the reeds and grasses that had replaced the rice and hoped it was too dense for caiman.

To our left we could see a strip of forest that ran adjacent to the rice field where the Raiolis River flowed. We couldn't use the embankment any more so being in the plantation made no sense and we cut left towards the tree line making noise to deliberately scare any caiman as we went.

The bright, white sunlight of the overgrown plantation was shut out by the old, dark trees and the cool, black freshness of flooded forest surrounded us. Up to our waists in brown water, the trees soon became spaced out enough for us to walk without too much cutting. The bright channel of the river was always visible on our left as we made great progress through our dark, private world.

We found a patch of land above the water for the night and although it wasn't much, our feet were on dry land. We strung our hammocks up between trees and knew that we were vulnerably close to the waterline but we had little option but to camp. We hoped that in the night it wouldn't rain upriver as we were only a couple of feet above the water level. As we crawled into our sleeping bags Cho called to me that the water had risen already; this was a bad sign. The feeling of inevitability seeped in with the water as slowly the whole ground that we had camped over became a sheet of water a few centimetres deep. Sleep was out of the question and we agreed that if the water rose another foot we would need to inflate the rafts, take down our hammocks, push out on to the river and find a community in the dark. But it didn't rise any more and at about 2 a.m. both of us slipped off to sleep in our semi-aquatic world.

The first river community on the Raiolis was Espirito do Santo. We were met by Arlindo, a chubby man with long hair and a scruffy beard. Arlindo was fishing with his son but had caught nothing. The immediately weird thing about Arlindo was that, to hold his ground on the river, he was paddling downstream. That meant that the river was either a different river that we'd mistakenly been following or it was flowing uphill, which I was pretty sure was impossible.

Arlindo took us to his house and allowed us to stay in his single-roomed hut on stilts above the floods. He had a long jetty protruding from his house out into the river and we sat in the sun and washed from the jetty with his many children playing and splashing around us.

Then the penny dropped. 'Does the river flow uphill twice a day, Arlindo?' 'Yes,' he replied, as if it were the most obvious question in the world. I smiled, happy I'd worked it out but, as a geography graduate, actually pretty ashamed I'd not done so sooner. Two months before the end of our expedition the rivers were already tidal and changed direction whenever the ocean tide came in.

Our progress had been good but I was worried about the forest on the south side of the Amazon itself. We still had to cross the neck of the whole delta and that could mean a lot of flood walking which would slow us down. We were now eleven days behind schedule, and we had flights to catch at the end of August.

The last three days of flooded forest walking were beautiful and open and we had little weight and enjoyed the beauty and the privacy of our secret domain. In the way that cavers relish the solitude and exclusiveness of their little-known, dark, subterranean universe so we had found our own unloved yet wonderful environment that we had adapted to and had grown to love. We eventually arrived at the mouth of the Raiolis and sourced a boat from the nearby houses and were whisked the 50 kilometres back upriver to Almeirim in a matter of hours. We'd now walked the estimated distance that we thought the river would drag us downstream and were ready to paddle across the main Amazon River channel for the very last time.

It was 11 and 12 June when we paddled across the Amazon from Almeirim. The total distance paddled was about 49 kilometres but I won't make a big story out of it as it was easy and nothing to worry about. The rafts were far more stable than any canoe and they just rose over any large waves effortlessly. We stopped in a house on stilts on an island about two-thirds of the way across as it was getting dark and then continued the next day to Vilazinho, a small village on the south bank.

We then started walking across the Amazon's jungle-covered delta towards the city of Belém, which was now just 400 kilometres away. In Vilazinho two cheerful fishermen walked the first hour with us until we found a logging path that they said would help us. It did help us greatly and over the course of the next five days we climbed to 71 metres above sea level. If you consider that Tabatinga (where we entered Brazil in April 2009, some 3,000 kilometres to our west) sat at only about 85 metres above sea level, this was unexpectedly high ground and we made excellent progress across surprisingly dry ground.

The NLP self-coaching that I had been practising worked very well. The simple knowledge that I had the power to decide what mood I was in was a revelation. I just coached myself and decided what mood would be the best for tackling the current situation. Was anger going to help? Of course not and I felt so much happier as a result. Each time I felt the onset of a period of feeling negative, low or angry I would coach myself back and I got a huge morale boost from the knowledge that I now had control over how I felt. It was self-perpetuating and I needed to coach myself less and less. Cho was no longer the focus of blame for things that went wrong. I took full responsibility for everything and focused on how positively to solve any problem.

I started to dream again of future expeditions. The idea at the time was to paddle the entire length of the Congo River, an extremely dangerous and exciting expedition that I was sure no one had done. I was wrong; an Englishman called Phil Harwood paddled the length in 2008 (with a little help from a sail) while I was beginning my expedition but the dream kept my brain focused on something positive for weeks.

The open, dry forest allowed us to stretch out and not just catch up our lost days but actually to get ahead of schedule.

In late June we were dragged back to a realistic pace by kilometres and kilometres of beautiful flooded forest. We were wading through water the colour of black tea that tasted acidic – vaguely lemony.

The Atlantic was still a fair way off in jungle miles but we exchanged childishly exuberant ideas for the future as if we were arriving home tomorrow. My head was wrapped up in future expeditions and Cho had his sights on being a demon winger on the rugby pitch on his arrival in Leicestershire.

It was great to be doing this last leg in real jungle. Our routine was restored, rice and beans were our staple, and the weight was dropping off us once more. We felt fit and healthy and had thrown off the sluggish monotony of the cattle-ranching roads.

We were still covered in ticks, my pack was still broken, Cho's boots were held together by threads and the BGAN had been repaired with duct tape and cable ties – but none of this seemed to matter any more. There was now a quiet feeling of accomplishment growing in both of us that would be very hard to knock. We still had over a month to go; could we keep up this positive momentum?

We crossed lakes and rivers at right angles as we cut south-east across the delta. On lakesides our mosquito nets would billow in the wind off the lake and our backs would be chilled through the thin hammock material.

I had a small botfly living in my head. I'd had them before and they were just a slight inconvenience, nothing more. Their eggs are laid on the underside of mosquitoes by the adult female botfly and then when the mosquito bites you the eggs fall off, stimulated by the warmth of your body. The parasites then grow inside your flesh, forming larvae that grow by eating your flesh. The sensation is just like a pinprick and it could be irritating, especially when I wanted to sleep.

To get a botfly out you have to kill it as the spines make it almost impossible to squeeze out alive. Suffocation was the simplest method. I had a small tube of superglue that I used to mend things and Cho simply dabbed a bit over the opening that the botfly breathed out of and the botfly was dead in a matter of hours. After breaking the skin with a tree spine the next day, as it had grown over, Cho simply squeezed and then gently pulled at the larva until it came out whole. That part was extremely satisfying.

After we hit Lake Caxiuana we broke for a rest in the small town of Portel but we could hardly sit still. We weren't tired and didn't feel the need to stay. We just wanted to walk.

By 24 June the going had been so fast that I brought the flights forward by three weeks, to 10 August. With only forty-seven days to go we powered through all types of jungle with momentum and purpose.

Often when we broke out on to a river there was no shop and so we could buy only what families were prepared to sell us. Normally this was just farine or rice but by then Cho and I were running on pure excitement and were happy with anything. We drank ice-cold acai by the bucket-load whenever we got the opportunity. This thick, purple drink is freshly ground from the locally harvested acai berry. It was abundant and the main staple when in season and it seemed to be packed with nutritional goodness.

Typically, after I changed the dates of the flights the forest became worse again and we spent many days in semi-swamp trying to keep the mileage up while our feet were being sucked down by the mud.

More than ever before we seemed to be able to ride out tough bits of jungle and maintain our humour. This far east in Brazil none of the rainforest we walked through was untouched. Most was brutally butchered – all the large trees had been removed and secondary growth was rampant. Deranged logging paths tempted us in different directions but we moved faster, sticking to a straight-line compass bearing and taking our chances with our machetes.

We crossed the River Camairapi and picked up a huge stretch of what appeared to be natural grassland as we headed east towards the Jacundá River. On 10 June we made 23 kilometres in one day but were being cooked by the sun again and would hide under the smallest scrub bushes when we breaked.

We had been using an electricity power line to move quicker but soon it altered direction and we were forced back into jungle. The following day was one of the worst in the whole two and a half years.

We wanted to reach the Jacundá River – just 11 kilometres from the electricity power line. A logging track started us off in roughly our direction but soon, as often happens, the path started to veer away from our course so we took a bearing for the river and plunged into the undergrowth.

At first it was just tangled and slow, like working our way through a giant barbed-wire obstacle. Then the ground sank away and we were cutting through swamp.

Our sense of humour failed us at this point – something to do with the easy days before seemed to have lessened our tolerance. Cho hated going back, so when I suggested regressing to the path and finding another route around the swamp he refused. I grudgingly agreed to continue.

But I was dumb to do so. After another hour of swamp we still had over four kilometres to go and we were completely committed.

We began snapping at each other, looking at one another to cast the blame. It was poor expedition behaviour but we'd lost perspective and I was immediately too far gone to self-coach myself back. 'Great decision, Cho – thanks,' I childishly provoked him as he tried to free his leg from sucking mud. Both of us were fuming and had lost our usual ability to lift ourselves and see the positives. He just glared back at me.

Our bad moods made the going worse – hour after hour of miserable work at a painfully slow pace. About a kilometre from the target river the swamp got deeper and we were swimming between clumps of gnarled trees.

The jungle became so thick that we had to take off our packs, hang them in trees above the water and cut a path ahead with our machetes. At 6 p.m. the already fading light was cut out by a storm cloud – lightning and thunder announced an almighty tropical storm. When the rain arrived it bit into us and we had to get out our head torches to continue.

Our bad moods evaporated. As much as we let ourselves slip into negativity we knew that things had become serious and we now needed to work together. For me the frustration was replaced by a real and chilling fear of spending the night shivering in a clump of reeds, rain cutting into our bodies through our thin, grimy clothes. We weren't panicking but we badly wanted to get out.

Camping was impossible. No trees big enough to tie hammocks to, and no hard ground. With small fire ants biting constantly and horseflies adding to our joy, we tried to keep our head torches out of the rain under our cap peaks and kept moving forward.

As it became really dark the jungle gave way to reeds and we knew we didn't have far to go. It was 7 p.m. by the time we inflated the rafts and with enormous relief were discharged on to the inflamed river. We had to scream at each other in the dark to be heard above the noise of the rain and wind.

With no idea if there would be people living close by, I marked our exit point to return to in the morning. A dim twinkle of light about a kilometre upriver gave us new energy and we paddled desperately towards it.

The occupants of the houses on stilts were scared of us at first and a man told me to keep paddling. Arriving after dark is a bad idea as communities shut themselves away and think badly of people who travel at night. I persisted (and slightly begged) and he gave way and let us climb up into his dry, warm house. Shivering, we thanked him over and over again and he informed us that Spain had just won the World Cup. Normality had returned – we washed, put on dry clothes and drank coffee.

It was at times like this that I doubted I would ever be able truly to convey how elated I was to have on a pair of dry shorts and hold a cup of sweet coffee on my hands. Cho and I never needed to apologise to each other – we had become almost like brothers and understood these testing times strained our behaviour; if it was mentioned at all we just laughed at ourselves for letting things get to us.

Completely content, as perhaps you can be only after feeling truly desperate, we slung our hammocks in a small wooden boxroom and fell asleep to the sound of the flowing water below us.

From the Jacundá River we needed to cut across to a highway that ran to Cametá. It was the last stretch of jungle of the whole expedition and we were now bound by quite a tight schedule. We had to host a journalist from the London newspaper *Metro* to come in for a few days' walking, and then make our way as fast as possible to the road.

I was now almost exclusively using Google Earth to navigate and I found a clear track that had been cut recently that would link us up with the Cametá highway. We arrived at the track, ready to kick off our jungle boots and slip on our road shoes when I saw my mistake. The white, thin line running north–south was an abandoned and overgrown telegraph line. The going was twice as slow as walking straight through secondary jungle. It had at one stage been a proposed road, but plans had been abandoned after Indians burned a bridge in protest against the intrusive infrastructure. The power line had once supplied the town of Oeiras with electricity but many of the posts had since toppled and the cables now lay knotted and interwoven with vines. Light had flooded into the linear space in the years of abandonment to form a 30-foot-wide, 30-foot-high, 50-mile-long razor grass bramble bush.

With just thirteen days to go, Cho and I settled into the challenge of speed walking through this green mess. There is nice rainforest and there is nasty rainforest. We were in the latter. It was a black sense of humour that was driving us now. Breaks were punctuated by knowing glances and a shared sense of amused self-pity that fate had handed us extra jungle time just when we thought we'd finished. The outcome was that we needed to increase the daily mileage when we hit the road network through and beyond Belém.

Surreal doesn't begin to describe the bizarre juxtaposition between crashing through the undergrowth in a concerted effort to make good ground and then doing a streamed video call with Cho to CNN in Atlanta. It was the first of many. The expedition's amazing publicist, Vikki Rimmer, had organised for them to interview me daily from that point from the side of the track or road until we reached the Atlantic. Until we broke free of the jungle the half-hour before these interviews was a time of panic as we tried to find a hole in the jungle canopy large enough to get a signal through.

There was a bit of us both that was actually quite pleased that the road didn't materialise and turned into more jungle days. The renewed urgency and the need to focus completely on our task had given us renewed zeal. 'There is no option,' said Cho with a smile. 'We have to get there.'

On 31 July the day started mutely at 5 a.m. when I silently fanned the embers of the fire into life and boiled rice in the dark. As the gloom lifted, we broke camp and tried to make some headway down the disused power line. The forest to the side was razor grass one minute, dense bamboo the next. We weaved between the two, searching for the fastest escape.

For most of the day we were aware of a river off to our left and we encountered local people regularly. At 9.30 we passed a house that gave us the sunny news that the bridge we'd been aiming for (the one that marked the beginning of civilisation) was only an hour away. We naively allowed our spirits to soar and our scepticism to doze.

After two disillusioned hours a kind man fixing a dugout canoe said that we'd be there in half an hour. An hour later a short, round lady told us exactly the same thing.

At just before 2 p.m. we sighted the wrecked wooden bridge and scaled the high, unramped buttress end to walk across into the land of generation 4 iPhones and two-finger scrolling.

The sprawling metropolis that is Belém loomed ahead, an unavoidably urban finish to our uncivilised journey. Cho and I were not complaining, however – we had had our share of rainforest for now – and the temptations of civilisation were most welcome.

The Tocantins River had to be crossed from Cametá and the paddle took us the entire day. We arrived on the Belém side in the dark at 7 p.m. We found a cheap hotel and looked at the map and the distances involved. We were now looking at 55 kilometres a day (a mere eleven or twelve hours' walking each day) to get us to the ocean in the remaining week.

Our excited energy was damped down by sheer exhaustion. Making the video after the day's crossing had me up until about two in the morning and we were up again at 5.30 to get more kilometres under our belts.

It became a bit like watching a clock for days on end. The road walking was punctuated by ticking signs that told us how many kilometres there were to go. One moment we are eighty-six from Belém. Twelve and a half minutes later – tick – eighty-five.

Parched by the equatorial sun, our lips were cracking and our T-shirts fading. We already missed the cool air conditioning of the rainforest shade.

In this state, Cho and I would normally have taken a break to recover but the time pressure meant that the daily mileage was unrelenting.

Keith Ducatel, the photographer who had come out in Peru, arrived to capture the end of the trip. Cho and I were both happy to have him back and, even though he had just slipped two discs and had been in hospital for a month, he was determined to get some great images. His complete involvement in the photography almost cost him his life. He had been lying in the middle of the road, taking photographs from the asphalt, when we heard a truck coming and moved to the side of the road. The truck was heading from north to south and Keith wanted to continue taking photos when it had passed. As soon as the truck passed him, he stepped back into the road, not looking to the south, and a motorbike had to swerve violently, missing him by less than an inch. He stood shocked at the near-death experience, laughed and put it down to a lesson well learned.

At 11.32 on 4 August, with just five days and 260 kilometres to go, I wrote my daily blog and set the alarm for 2 a.m. to start walking again. The final march was becoming gruelling as we wore our bodies out in the day and then didn't get enough sleep to recover at night. The previous night I'd not even managed to get into bed, let alone sleep, having picked Keith up from the airport at two in the morning.

The problem was that, unlike the jungle, the road was all urbanised and privately owned and we couldn't just camp in people's gardens. I'd made the decision to base ourselves out of

Belém in order to solve this problem and hire a car that would take us in and out to do the walking each day. I'd not reckoned on the length of the car journeys, though, and the combination of twelve-to fourteen-hour walking days, four-hour round journeys and interviews, blogs and videos to edit meant that sleep was invariably the luxury that was skipped. If I did it again I think I'd have hired a camper van with a driver for a week and just collapsed in the back at the end of each day.

The next day was the same: up at four, started walking at seven, finished walking at Porto do Arapari at ten, with emails and admin finally got to bed at 1.27 a.m.

From Porto do Arapari there was a stretch of water that we had to cross to arrive in Belém before walking onwards to the Atlantic coast. The long detouring road was too far out of the way to be a viable alternative so out came the pack rafts one last time.

'The tides are dangerous around Belém,' we'd been warned. 'The water level fluctuates greatly and the currents can be very strong.'

Cho and I acknowledged and ignored the advice simultaneously. We'd listened to so much melodramatic negativity over the last two years together that our response was weary and somewhat dismissive.

The other reason we ignored it was because we had no option if we were to make our deadline of 9 August, so at dawn the next day we embarked on the final river crossing of the expedition.

It was 6 August and the new sun was half hidden by the horizon, casting a softening warmth over the water. 'See – it's easy,' smiled Cho as we moved slowly away from the south bank. But as we stopped paddling for two minutes to apply factor 30, the GPS inter-rupted our peace to inform us that we were going backwards – fast.

We paddled strongly to break through the area of backwards current. Some three kilometres of fierce paddling before the going grew easier once more, our speed picked up and we relaxed into the remainder of the 10-kilometre crossing.

But as the last part of the crossing lay ahead, the satellite navigation's estimated time of arrival started to climb. 1 p.m. . . . .

2 p.m. . . . 3 p.m. . . . The current seemed to have shifted again. We were heading out to sea, fast.

Without thinking, I changed our course and made for the closest far bank rather than our desired port. Cho followed and we were treated to an impressive demonstration of the power of nature versus the fragility of man. Belém whizzed from left to right in front of us while we hurtled out to sea like two little corks in a flooded gutter.

With Herculean effort, we dug our way closer to the far bank. The city was disappearing to the right and the beaches and rocks running towards us from the left. With chests and arms burning, we broke through into a patch of relative calm and managed to land in a silty mudflat covered in litter. We panted hard and looked at each other in silent relief.

'I told you. Easy,' smiled Cho.

The final obstacle of any substance was now behind us but we had to keep walking that day and make as many kilometres out of the city as we could. We packed up the rafts for the final time and headed north through the vibrant city streets that were still decorated in gold and green left over from the World Cup.

On Saturday 7 August the plan had been to push on all night to give us some rest in Maruda on Sunday night – just short of the final beach arrival on Monday morning.

At 3 a.m. on Sunday we still had 85 kilometres to walk. I started to fall asleep while walking – similar to the sort of terrifying sensation you sometimes experience when driving a car feeling utterly shattered. I figured that if we stopped and lay down at the side of the road for twenty minutes I would recover.

While lying down I started to itch furiously. I began scratching frantically but the itching became maddening. I came out in a total body rash and was unable to walk or lie still.

It was a surreal, dream-like experience and for about an hour I lay by the side of the road asking for help to be called. I was too tired to think about the remaining miles ahead and as time went on I passed out in a state of utter exhaustion with my head on the road.

When I passed out, Keith was called to come and pick us up in the hire car. After just a few minutes of sleep the symptoms had all but gone and I was left drained but clear-headed again.

It was decided that three hours' proper sleep was needed and so we headed for the hotel in Maruda where I woke up from the enforced rest feeling like a new man. I wrote the daily blog, then we made our way back to the point of collapse in the hire car.

Cho and I started walking again at midday and there was now no option but to walk all afternoon and night to complete the remaining 85 kilometres – arriving at the beach, we hoped, for sunrise. We'd never gone that far in a day before, let alone with those time pressures or in that physical state. A car of Brazilian journalists was following us.

I felt slightly humbled that my system had just decided to shut down so close to the finish. That day – the last day – would be the longest of the whole expedition.

The night was indeed long and although we started at a great five kilometres per hour we slowed as the early hours wore on. Before dawn I got a call from Clive, our Irish friend from Manaus, who had come to see the finish, saying that he had news teams that wanted to come and film me but that he was holding them back as he didn't want them to slow us down.

Associated Press and Reuters were there, two of the biggest press organisations in the world, as well as several Brazilian channels.

As the sun started to rise, Cho and I were numb and our legs were so taut that at any point I felt as if I might tear my calf muscles. Then Clive released the news teams.

They swarmed in like commando units in the pale morning light. Halogen top lights blinded us as we walked and paparazzi-style flash photography disorientated us further. Nobody said a word. The crews had been briefed not to interview us until we turned the corner to Maruda beach, which would be at about 8 a.m.

The presence of the press and the fact that people were now watching us lifted us and we almost floated down the road. As it got properly light the crews took turns to walk with us and interview us. It was incredible to experience and it didn't feel real, but the rush of all these people being so interested in what Cho and I had done gave us a big sense of pride.

For about four kilometres we were joined by a few friends who were all as excited as we were, and we walked in a group of about ten until we had around 500 metres to go, when they left Cho and me to complete the last part on our own.

We could tell we were close because we could smell the salt in the air and then we could hear the waves crashing in the distance and then we rounded a corner and could see our friends and the crews all waiting for us at the top of the beach and behind them, through some tourist parasols, was the Atlantic Ocean.

As we reached the parasols the owner of the hotel we were staying at tried to introduce me to someone but I had to make my excuses. With just 50 metres of sand to go, Cho and I dumped our rucksacks and started running. With grins as wide as they had ever been, we tore down the beach and, somewhat bizarrely, ran into the sea holding hands until the waves tripped us and we plunged into the salt water.

We hugged each other, somewhat unsure what to do next. I was so happy and the look on Cho's face was one of pure happiness too. Born in central Peru, he had never seen the sea before. What a way to experience it for the first time.

Keith took us deeper into the sea to take some pictures and told us to dive into the waves and mess around. In my stunned, emotional state, I was delighted to be told what to do.

I took my video camera off on my own to record my last video diary of the expedition and away from everyone, confiding in my digital friend for the last time. I was almost overcome with emotion.

Cho and I did a photoshoot with the huge expedition sponsors' flag on the beach and then Clive gave us a bottle of champagne each. Then, after I'd given Cho a quick lesson on opening, we shook the bottles like Formula One racing drivers and poured the contents all over each other with cameras snapping all around us.

It was over. Nine million-odd steps; over 200,000 mosquito and ant bites each; over 8,000 kilometres walked over 860 days, 733 of them with Cho, about 600 wasp stings; a dozen scorpion stings; 10 HD video cameras; six pairs of boots; three GPSs and one Guinness World Record. My chest swelled with pride and satisfaction. It was a day I will never forget for the rest of my life. No one would ever take that away from us.

Epilogue

By 9 August, more than 900 articles had been written worldwide about our achievement. I came back to London to a hero's welcome and bounced around various TV and radio stations for the first fortnight. I was invited to speak at the Royal Geographical Society and made a fellow of the Society as well as a trustee of Sir Ranulph Fiennes's Transglobe Expedition Trust.

On reflection, I am proud of what was achieved. The total amount raised for charity was only £27,000 but the link to schools around the world worked better than I could have imagined, and that is largely thanks to the Prince's Rainforest Project site for which I did a fortnightly children's blog. Linking with schools is something I hope to develop in future expeditions. In January 2011 I did a schools tour of the UK and could see the excitement in the faces of the children about the Amazon and their keenness to tell me all they now know about this mysterious, faraway jungle.

This book was completed in February 2011, six months after the end of the expedition. At the time of writing, Cho's visa application has been granted and he should be arriving in England in six days' time. His plans are to live with my mum up in Leicestershire, learn English and play rugby for my local team, Stoneygate. His new adventure is about to start.

I am living in London and, having now written my first book, I am planning future ventures. I currently make a living by doing motivational speaking internationally.

The whole experience has changed me in a way I didn't think was possible. I'd been in the military, worked with the UN in Afghanistan and led expeditions to various parts of the world. Surely one expedition wasn't going to have much of an impact on my character in that context? In reality, although the sum of my experience before I started the expedition helped me achieve my mad dream, it paled into insignificance in comparison to the experiences and events contained in this book. I now find myself in the pleasant position of being calmer and happier with the world about me. My confidence now comes from within rather than from the opinions of others. I now know who I am and what I am capable of. I have faced my many and various weaknesses time and time again and, on the whole, have learned to manage them so that they don't drag me down.

The Amazon is still being cut down and the authorities are still not enforcing logging restrictions as well as they might. In two years and four months I never saw a single authority actively policing logging restrictions in the Amazon. Not one.

I am optimistic, however, that things are changing. The expression 'lungs of the planet' was quoted at me by children across Peru, Colombia and Brazil and the educated among the population are proud of their forest and passionate about preserving it. As this popular voice rises, and attains positions of power, I am hopeful that these good values will prevail. Globally, I believe we are beginning to care enough to ensure that happens.

Kit list for Walking the Amazon

This is what Cho and I evolved to carrying after developing the best practices over 28 months:

Sony HVR-AIE camcorder (x 2) with spare batteries (x12), tape stock (x30), cleaning kit (x1) and charger (x1)

Macpac Cascade 90 (x 2)

Ortleib XL 100 litre waterproof rucksack liner (x 2)

Ortleib dry bags (various sizes) for individually waterproofing each electrical item (multiple)

Silica gel sachets for putting in electrical kit dry bags to extract moisture from the trapped air (multiple)

BGAN Thrane and Thrane Explorer 500 with LAN cable for Internet, a standard UK household telephone handset, charging cable, and 2 x spare batteries.

Basic white Macbook (x 1) with spare Macbook batteries (x 2) and power cable (x 1).

Local cell phone and charger for areas with reception (x 2)

4-way adapter (x 1) (so multiple items can be charged off one generator)

Machete 18" (x 2) any decent brand, ideally wooden handle. Metal file (x 2)

Top pocket of pack (x 2) (e.g. is Ed's. Cho's was similar): Garmin GPSmap 60CSx, 1st head torch (Petzl Zipka Plus), map, Leatherman Wave, small tube sun block, Deet 50% (repellent), notepad and pencil, gaffer tape, loo roll, lighter, tree resin for fire lighting, Vaseline, udder cream, paracord, Speedy Stitcher sewing awl, chlorine purification drops.

Fishing kit (x 1): Gill net x 2, various grades of strong hooks, two reels of line, wire for making wire leaders to stop piranhas biting the hooks off the line.

Alpacka 'Yukon' packraft (x 2) and inflator sack (x 2).

AquaBound 4-piece carbon fibre paddles (x 2).

Boat-mending kit (x 1) procured by Jason Warren: For quick repairs on the move: 3 x rolls of tear aid Type A and some Stormseal. For more permanent repairs: a large square of polyurethane coated 7 oz Nylon that could be cut up and fixed over the largest of holes with two part marine adhesive. Bomb proof.

Medical kit (x 1): Antibiotics (two full courses of Metronidazole, Flucloxacillin, Ciprofloxacin, and Amoxicillin) Tramadol, Ibuprofen, Paracetamol, dressings, and iodine tincture.

Night bag (x2): (e.g. is Ed's. Cho's was similar) 2nd head torch (Petzl Tikka Plus), book, Rite in the Rain journal, pencil, pen, LED micro light, medicated talc in 'foo foo' bag (bag you can put whole foot in to avoid wastage/spillage), earplugs, 'housewife' (sewing kit), Superglue, 3 x AAA batteries for head torch, iPod Nano, PowerMonkey power reserve for powering and recharging iPod, laminated photo of Chloë, vitamin tub of pills including: antihistamines, multi vitamins and minerals, personal medication and doxycycline (malaria prophylaxis).

Wash bag (x 2): (This is Ed's. Cho's was similar): Nivea for men small can of deodorant, toothbrush Colgate 360, Sensodyne toothpaste and Protex antibacterial soap in a small lock and lock box.

Sleeping system (x 2): Large parachute silk double hammock, custom made mosquito net with Guyana-style 'wizard's sleeves' for hammock to pass through, Hennesey Hex Fly, ultra-lightweight Macpac down sleeping bag, silk sleeping bag liner.

Clothing day (Ed's): peaked baseball cap, loose-fitting T-shirt with some stretch in it so that it was easy to slip on and off when soaking wet, lightweight loose-fitting trekking trousers, Bridgedale medium weight trekking socks, no underwear. Compass round neck. One spare pair socks in pack. (Cho's variant was he always preferred long-sleeved tops)

Clothing evening (x 2): shorts only in the end

Clothes town (x 2): Clean, dry extra T-shirt and shorts each for arrival in town when all clothes go to get laundered.

Footwear (x 2): Altberg jungle boots (custom made with open eyelets replacing the standard 'valves'). Crocs for washing in, and around camp in evening, and road walking. Locally bought rubber wellies when leather boots wore out

Spare Kit bag (x 2): 6 x AAA batteries (for head torch), 4 x AA batteries (for GPS), 2 x Deet 100%, spare journal, spare pen and pencil, spare thread for sewing awl, spare loo roll, spare lighter and tree resin.

Cheapest Casio watch (x 2) with light and alarm

Nalgene 1-litre water bottle (x 4)

Metal mug (x 2)

4-piece REI cookset (two small pots and top small lids that fit inside each other)

Learn English book (x 1) (Cho's)

Bible (x 1) (Cho's)

Large bags for food (x 2)

Lock and lock lunch boxes (x 2) for eating out of, carrying food that was cooked at breakfast for lunch, using to bail water over self to bathe. About 1-litre capacity.

Food (per man per day) 125g dried beans, 500g rice, bag of various condiments: garlic, salt, oil, vegetable stock, and mixed herbs. Brew kit: Coffee, milk powder, sugar (and 'zero-cal' sweetener for when sugar ran out). Flour on short legs as a treat. Fish only when caught. Occasionally took cured or dried meat if likelihood of fishing was low.

Acknowledgements

I would like to thank to those who donated money to the expedition to keep the whole thing going when sponsorship funds ran out. Between them, with donations from £5 to £6,000, they donated nearly £48,000. Any missed off – apologies: this means that either Ba Stafford (my mum) wasn't notified or I messed up somewhere in my post-expedition tiredness.

In alphabetical order: Lynn Adlington, Ralph Alcocer, Douglas Alexander, Magnus Anderson, Velma Anderson, Sheila Astbury, Richard Atkins, Steve Backshall, Jon Bailey, Mark Barrowcliffe, Caroline Baugh, David Baugh, Raymond Belair, Mike and Sue Berry, Rachael Bibby, Elizabeth Bilton, T. C. Binstead, Dan and Rebecca Birch, Sharon and Simon Bird and family and friends, Andy Blake, Lisa Boggs, Richard Booth, Mike and Joan Bosworth, Jean-Philippe Boudreault, Peter Bowker, Carl and Sally Bradshaw, Mitchell Brass, John and Lesley Bray, Euan Brodie, Giles Brookes, Gill Brown, Crispin Busk, Katie Carter, Pete Casey, Tim Chalmers, Charlie and Lesley Chivers, Robin Cleaver, Sue Clement, Adrian Cole, Richard Comber, Phyllis Constant, Mike Corwin, Alison Cox, Laura Cox, Sven Crongeyer, McDowell Crook, Ralf Darius, Sylvia Davis, Rob and Pauline Dawes, Susannah Day, Andrew Diamond, Richard Dodwell, Nick Dombrovskis, Shawn Douglas, Mike Doyle, Leigh Driver, Ann and David Eardley-Wilmot, Gina Ebole, Joanne Edward, Jonathan Ellison, Lesley Farmer, C. Farrow-Ryue, Anthony Fernandisse, A. J. Firth, Mark Furber, Roger Forrow, Gabe, Di Gaetano, Kieran Gaffney,

Gerard Ginty, Kris Girrell, Dan Glasuer, Ann and John Golding, Charli Golding and Tim Williams, Mandy Green, Liz Greenham, Ted Gurbac, Sylvia Halkerston, Robert Hall, Tina Hamilton-James, Philip Hammond, Roger Harris, Karla Hart, Steve Heald, Timothy Heck, Lisa-Mae Hill, Lakota Hillis, Amanda Hilton, Chris and Vonnie Hilton, Ross Hippeley, Cindy Holdorff, Jon Huston, Megan Irving, Chrissie Jackson, Michael Jackson, David Janke, Tan Jingyi, Kenneth Joyner, Andrew Kelly, Frank Kelly, Jonathan Kemp, Sarah Kemp, Steven and Jos Kemp, Fiona Kennedy, J. S. Kent, Joseph Keogh, J. Kratsky, Martin Kratz, George Lamb, Kellyann Lamb, Sue Lardner, John Leen, Matthew Lehmann, Dan Leinenger, Lena from Palo Alto, Devora Leogrande, Sergio Leunissen, Craig Lundeen, Guy and Vicki Macken, Nadine Manning, Mautner Markhof, Mrs S. M. Martin, Carrie Mayor, Barry McCarthy, Cameron McFee, Claire McFee, M. McKenzie, Janet Meek, David and Liz Mitchell, Jodie Mitchell, Mary Mitchell, Charles Montier, Jamie Morris, Leah Morris, Edward Morrison, James Moy, Andy and Robert Nasreema, Sue Nash of GLCS, Huy Nguyen, Mark Noltner and the class of 2-4, Vern Nicholson, Shah Nishit, the 4th Grade of Dryden Elementary, Arlington Heights, Kevin O'Brien, Jon Orantes, OrgoneCrystals.com, Javier Ortez, Matt Ostiguy, Robert Ousey, Rita Partlow, John Phillips, Susan Phillips, Michael Pike, Anthony Polley, Clare Procter, Richard and Penny Pursey, Mrs C. Quinn, Paul Randle, Amy Rawson, Robert Rees, Tim Rees, ReGet Software, Joan and Faber Richardson, Michael Richman, Stephen Ridgway, Tony Ritchie, Tom Rogers, Roy Rollo, Michael Rowton, Mitchell Rowton, Phillipa Rudge, Richard and Susie Russell, Tim Russell, Michael Salguero for Karlene and Shawn, Jerome Scanlon, Bryan Schneider, James Scott Hosking, Oliver Seeler, Vijay Shah, S. Shanagher, Lisa Shaw, Marla Silverman and P.A.N.D.O.R.A., John and Paula Simon, Caroline Sims, Cyril Sirk, Sky 2 Sea International, Cynthia Smith, J. Snow, A. Southgate, Spratton School, St Mark's Catholic Primary School, Dave Stevens, Edmund Stewart, Georgina Steytler, Stoneygate Rugby Club, Emma Summers (sorry about the flag, Emma), Szesciorka, Tony Talbot, Denise Thorpe, William Throndset, Andrea Thrussell, Tilton-on-the-Hill

Produce Show, Jamie Tinker, Ingrid Toppe, Carolina Torres, Richard Tyler, Dirk Van de Werff, Guy and Sue Wakeham, Mike and Sally Wakeham, Jason Warren, Pat Warren, Harry Wass, Moya Webb, Ron Wedel, Guy Weller-Pooley, Chloë Wells, Fiona and Ian Widdowson, Wild Lodge School, Patricia Williams, S. Willingale, Carol and Meg Willis, Emma Wilson, Gillie Wilson, Wendy Wilson, Winsp and Mack, Sue Wojcik, Kandy Wong, Sean Woodward, Time Wright, E. Zindy.

Thanks, too, to the following expedition sponsors who gave kit or money to make the expedition happen:

Jonathan Stokes of JBS Associates, main sponsors, who gave more than £34,000 to get the expedition off the ground and keep it running for over a year; Scott Cecil of Save Your World for sponsoring the interactive map; George Meek of Unicorn Media for sponsoring the video blogs; Tracey Harris of AST Satellite Communications for lending me three very expensive BGANs; Clare and Simon from The Energy Brokers for sponsoring the blogs; Anton Bowring, Sir Ranulph Fiennes and all the trustees at the Transglobe Expedition Trust who gave me grants and encouragement; the Sculpt the Future Foundation who donated funds; Macpac – official rucksack, sleeping bag and tent suppliers; Red Flag Recruitment who sponsored us; Altberg – official boot supplier, Rite in the Rain who supplied waterproof notebooks for my diary; Rory and Andy at Embado who helped with the website; Sheri at Alpacka rafts for giving me a good deal; Bruce Chapman for flooded rainforest data from NASA; Ged and Dai from Ex-Med for their training and advice; Tom and Ann from Hennessy – official hammock suppliers; Ralph Martindale – machetes, and Sam Crossley of Nightstar UK – torches.

Thanks also to all those men and women who guided us for short periods and to everyone whose village we stayed in, whose food we ate and whose houses we strung our hammocks up in. Without such hospitality, kindness and understanding we could never have completed this journey.

Special thanks go to Julian Alexander from the Law Agency and

Clare Wallis at Virgin Books respectively for their help in getting the book published and support whilst writing, the rest of the team at Virgin for all their work. To Ash Holland for the photos on the original website; Clive Maguire for free board and friendship in Manaus; Mandy Pursey for her help with money-raising ideas; Mel Gow for getting me up and running with social networking; Julio Garro for helping with the Peruvian visa situation; Sam Dyson for coming and walking for a bit and putting up with me; Luke Collyer, without whom I wouldn't have started the whole expedition; Jason Warren and Clare Proctor for help, advice and friendship in different parts of Peru; Phil Parker for invaluable NLP coaching via satellite phone; Carole and David from Project Peru who, with my mother, who is a trustee of the ME Association, organised the boat party on the Thames before we left; Janet Meek for organising the homecoming party; Nadia Nassif for translating all the blogs and website into Portuguese; Will Mather for designing and making two websites for peanuts and making constant updates and alterations; Oswaldo Teracaya Rosaldo, my original guide; Alfonso and Andreas Dongo – the Asheninka brothers; Raul Inuma Ojanama and Jorge Huayambahua Shuña, who walked with me from Orellana to Nauta; Moises 'Boruga' Soria Huane and Juan Rodriguez da Silva who walked with us from Pebas to Colombia; Jeremy Boanson-James for photography in the UK and helping to make the sponsors' flag; Janie Boanson-James for helping with the Facebook page and being an ace sister who I love very much; Marlene Lopez B for logistics, friendship and translating the whole website into Spanish and translating *all* the blogs; Keith Ducatel for investing his own time and money to come out, take photos and sort my head out; George Meek for helping with the sponsorship and for being a loyal friend to chat to in times of need; Craig Langman for being my link to all things TV and for hours of unpaid, thankless work editing the earlier blogs and dealing with TV companies; Vikki Rimmer at Press Contact for doing the entire expedition's PR for free (because she is so lovely) and achieving a monumental amount of publicity at the end; and Chloë Wells for understanding me better than anyone in the world.

The two people I owe the most to are my mum, Ba Stafford, for *everything*: love, support, financial help, bookkeeping, advice, and huge amounts of hard work and dedication raising additional funds that kept the expedition going; and, lastly, Gadiel 'Cho' Sanchez Rivera, the least selfish and most patient person I have ever met.